Aerial Gunners:
The Unknown Aces
of World War II

Also by Charles A. Watry

WASHOUT! The Aviation Cadet Story

Aerial Gunners:
The Unknown Aces
of World War II

by
Charles A. Watry
and
Duane L. Hall

California Aero Press
Carlsbad, California

CALIFORNIA AERO PRESS
P.O. Box 1365
Carlsbad, CA 92008

Library of Congress Catalog Card Number 85-91368
ISBN O-914379-01-1

Printed in the United States of America

Contents

Introduction

Sometimes the germ of an idea begins in strange places. The idea for this book started in, of all places, the base exchange at March Air Force Base, Calif. There, a chance encounter with John Caputo, former tail gunner on B-26 Marauders, spurred my interest in writing a long overdue book on American aerial gunners in World War II. Along with Charlie Watry, former Air Force pilot, and a lifelong friend, we have had some fascinating interviews and researched some of the most exciting accounts of World War II aerial combat.

Without the help and interest of a number of former gunners, this book would have been much more difficult to compile. We especially thank Dan Brody, John Caputo, Jim Ferris, John Foley, Van Gasaway, Sam Miller, Leo Nadeau, Jack Penn and William Wolf for their valued assistance.

Although he was speaking about Army Air Force aerial gunners, Winston Churchill's words apply to aerial gunners of the Navy and Marine Corps as well. He said, "They never flinched or failed. It is to their devotion that in no small measure we owe our victory."

DLH
Chula Vista, Calif.   January 1986

When Duane Hall telephoned me one evening in early 1984 about collaborating on a book about aerial gunners, he immediately got my attention. When he said, "Let's write a book and here is the title," he had me trapped. In the same way my book about the Army Air Forces aviation cadet program filled a gap in WWII military history, I knew that a book on American aerial gunners in WWII would do the same. I dropped all other writing projects and eagerly went to work on this one.

The experience has been rewarding. Hearing and reading about the exploits of aerial gunners in combat has made me appreciate their enormous contribution to the final outcome of the war. Their actions were truly "above and beyond."

CAW
Carlsbad, Calif.   January 1986

I

1. A Shaky Start

In the vast air armada that the United States was able to mount during World War II, the aerial gunner played a critical role in helping to defeat the nation's enemies. Were it not for the determination and grit of these men, the war would have been even more difficult to wage than it was.

Consider that in a typical Army Air Force heavy bomber crew of ten men, eight of them had undergone gunnery training and were assigned gun stations for combat. Nearly all of the enlisted crew members were trained in gunnery, and most had another technical specialty as well. Most bombardiers and navigators, while officers, were trained gunners and had assigned stations from which to defend against attack. In the Army Air Forces alone, some 297,000 gunners received schooling at gunnery schools, more than any other specialty except aircraft maintenance.

Aerial gunners were an integral part of the flying fleet of each service, and they served in all of the far-flung theaters of operations. In the AAF they manned heavy bombers, medium bombers, attack aircraft and night fighters. In the Navy gunners served on torpedo bombers, dive bombers, scouts and patrol bombers. In the Marine Corps they manned dive bombers, torpedo bombers and patrol bombers.

While pilots and navigators were sometimes assigned to non-combat flying duty, such as transport units, the ultimate destiny of every gunner was to train for, or participate in, combat!

The art of aerial gunnery at the start of World War II, in the Army Air Forces, at least, was in a state that could only be described as shaky, at best. Gunners on the Tokyo Raid had never fired the turrets on their B-25s; early gunners of the Eighth Air Force were scoffed at by Royal Air Force gunners, who pitched in with equipment and instruction to raise the proficiency of the Americans; gunners on U.S. bombers early in the Mediterranean theater of operations were taught by an RAF gunner who went along with them to show them how it was done, directing their actions from the top turret of a B-24 while personally downing a score of the enemy. The fault of the early gunners was not theirs, however. The first formal training for gunners did not begin until December 9, 1941, two days after Pearl Harbor! The early training of gunners had been limited to that of their technical specialties, whether as mechanics, radio

1

operators, armorers, or engineers. They picked up what knowledge they could of their assigned weapons and shooting techniques on their own.

This situation would not always be, and training in weapons and in firing them would rapidly progress as later gunners mastered increasingly complicated turrets, gunsights and, eventually, with the B-29, a computerized, remotely controlled, integrated fire control system.

In the beginning, flexible aerial gunnery was quite primitive. With the advent of flying machines, military men, quite naturally, began thinking of different ways to employ airplanes in battle. Just nine years after the Wright brothers' first flight a machine gun was first carried aloft and fired. It was at College Park, Maryland on June 7, 1912 that a Lewis gun cradled between the knees and feet of Capt. Charles De F. Chandler became airborne in the open-air right seat of a Wright Model B biplane piloted by Lt. De Witt Milling. The Wright biplane struggled to a height of 300 feet, whereupon Capt. Chandler fired the full drum of 47 bullets at a canvas sheet on the ground, scoring 12% hits. Not too bad a beginning for Chandler, the world's first aerial machine gunner!

The Lewis gun was to become a standard weapon in many of the worlds' air forces for the next 30 years. It was developed by another American, Col. Isaac N. Lewis. He made improvements in the gun, lightening it for airborne use. The gun was also adopted by the U.S. Army for ground use as well. The Lewis fired .303-inch caliber rounds from a 47-round drum. It weighed 26 pounds and had a rate of fire of 560 rounds per minute.

A year earlier, in 1911, saw what was possibly the first aerial battle using "flexible gunnery": that is flexible arms and flexible hands brandishing pistols. And the honor of being on of the first participants in this aerial battle goes to another American, 22-year-old Dean Ivan Lamb. His opponent was a Mexican Army pilot, who actually fired the first shot.

It happened this way. The Mexican Army in trying to subdue the legendary bandit Pancho Villa had decided to employ an airplane in its chase. They shipped by rail from Mexico City to the northern state of Sonora a Curtiss pusher biplane. To counter the threat, Villa acquired a Curtiss pusher biplane of his own and was looking for someone to fly it. Lamb, working as an Arizona cowboy, heard about Villa's search and, since he knew how to fly, decided to apply.

When he located Villa, Lamb was in for a disappointment. Villa ridiculed Lamb's slight physical build, saying that he was so skinny that the wind would blow him away. Villa gave Lamb a shove that sprawled the youngster in front of the rest of the laughing bandidos.

Lamb jumped up and threw a punch at Villa's face hitting him in the mouth and drawing blood. He could hear the bolts of the men's rifles click into battery. All was still.

Then Villa spoke. He said to Lamb that he was a fighter as well as a pilot and that he had the job.

For three days Lamb patrolled the deserts of Sonora in his pusher, without sighting the other plane. On the fourth day, while cruising along enjoying the beauty of scenery from the air, he suddenly saw the other plane bearing down on him from his left. While he looked there was a puff of smoke and something thudded into his right wing. He quickly turned toward the other craft, barely missing it. Then he pulled his own revolver and fired a round at the attacker. It missed.

Now the two planes were flying beside each other, line abreast. The Mexican pilot gave a little wave of his hand, then fired a few more rounds at Lamb. Lamb retaliated. In a few minutes both flyers had exhausted their ammunition and each went his own way. It had been history's first aerial battle and it had ended in a draw. While Lamb could not claim a victory, he had done the job Pancho Villa had hired him to do. The Mexican Army Curtiss never again flew in seach of the bandit.

For Lamb it was only the beginning of a life of aerial adventure. He found he could sell his flying and fighting skills in other places, as well. In South America he took part in putting down two minor revolutions and served with the armies of Honduras, Paraguay, Nicaragua and Colombia. When the United States entered World War I he returned and was accepted as a pilot by the Army. As a second lieutenant he was attached to the Royal Flying Corps in England and is said to have been the first to down a plane over Britain, a German Gotha bomber.

Following the war he barnstormed, then it was back to South America, where he had several flying "firsts." Back in the U.S. Lamb was one of the early mail flyers, and flew in various other jobs for the next 16 years.

When World War II came along, he managed to reenter the Army Air Forces, and flew as a cargo pilot in India and China. He retired as a colonel in 1953.

The honor of being the first to down an enemy by gunfire goes to a young English pilot named F. Vessy Holt, who, like Lamb, used a pistol. It was early in the first World War. Holt was on a routine reconnaisance mission, which is mainly what airplanes had been used for up to that point. He spotted a German observation plane below him and rolled his scout into a vertical bank firing over the side of the cockpit with his pistol. He missed, but the German was so shaken by the attack that he landed in the first available field and gladly surrendered to allied ground troops.

Soon other pilots and observers were carrying pistols and rifles and using them to intimidate and interfere with the other side's aerial mission. Other missiles, such as bricks, and hand grenades were also dropped from higher altitudes on unwary enemy planes. Among the deadliest of these were small metal pellets which were dropped by the bagful. Even though the pellets were small they could shatter wooden propellers, destroying the airplane.

The first true victory as the result of aerial gunnery is acknowledged to have been as a result of the accuracy of a French Air Service gunner, Corporal Louis Quenault. A member of Escadrille VB24, he and his pilot, Sergeant Joseph Frantz, were flying their Voisin III pusher-plane on a bombing raid. It was October 5, 1914. In the Voisin, the gunner's position was in the front of the plane and he stood up in the open to fire his pedestal-mounted machine gun. This was not such a hardship as the Voisin's top speed was only 69 mph!

When pilot Frantz spotted a German Aviatik he gave chase. Gunner Quenault opened up with his machine gun and soon the enemy plane headed down in flames, killing the crew. The victims of this first air-to air combat victory were Wilhelm Schlicting and Fritz von Zangen.

Placing the gunner in the front of a pusher-type airplane was a development of tactics that grew out of early encounters after machine guns were installed in combat craft in World War I. Since the early machines were unable to fire forward through the propeller, the gunner/observer in the rear cockpit of front-engined planes did the firing. To down an enemy, the pilot maneuvered in front of the other aircraft to give the rear gunner a clear field of fire.

With the development of pusher aircraft with the gunner in front the tactic of shooting at an enemy flying behind no longer was feasible. Later, of course, interrupter cams would allow forward firing of machine guns through the propeller.

One of the pusher-type fighters developed by the British was the FE-2B. Manned by a pilot who sat behind the gunner/observer, the fighter had a good record of victories in the early part of the war. Often the gunner/ observer was an officer while the pilot was an NCO. The gunner sat in an open pit and a Lewis gun was mounted on a pedestal. He was surrounded by stacks of ammunition drums. The gunner kneeled or stood up to fire the forward-firing Lewis gun, held in the aircraft only by his grasp of the weapon. The coaming on the side of the "bath tub" cockpit came to about his knees.

Later models added a second Lewis gun mounted on a tall pillar behind the gunner. When the FE-2B was being attacked from the rear, the gunner stood up on the sides of the cockpit to fire at the enemy over the top of the wing. Again, he was held in only by his grip on the gun. There were no straps to retain him in the cockpit, nor were there parachutes.

An aerial gunner who made a name for himself flying in the FE-2B fighter was an American, Fred Libby of Sterling, Colorado. Libby worked as a cowboy and happened to be in Canada when World War I broke out. He immediately enlisted in the Canadian army and by 1916 was fighting as an infantry private in the trenches in France.

Periodically the British Royal Flying Corps sent out bulletins to those in the trenches calling for volunteers to fly as observer/gunners. It was suggested that those who could qualify could end up with a commission as second lieutenant. Libby saw this as a chance to escape from the muddy trenches as well as a chance to better himself as an officer. He was unaware that the reason for this opportunity was the fact that the average life expectancy of an observer was just ten combat flying hours! That was why so many were needed. And the number of observer/gunners who survived to become commissioned as a second lieutenant was very small.

When Libby arrived at the RFC's 23rd Squadron, no time was wasted in getting him ready for combat. Although he had never been in an airplane nor fired a machine gun, he was sent on his first day in the squadron to a ground practice range for a half-hour of training in the Lewis gun. As he returned from the range, a plane was being readied for his first training in the air.

In the air, the target for his Lewis gun was a fuel can on the ground. He had not been issued goggles yet, so on the first pass by the can he could not even see it for the tears in his eyes. He wiped his eyes and on the next pass he was able to see the can and he hosed off the entire drum of 47 rounds at it. It kicked into the air and Libby knew his bullets had found their mark. On the third pass Libby again squeezed another entire drum and the can went rolling across the field. When the FE-2B landed Libby was congratulated by his commanding officer for his marksmanship.

Libby had lunch and then went to his tent where he stretched out for a nap. His period of relaxation was short, however, because an orderly carrying an armful of heavy flying gear came to his tent and told him he was scheduled to fly again at three o'clock in the afternoon. Libby assumed the flight would be another training flight, but soon found out that he would be going on a combat mission, just hours after he had arrived at his squadron.

He was assigned to fly with a pilot whose observer/gunner had just been killed. The pilot congratulated him on his good shooting that morning. They were assigned to fly as top cover for the five FE-2Bs in the formation, above and behind the others. It was a vulnerable spot.

When they were over the front lines Libby looked down to see the trenches that he had been in the previous day, then from the right a German plane came at them, guns smoking. The fabric on the top wing of the FE-2B began to rip. Libby quickly grabbed the Lewis gun from it stowed position and hurried to install it in the front mount. In his haste he fell over backwards with the Lewis gun falling on top of him. He struggled to get up and install the gun in its mount.

When he did, he saw that the German plane was passing in front of his fighter in a steep bank. As he had done on his morning training flight, he gave the enemy plane the full drum of ammunition. Now, momentarily, he was without ammunition to defend against another attack, so he was pleased to see the German plane begin a dive beneath them. Quickly, Libby placed another drum of ammunition on his gun, in case the German came back.

Soon their mission was over and as they turned for home, Libby felt a slap on his helmet. It was his pilot hitting him with his glove to get his attention. Then the pilot held out his hand to shake a puzzled Libby's hand.

When they landed, some senior British officers had assembled by the hangars and an NCO met the plane to say they wanted to see Libby. When he approached the group, the wing commander held out his hand to shake Libby's, as his pilot had done. He was being congratulated for shooting down the German in flames, a feat he had been unaware of. Artillery observers near the front lines had witnessed the victory and had telephoned to the airfield at once with the good news.

On his first day in the squadron, Libby had been introduced both to machine guns and to flying and had flown his first operational mission on which he had downed his first enemy aircraft. All this between ten in the morning and four in the afternoon.

Libby, who maintained that aerial gunnery was 90 percent instinct and ten percent aim, went on to become the first American to shoot down five enemy aircraft. He continued flying, sometimes two and three missions a day, until he had downed ten of the enemy as an aerial gunner. He was then awarded the Military Cross, one of Britain's highest decorations, by King George V in person at Buckingham Palace.

But combat flying was not over for Fred Libby. He had qualified for pilot training and soon had his wings. He repeated the feat he had performed as a gunner by downing an enemy Albatros fighter on his first combat mission as a pilot. He went on to score a total of 14 victories as a pilot, making his grand total for the war 24 kills, nearly equalling the score of Eddie Rickenbacker.

Although Fred Libby downed more than five enemy aircraft as a gunner, he was not considered an ace, an unofficial term most sources reserve for pilots, until he had downed five enemy aircraft as a pilot. That gunners are excluded from the elite fraternity of acedom seems wrong to a lot of people. One exception in World War II to the rule was Marine Corps gunner Warrant Officer Henry B. Hamilton, of Larue, Texas, who is credited with seven assists by his service.

The other exception were gunners (and radar operators) of two and three-men crews of Army Air Forces night fighters. While each crew member received credit for downing an enemy plane, no gunners accumulated enough victories to qualify them as aces. (Three radar operators in night fighter units were credited with more than five victories, however.) A chapter on gunners crewing night fighters appears later in this book.

In the Army Air Forces during World War II rules for victories in combat were determined by each individual numbered Air Force. The rules varied from headquarters to headquarters. For example some air forces allowed shared kills, while others recognized only whole kills by a pilot or gunner. Some air forces counted aircraft on the ground destroyed, while others did not. (The Navy and Marine Corps counted shared kills but did not give credit for aircraft on the ground destroyed.)

In the same fashion some air forces recognized gunner victories in official published orders, while most did not. In the 12th Air Force four gunners appeared on its list of those credited with five or more victories. They were Tech. Sgt. Robert M. Brunner, Dixon, Calif. (six victories), Staff Sgt. Jack D. Guerard, Beaufort, S.C. (six victories), Sgt. Fred E. Bowker, Oak Park, Ill. (five victories) and Staff Sgt. Joseph R. Myshall, Millinocket, Maine (five victories).

In the Twelfth Bomber Command, Staff Sgt. Benjamin F. Warmer, San Francisco, Calif., was credited with nine victories. More on Staff Sgt. Warmer's exploits later in this book.

In the China-Burma-India theater of operations, two gunners made the list of five or more victories. One was Staff Sgt. Arthur J. Benko, Bisbee, Ariz., who had nine victories in the air and nine more aircraft destroyed on the ground for a total of 18 credited victories. Tech. Sgt. George W. Gouldthrite, Spokane, Wash., was credited with five air-to-air victories.

All the variances among World War II credits for kills have been laid to rest, at least for Army Air Force flyers, by the publication in 1978 of a 685-page study (USAF Historical Study No. 85) which officially credits victories over enemy aircraft. The only gunners listed are those on night fighter crews. In spite of this, those other gunners who are certain that they downed enemy aircraft can feel that their skill contributed as much to winning the war as the fighter pilot who did the same thing. And those gunners who are certain they downed five or more enemy aircraft, since the title is only honorary and not recognized by the U.S. and most other governments, can consider themselves to be aces.

The derivation of the term "ace" for those who achieved a certain number of victories over enemy aircraft has been attributed to French flyers at the time of the First World War. They took the name from the top card in a playing card deck. By some accounts, the figure for qualifying for the title was, from the start, five kills. Other accounts say the French established ten kills as the criteria and it was accepted by both the Germans and the British. This version holds that when the Americans entered late in the war it was feared that U.S. pilots would not be in combat long enough to down ten of the enemy. Since heroes were needed to bolster support for the war effort back home, Americans, it is said, determined that five kills would qualify a U.S. pilot for the title. The French, Germans and British followed suit.

To compile an accurate listing of confirmed kills by World War II gunners would be a monumental if not impossible task. In the Army Air Forces, especially, the heavy bomber formations were designed to provide mutual protection by having as many guns as possible able to bear on attacking fighters. As many as a dozen or more gunners could fire at an attacker at the same instant. And, if the enemy plane were seen to go down, who could say which gunner's fire delivered the fatal blow?

Another problem with regard to crediting gunners is the lack of gun cameras. Gun camera film was one of the best ways to confirm kills for fighter pilots. About 40% of the World War II kills by pilots were verified by film. Gunners, with the exception of those manning a few models of power turrets, were not equipped with gun cameras.

A further difficulty in accurately assessing gunners' claims is the type of combat action they faced. Fighter pilots, in the main, concentrated on one enemy airplane at a time. Therefore a wingman was usually able to act as a witness if gun camera film was not available. Gunners in bombers were many times under attack by hordes of enemy fighters, and those who could act as witnesses to downings, usually another gunner, were often too busy to watch the enemy plane until it hit the ground or water.

The difficulty in verifying kills by gunners can be illustrated by the exaggerated claims made by gunners in comparison to the actual losses as recorded by the enemy. These exaggerations are primarily the result of double or triple, or even more, claims by gunners shooting at the same enemy airplane. In the Schweinfurt/Regensburg raid of August 17, 1943, Eighth Air Force gunners claimed 288 enemy aircraft destroyed. The figure just about equals the total number of German fighters that participated in the battle. These claims were later reduced to 148 with another 100 or so chalked up as probably destroyed or damaged. Following the war, the German records for the day in that area revealed just 25 of their fighters were lost. There are those who question the method the Germans count losses (some say that if the pilot survived the downing the Germans did not consider it a loss), but even allowing for those circumstances, the top number of German planes downed in the raid would not exceed 35.

In an earlier Eighth Air Force raid against Romilly-sur-Seine, France, gunners claimed 53 kills, a figure later reduced to 21 destroyed and 31 probables. Postwar German figures show five of their fighters were downed. In a later massive raid against German aircraft factories, 183 kills were claimed by gunners. One group, the 390th, claimed 62 by itself. One B-17 crew claimed 12 enemy fighters downed and another crew claimed 11. The true figures revealed by Germany following the war were 22 fighters destroyed and five damaged. But, since the bombers had fighter escort, no doubt a number of those enemy aircraft fell to U.S. fighter guns.

So, while most aerial gunners of World War II with five claims will probably never be credited with ace status, this book will attempt to tell the story of the valiant effort gunners put forth, whether they had five victories, one victory, or none.

2. Top Guns

One gunner ace who was able to make it into official records was Staff Sgt. Benjamin F. Warmer of San Francisco, California. Warmer not only downed his five enemy aircraft, but established the incredible record of shooting down seven on one mission, a feat exceeded by only one American fighter pilot.

For a feat that was bigger than life, it took a man bigger than life to do it. Warmer looked like the typical American fullback — the football player who is called upon to punch through the line for a first down or through a determined goaline stand by the opposition. A fullback is what Warmer had been. At six feet six inches and 275 pounds, Warmer had charged opposition college team lines playing for the University of California. Later, in 1937, he had played professionally for the Golden Bears professional team. His size stood him in good stead in another way; serving as a bodyguard for Henry Morgenthau, then the Secretary of the Treasury for the U.S.

His size worked against him when it came time to do his service in World War II. When he joined the Army Air Forces to become a pilot he found that he was considered too big to fit into the cockpits of its planes. Because of his athletic background he was made a physical training instructor. This assignment was not Warmer's idea of how to fight a war — he wanted to fly, and found that the only way he could do it was to become a gunner.

In flexible gunnery training, manhandling a big, heavy .50-caliber machine gun can get the best of a man, especially if his build is slight. Not so with Warmer. He handled those machine guns as if they were pea-shooters — and his training scores reflected his mastery of the weapons.

Assigned to a B-17 crew, Warmer took his place as the right waist gunner. Here again his strength stood him in good stead — the waist gun positions were probably the most difficult positions from which to bring firepower to bear upon an attacker. In the nose and in the tail, gunners were shooting into or away from the slipstream of the bomber, with side forces being at a minimum. In the upper and lower turrets, gunners had power assistance to help them swing their guns into the slipstream. The waist positions, however, required brute strength to battle against slipstream forces which were constantly trying to pull the guns to the rear. Warmer was more than a match for these forces, and aimed his single fifty at will.

Warmer joined the 99th Bombardment Group in North Africa. It was the Spring of 1943 and the war in North Africa was winding down. Warmer flew a few missions at the remaining targets in North Africa and the island of Pantelleria before the attacks against targets in Italy and Sicily were mounted in preparation for the invasion of Sicily, and eventually of Italy. Warmer had logged twelve combat missions by June 1943 when the campaign began. On one of those 12 missions, Warmer and the rest of his crew had had to bail out of their B-17 over North Africa after a raid. Their bomber was limping home with two engines out and third flaming when it seemed that the best thing to do was to get out of it. A new bomber got them ready to go again.

Warmer had fired at a number of attacking fighters and was given credit for some "damage" claims. But he had yet to shoot down a German. Then came a raid on Naples, part of the softening up plan. On that mission Warmer claimed two kills against German fighters and the claims were verified. He now felt he had the technique down pat.

Warmer's next mission, on July 5th, 1943, was to be a momentous one. Part of the preparation for the invasion of Sicily was to try to eliminate aerial opposition from the Germans. This meant attacking their airfields on Sicily. A big raid was mounted to hit Gerbini airfield and its satellite fields. Up to now, German fighter activity against the bombers had been light. But, on July 5th, more than 100 fighters tore into the attacking bombers. Warmer's unit, the 99th, was the first over the target with 30 bombers, thus drawing the first onslaught of the Germans.

First came the twin-engine fighters, the Messerschmitt-110s. The first one to attack Warmer's plane came in from a wide pusuit curve, firing at the bomber well out of range. Warmer held his fire until the fighter was close enough, opened up and scored with his first burst. Pieces fell off the attacking plane, then flames came from the fuel tanks in the wing, finally exploding the aircraft in a fireball. Chalk up one kill.

The next Me-110 took Warmer's bursts in an engine then kept coming on a collision course as if piloted by a dead man. With one engine out it suddenly flipped on its back, then spun crazily to the ground. Warmer had his second of the day.

Now it was the single-engine fighters' turn. From 2-o'clock high came an Me-109 and Warmer hit it with short bursts. The fighter rolled, smoking a little, and headed into a dive. It looked as if this one had gotten away. But then the ball turret gunner, who had been following the fighter down, reported it had exploded and the explosion could be felt in the bomber. Three for Warmer.

Warmer's B-17 was not getting off scot-free, however. Holes appeared in the wings and fuselage and a small blaze broke out in the cockpit which someone put out with a fire extinguisher.

Then, another Me-109 came at the bomber from Warmer's position. Diving from three o'clock high the fighter took Warmer's long burst and immediately exploded, pieces flying wildly. Number four.

The tail gunner fired at the next attacker coming in from four o'clock, but his tracers trailed behind the attacker. When the enemy came in Warmer's view he fired a long burst hitting the fuselage at the wing root. Then when the fighter pilot tried to roll away the wing separated from the fuselage and the airplane flopped wildly down. Five for Warmer.

Warmer tracked the next attacker and when he zeroed in on it, pressed the trigger. The gun spit out a few rounds, then went silent. Warmer was out of ammunition. He scrambled around, slipping and falling on the spent ammo casings that were strewn around the belly of the bomber, and finally loaded another belt of ammunition. While he was occupied with reloading the bombers were on their bomb run, and the enemy fighters pulled off while the B-17s flew through the flak that came up from their target at Gerbini. Once past the target, the flak ceased and the fighters came at the formation again. By now, Warmer was ready for them.

This time a lone Messerschmitt made a diving attack from above at the nose of Warmer's B-17. The forward-firing guns of the bomber had been knocked out, so the German pilot scored heavy hits on the Fortress. The fighter broke off its attack on Warmer's side of the plane so when Warmer picked it up he fired a long burst into the engine and back through the cockpit. The fighter snapped into a spin and went down to the deck. Warmer had his sixth.

The final attack on Warmer's bomber was made by two Me-109s in formation, coming at the B-17 from behind and below. The tail gunner hit one of the attackers and it left smoking. The second fighter kept coming slowing as it climbed. Warmer got off several short bursts at it, getting hits in the engine. Suddenly the propeller jerked to a stop and black smoke poured from the engine. Then Warmer gave the crippled fighter another long burst and it spun away, hitting the ground in a fiery explosion as the crew watched. Lucky number seven for Warmer.

A feat such as Warmer's deserved the attention it got when the bomber formation returned. All crew members in the formation were questioned, and itelligence officers went over and over with witnesses their accounts of the action, to eliminate duplication and mistakes. When the exhaustive interrogation was completed, all were satisfied that, indeed, Warmer's claims for seven kills could be confirmed. Twelfth Bomber Command issued orders designating S/Sgt. Benjamin F. Warmer as an ace with nine confirmed kills, seven in one day. He was awarded the Distinguished Flying Cross and later was commissioned as an officer. The fullback had punched through the German fighter defense.

Perhaps the highest scoring gunner to be officially recognized as an ace by his command was Tech. Sgt. Arthur P. Benko of Bisbee, Arizona. Benko had always been an outdoorsman, growing up in the wide-open spaces of the West. He had done a lot of hunting as a youth and had a love for firearms. One of his favorite diversions was what he called "ink shooting": that is, throwing tin cans into the air and firing at them without using gun sights. Before his entry into the AAF he had been a champion rifle shot in Arizona. It was, almost certainly, this early training that allowed him to score well against Japanese aircraft.

By the autumn of 1943 Benko, a slightly graying, quiet man, was plying his trade as a turret gunner in the China-Burma-India Theater of Operations. We do not know his group nor the type of bomber on which he was a crew member.

On October 2, 1943 he got into a scrap on a mission near Haiphong in French Indo-China. He told reporters later that he had never worked a turret so fast in his life. His guns jammed twice during the battle, which people told him lasted forty minutes, but he was able to clear them. He said the fight seemed like just a minute long to him, and he had to be alert every second.

When the battle was over Benko had downed seven Japanese fighters, and, like Warmer, had a one-mission claim record that was bettered by only one American fighter pilot in World War II.

Official CBI records credit Benko with a total of 18 enemy aircraft destroyed; nine downed in the air and nine destroyed by strafing aircraft on the ground.

CBI records also credit another gunner ace, Tech. Sgt. George W. Gouldthrite of Spokane, Washington with five victories, all aerial kills.

Another ace gunner, but one who was not recognized on published orders was Staff Sgt. John P. Quinlan, of Stormville, New York. Quinlan was the tail gunner of the famous B-17F *Memphis Belle*, which is probably the best-known combat aircraft of the war in Europe. *Memphis Belle* was the subject of a full-color 45-minute documentary film which recorded aerial combat over German-held targets in Europe. Hollywood – director William Wyler went along on five of *Belle's* missions to get the combat footage, which received wide acclaim when it was shown to wartime audiences in the U.S. during the war. *Memphis Belle* was also the first bomber to complete a 25-mission tour of combat and was returned to the U.S. to make a war bond sales tour, so many Americans were able to see the actual plane and its crew after having seen the film.

Memphis Belle flew its combat tour between November 7, 1942 and May 17, 1943, when only four heavy bomber groups were active in the Eighth Air Force. The bomber and its crew were assigned to the 324th Bomb Squadron of the 91st Bomb Group based at Bassingbourn, England. Gunners of 91st Group Fortresses claimed more enemy aircraft destroyed, 420, than any other bomb group in the VIII Bomber Command, but the group also suffered more aircraft losses, 197, than any other group.

Gunners on the *Memphis Belle* claimed eight kills during their 25-mission tour. Five of these fell to Staff Sgt. Quinlan's tail guns, so he became an ace on his first combat tour. Quinlan was included in the crew members who would fly the *Memphis Belle* back to the United States, the first VIII Bomber Command to be returned with crew. Before leaving Bassingbourn, however, the crew of the *Memphis Belle* was visited by the King and Queen of the U.K. who toured the bomber and congratulated the crew members on their combat achievement.

Once back in the U.S. the plane and crew were joined by the young lady for whom the *Memphis Belle* had been named: Margaret Polk, of Memphis, who was the wartime sweetheart of the ship's pilot, Capt. Robert K. Morgan. Also along for the tour was a small dog named "Stuka." The War Bond Tour lasted for three months, which was about a month longer than usual for such a tour. Then the crew broke up, as did Morgan and Miss Polk — she never married and still lives in Memphis. So does the *Memphis Belle*, which was rescued from the boneyard by a Memphis citizen, endured 22 years of outdoor display and deterioration, and is undergoing extensive restoration in an Air National Guard hangar at Memphis International Airport.

Just two members of the crew of the *Memphis Belle* volunteered for more combat flying. One was the pilot, Capt. Morgan, who went to the 20th Air Force to fly the B-29 Superfortress. He began flying them out of the China-Burma-India Theater of Operations before moving to the Marianas. He flew the lead aircraft on the first mission of the 20th Air Force which bombed Tokyo.

The other *Memphis Belle* crewman to volunteer to fly more combat was Staff Sgt. Quinlan, who also became a member of a B-29 crew.

Quinlan, who had been the only member of the *Memphis Belle* crew to receive a Purple Heart, now flew in a Superfort named *Marietta Miss Fit*. He downed three more enemy fighters, this time Japanese, to give him a wartime score of eight kills. On what turned out to be his last mission, he was forced to bail out of his B-29 over occupied China. He was captured, then he escaped and walked to friendly territory.

3. They Fought With Honor

Of the four enlisted airmen in World War II who were awarded the Medal of Honor, the nation's highest decoration for bravery, three of them were gunners of the Eighth Air Force flying missions from England to targets on the European continent. The three were Sgt. Maynard H. Smith, Tech. Sgt. Forrest L. Vosler, and Staff Sgt. Archibald Mathies. Staff Sgt. Mathies' Medal of Honor was awarded posthoumously. The fourth enlisted man to receive the MOH in WWII was Staff Sgt. Henry E. Erwin, who was a B-29 radio operator but not a gunner.

Sgt. Maynard H. Smith, inevitably known by the nickname "Snuffy", was born in 1911 in Caro, Michigan. He was the son of a circuit judge. He enlisted in the AAF in 1942 receiving training at Harlingen, Texas as a "career" gunner to operate the ball turret on a B-17. He went overseas to England in the spring of 1943 as a replacement gunner and was assigned to the 423rd Bomb Squadron of the 306th Bomb Group, based at Thurleigh.

On May 1st, 1943, Smith was to fly his first mission in B-17F number 42-29649. At 32 years of age he was the oldest member of the crew by about ten years.

The targets for Smith's first mission were the German submarine pens at Saint Nazaire, France. In the early days of the air war in Europe the sub pens along the western French coast in the Bay of Biscay were frequent targets for the budding Eighth Air Force. They were also frustrating targets because the AAF lacked the the type of heavy ordnance that could punch through the eleven-foot-thick reinforced concrete roofs that shielded the submarines. In addition, the Germans were highly protective of their submarine fleet and the pens were heavily defended by both anti-aircraft artillery and by fighters. Saint Nazaire was known to the crews of the bombers as "Flak City."

It was to be a bad May Day for Smith's unit. First, the targets were obscured by a seventh-tenths cloud cover which limited the effectiveness of their bombing. Then a navigational error on the return flight put the 306th Group closer to the French coast than had been planned. When the Brest peninsula was sighted through the clouds, it was assumed to be Land's End in England and the formation began to descend from its high bombing altitude. This made the formation sitting ducks for the accurate flak that was thrown up at them from the considerable defenses around Brest.

Smith's B-17 received several hits from the barrage and fires started in the radio compartment and in the waist section. The intercom system was shot away as was the oxygen system. Smith, in the ball turret, found that it ceased to operate because power was lost. He climbed out of it just in time to see both waist gunners and the radio operator bail out over the sea. Seeing the more seasoned combat veterans leaving the stricken bomber might have induced Smith to jump as well. He had no way of knowing whether those in the forward part of the plane had also jumped. He did see that the B-17 was holding its place in the formation so he decided to stay.

First he had to cope with the intense fire in the radio compartment. He wrapped his face in a sweater to provide some protection from the smoke, then with a hand fire extinguisher struggled to contain the fire.

Next, Smith turned his attention to the other fire farther to the rear of the plane. When he approached it he found that the tail gunner lay outside of his compartment seriously wounded in the chest. He gave first aid to the gunner and then went back to the fire in the radio compartment, which, fueled by escaping oxygen, continued to blaze.

By now, German FW-190 fighters had joined the attack on the formation, so Smith alternated firing both waist guns, tending the wounded tail gunner, and fighting fires.

Then, ammunition stored in the radio compartment began exploding from the intense heat. Smith, a slight man, as were most ball turret gunners, heaved the heavy ammunition boxes through a large hole which had been burned through the side of the fuselage.

When the Focke-Wulf attacks ceased, Smith turned his full attention back to the fires. When he had used up all of the fire extinguishers he tried smothering the fires with some clothing that he wrapped around his hands. He fought the fires for a total of ninety minutes.

Feeling that the fires had seriously weakened the fuselage, as the formation neared the English coast, Smith began throwing out all pieces of equipment that he could to ease the strain during the landing. The plane made an emergency landing at the first available base, Predannack, near Land's End. The fuselage held together but the airplane would never fly again. The fire had been so intense that metal parts of the camera, radio and even the gun mounts had melted. There was also battle damage from the fighters and flak to the propeller, engines, top turret, nose, wing flaps and fuel tanks in addition to that caused by the two fires that Smith fought.

Six weeks later, Sgt. Maynard H. Smith became the first enlisted airman to be awarded the Medal of Honor. It was given to him by Secretary of War Henry L. Stimson. Smith's valorous actions had certainly saved his ship and probably the lives of his crewmates as well. Smith flew just four more missions before being given a ground job, and was returned to the United States a short time later.

☆　　☆　　☆　　☆

Tech. Sgt. Forrest L. Vosler was born on July 29th, 1923 in Lyndonville, New York. After leaving school in 1941 he worked as a drill press operator for a year before enlisting in the AAF. He received radio operator training at Scott Field, Illinois and completed aerial gunnery training at Harlingen, Texas. It was the summer of 1943 when he was sent to England as a replacement crew member. He joined the 303rd Bomb Group, called the "Hells Angels" and flew from Molesworth airfield.

By the winter of 1943, Vosler had flown three missions as a radio operator and gunner on B-17s. The bombing weather for targets on the continent got worse as the winter progressed. The Eighth Air Force had to resort to radar bombing with a primitive unit called "Mickey". Many of the targets assigned to the bombing forces were seaport facilities in northern Germany, such as Bremen and Emden, because the targets provided a good land/sea contrast for the radar operators.

On December 20, 1943, Vosler and the rest of the crew of B-17F *Jersey Bounce Jr.* were assigned to attack Bremen. Over the target the bomber was hit by flak and was unable to keep up with the formation. A lagging bomber, naturally, attracted fighters and the *Jersey Bounce Jr.* began a fight for its life that it was going to lose.

Vosler, manning his machine gun in the radio room, was hit by fragments from an exploding 20-mm cannon shell early in the fight, sustaining shrapnel wounds to his legs and thighs. He stayed at his gun, however, battling the attacking fighters.

Another 20-mm slammed into the radio room, and this time Vosler was seriously wounded in the chest, face and both eyes. Streaming blood from his face, Vosler had only partial vision, able to distinguish only large shapes. But, he refused first aid and carried on with his crew tasks. He even repaired a damaged radio using just touch to make the repairs. From time to time he would pass out from the pain of his wounds.

Eventually the *Jersey Bounce Jr.* made it to the safety of the North Sea, but the plane's wounds were so severe that it would not make it back to

Molesworth. The pilot had to ditch the bomber in the North Sea off the coast of East Anglia.

Vosler, even without his eyesight, clambered out onto the wing on his own. While the others in the crew were readying the life rafts, Vosler held another severely wounded crewmember to prevent him from falling off the wing and into the sea. The crew was shortly plucked from their life rafts by a passing merchant vessel.

The account of Tech. Sgt. Vosler's actions on the mission by his crewmates became the basis for awarding him the Medal of Honor. He was returned to the United States and hospitalized while he recovered from his temporary blindness, but it was six months before his sight returned. During his recovery he was awarded his Medal of Honor at the White House by President Franklin D. Roosevelt. After ten months of hospitalization, Tech. Sgt. Vosler was discharged from the AAF.

☆   ☆   ☆   ☆

Staff Sgt. Archibald Mathies was born in Scotland in 1918 from where his parents relocated to Pennsylvania in the U.S. After Mathies enlisted in the AAF he went through aircraft mechanic school at Chanute Field, Illinois. Following that he became an aerial gunner, training at Tyndall Field, Florida. He was sent to England as a replacement engineer/ball turret gunner and was assigned to the 351st Bomb Group, based at Polebrook.

Mathies arrived in the UK in early 1944 when the weather that had been so bad in the last few months of 1943 continued. Bombing weather over the continent continued to be poor also, so many of the missions were flown using radar bombing from pathfinder planes. When the weather permitted, the Eighth Bomber Command flew missions against V-1 buzzbomb launching sites that were located just across the channel from England.

On the 20th of February, 1944, the weather was forecast to be poor in Germany, so radar bombing missions to industrial targets deep in Germany were ordered. This was to be Staff Sgt. Mathies' second combat mission. The target assigned to his B-17G was an Me-109 factory in the industrial city of Liepzig. The weather in Germany was better than had been forecast, so German fighters were up in force. Allied fighter escort fended off many of the attacks, but a number of enemy planes got through.

As the force attacking Liepzig turned away after its bombing run it was met by head on attacks from fighters. Mathies' B-17 took a direct hit through the right windshield, killing the co-pilot and severely injuring the pilot, who became unconscious. Seeing the wreckage in the cockpit and the dead co-pilot, the bombardier felt that the ship would go down, so he gave the call for the crew to bail out. The bombardier then bailed out, but the rest of the crew, in spite of the severity of the attack to the cockpit, hesitated to jump.

It was Staff Sgt. Mathies who was first to reach the cockpit, coming from his ball turret position in the waist. He brought the big bomber under control, leaning over the bodies of the pilots. He was soon joined by Second Lt. Walter E. Truemper, the plane's navigator. In spite of the sub-freezing rush of air through the windshield, they decided to try to see if they could get the airplane back to England. While other members of the crew struggled to get the dead co-pilot's body out of his seat, Mathies and Truemper took turns controlling the plane using the control wheel alone.

While neither Mathies nor Truemper had ever landed any plane, both had some piloting practice in the air. When the co-pilot's body was finally removed, Mathies, who had a bit more flying experience, took the co-pilot position, sitting in the frigid blast of air through the shattered right windshield. He was relieved at his position periodically by Truemper and other crew members when he could no longer stand the numbing of his body. When the B-17 had descended to the more moderate temperatures of lower altitudes, Mathies maintained the co-pilot position.

Mathies and Truemper decided to head for their home base at Polebrook and get advice over the radio about what to do. Since the pilot was still unconscious, the other crew members were ordered by the base to bail out when the bomber reached Polebrook and Mathies and Tuemper voluntarily would try to land the plane. The group commander took off in another B-17 to try to talk the two crewmen through the landing. Radio contact between the bombers, however, was never established, and the erratic flying of the inexperienced crewmen prevented the group commander from flying close enough formation to give visual signals. Seeing the erratic flying, the group commander told the control tower to have the two head the bomber for the sea and then bail out. Mathies and Truemper refused because their unconscious pilot was still alive.

Given permission to attempt a landing, with instructions from a pilot in the control tower, the two made their approach. On the first attempt the plane was too high. The second attempt was the same. On the third try, the airspeed fell off too much and the big bomber stalled out and crashed in a field. Both Mathies and Truemper were killed in the crash, but the pilot they were trying to save was still alive. He died a short time later.

Both Staff Sgt. Archibald Mathies and Second Lt. Walter E. Truemper were awarded the Medal of Honor, posthumously, for their valor in combat.

The Distinguished Service Cross ranks just below the Medal of Honor for gallantry in combat against an armed enemy. Tech. Sgt. Maurice V. Henry, another Eighth Air Force gunner, proved his bravery and leadership and was awarded the DSC, albeit posthumously.

It was the fall of 1943. The weather was bad both in the UK and on the continent. The 384th Bomb Group, equipped with B-17 Flying Fortresses, was part of the Eighth Bomber Command and was based at Grafton Underwood. Tech. Sgt. Henry was a top turret gunner in the group.

On November 26th the 384th was sent to a target at Bremen, Germany and a B-17 named *Barrel House Bessie*, with Henry as part of the crew, participated in the attack. Bombing had to be done with planes dropping on the mark of pathfinder airplanes who used radar to find the target. 427 planes, both B-17s and B-24s took part in the raid. They were opposed by more than 100 German planes, including some four engine bombers (thought to be either FW-200s or Ju-190s) that dropped bombs into the American formation from above.

Nearing Bremen, *Barrel House Bessie* lost the number one and number four engines and quickly fell behind the formation. The pilot ordered the bombs to be jettisoned to lighten the plane, but one bomb refused to release and remained fully armed dangling in the bomb bay. At that moment attacking fighters pounced on the straggler and the pilot was forced to take evasive action. Meanwhile, Henry had left the top turret and entered the open bomb bay to try to release the hung bomb. Working in the cold of a pitching open bay, Henry managed to clear the bomb from the plane. Just as he was returning to his top turret, the number three engine was damaged by cannon fire.

Back in his turret, as the attacks became more vicious, Henry was able to shoot down one of the attackers and damage another. Now the B-17 was receiving more damaging hits. Some of the pilot's controls were lost, the oxygen system was taken out, and electrical power was gone from the entire plane. Henry's top turret became inoperative.

Then, an incendiary round smashed into the cockpit, wounding the pilot slightly and setting a fire, which Henry put out. Losing altitude, the ailing bomber entered the clouds, which put an end to fighter attacks for the moment. Since the intercom system was inoperative, Henry made frequent trips to all parts of the ship, passing instructions from the pilot to jettison equipment.

Bessie broke out of the clouds at 6,000 to find herself directly over the heavily defended port of Emden. *Bessie* immediately began drawing heavy and accurate flak which further damaged the already wounded plane. Once over the sea the flak stopped, but by now all of the engines were either losing power or out. The B-17 was going to come down in the icy North Sea. Henry quickly assembled most of the crew into ditching stations in the radio compartment.

As they glided toward the water, the pilot spotted a small boat and Henry fired a distress signal with the Very pistol. When the pilot set the airplane down near the vessel, the shattered bomber broke in half aft of the radio compartment.

Henry assisted the others in getting out of the sinking plane and was the last one to leave because he was searching for the emergency survival radio. He found it and clutching it climbed out of the plane. As he entered the water, he was carried away from his crewmates and perished.

Just ten minutes after the bomber sank a rescue boat arrived and seven of the crewmen that Tech. Sgt. Maurice V. Henry had struggled to save were rescued and returned to England.

Another Eighth Air Force gunner who received the DSC was Tech. Sgt. Arizona T. Harris. Like "Snuffy" Smith, Harris was assigned to the 306th Bomb Group based at Thurleigh. And also, like Smith, he distinguished himself on a raid to the St. Nazaire submarine pens.

The date was January 3, 1943 and it was the first raid of the VIII Bomber Command for the year. Leading the mission was Col. Curtis E. LeMay's 305th Group, and the entire formation of 85 B-17s was employing the new formation boxes developed by LeMay. The formation flew at altitudes between 20,000 and 22,000, which was high enough to affect the accuracy of flak gunners. But the anti-aircraft gunners at St. Nazaire were proving more proficient than other German batteries.

The skies were clear and the visibility was excellent. That made for good bombing accuracy, but it also aided the ground gunners in zeroing in on the bombers. Added to this was the fact that the bomb run was directly into very strong head winds, which we now identify as a jet stream. This doubled the time that the formation was over the target area and for more than nine minutes the bombers were exposed to a predicted barrage type of flak attack that was described as "heavy, intense and accurate." Experienced crewmen said it was the worst flak they had encountered. More than half of the force received hits from the flak and three bombers went down in the target area.

As the force turned for home, the fighters hit. They would claim four more of the B-17s. The formation of bombers let down over the English Channel to get under the radar coverage and to stave off attacks from below. They flew at 500 feet above the water.

The B-17 *Son of Fury*, on which Arizona Harris was top turret gunner, had been badly damaged by flak and was operating on only two engines. Its pilot did not want to take chances down as low as 500 feet and he remained at 1,500 feet trailing the formation. The bottom of the nose had been blasted away and with the damage had gone both the bombardier and the navigator.

When *Son of Fury* was 40 miles north-west of Brest, it was jumped by six Focke Wulfe-190s. The tailgunner of the B-17 *Banshee*, Sgt. P. D. Small witnessed the battle between the fighters and the doomed *Son of Fury*. On the first pass by the fighters, Small saw the parachutes of four of the crew open. Then the Fortress began descending toward the water until finally it hit. As it was starting to sink, the FW-190s appeared to be strafing the bomber. Then, Small saw that the top turret, as the last part of the plane to go under, was firing back at the German fighters. Arizona Harris went to his death still manning his guns. For that he was awarded, posthumously, his nation's second highest decoration.

II

4. Earning Their Wings

The status of aerial gunnery in the early days of combat in World War II was far from satisfactory. In the Army Air Forces, formal training in aerial gunnery did not begin until after Pearl Harbor. Gunners were on their own to familiarize themselves with their equipment and had only vague notions about the techniques of tracking an enemy fighter.

In April 1942, for example, aerial gunners manning the sixteen B-25 bombers which attacked Tokyo under the command of Jimmy Doolittle had never fired their turrets before embarking on the *USS Hornet*. The only firing of the turrets before the raid came when kites were flown from the stern of the aircraft carrier and gunners were allowed to shoot at them from the deck of the carrier.

In June 1942 at the Battle of Midway, gunners aboard the AAF B-17s had had almost no practice in the several months before the battle because their B-17s were used to patrol Pacific waters instead of being allowed to train with the newly acquired bombers. Even at that, B-17 gunners were able to account for eight Zeros in the three-day battle. (A gunner aboard one of the four B-26s participating in the Midway battle accounted for another two Zeros).

In July 1942, gunners in the first heavy bombardment group to reach England had little or no practice in shooting at targets in the air and many had never operated a turret in the air. In the haste to get the 97th Bomb Group into combat with the Eighth Air Force, the crews had been given just enough training in their recently assigned B-17s to enable them to be safely ferried to England. It was not only the gunners who lacked the skills for combat, but the pilots had had no training in flying tight formation, particularly at high altitudes, and many radio operators did not know the Morse code. But it was the lack of proficiency on the part of the gunners that caused the concern of the leaders, because upon them would depend the defenses of the bombers against the fighter attacks that were certain to come. So began an intensive training period to upgrade the skills of the gunners. Gunnery training facilities and tow-target planes were borrowed from the British, RAF instructors pitched in to help, and American instructors were sent to RAF gunnery schools to study their instruction methods. In the meantime, pilots practiced formation flying and became acquainted with the procedures for flying in the U.K. But, the planned two weeks for this familiarization and gunnery training stretched into four weeks before there was enough confidence in the crews to send them on their first combat mission. Even at that, gunnery skills cannot be learned overnight, and the results of training against aerial targets continued to be disappointing.

In the pre-war days there were no specialized Air Corps gunnery training schools. It was the fall of France to the Germans in 1940 that generated planning for an expansion of all combat crew training, including that for gunners. Three gunnery schools were planned and built, the first at Las Vegas, Nevada, a second at Harlingen, Texas and a third at Tyndall Field at Panama City, Florida. All were in being at the time of Pearl Harbor, but, except for training a few instructors, no students had been trained. The order came to get the program rolling and in January 1942 both Las Vegas and Harlingen graduated some gunners. Tyndall Field turned out a class in February 1942.

The first three schools had the help of the RAF in setting up their training programs. Two U.S. Air Corps officers, Major William L. Kennedy and Major D. W. Jenkins, went to the U.K. in the summer of 1941 to study both British training and the performance of British gunners in combat. The RAF sent Wing Commander E. B. Beamish, a gunnery expert, to the U.S. to tour the three bases, advising on training methods and helping set up training programs. He also gave formal training to gunners who would be instructors at the first three schools. The Royal Canadian Air Force also helped, supplying training outlines to Air Corps officers who visited their schools.

After the war began for the U.S., four more gunnery schools were built. They were at Fort Myers, Florida; Laredo, Texas; Kingman, Arizona; and at Yuma, Arizona. By August 1944 the seven schools were turning out graduates at the rate of 3,500 per week or about 180,000 a year. By September 1944 a total of 214,826 gunners had been trained, even though problems such as a lack of planes, training gear, cameras, turrets, sights and a shortage of qualified instructors seemed to be endless hurdles to be surmounted. 1944 was the high point of the gunnery training program.

Taking their training at the high point were Sgt. Duane L. Hall, Glendale, California and Corporal John H. Penn, Santa Monica, California. The war ran out before these two gunners made it to combat, but their recollections of their training are clear. Hall trained at Yuma while Penn trained at Las

Vegas. Both later went through B-17 Operational Training Units and Penn also trained in B-29s. Hall had competed radio operator technical training before entering gunnery school while Penn was a "career" gunner. Both had entered the pilot training program but both were eliminated before getting to flight training.

Physical qualifications for entering gunnery schools varied throughout the war. The age limit was gradually raised so that later in the war, men up to 35 years were being accepted. The height limitation increased to six feet, while the weight limit was upped to 180 pounds. Hall was 5' 10" when he entered gunnery school, but continued to grow and by the time he was on a B-17 he stood at 6' 1", taller than the limit. But, as a radio operator he manned the right waist gun, where height was not a problem. (The radio room flexible gun had been eliminated by the time Hall was assigned to Fortresses). Penn was 5' 7½" and weighed 134 pounds, which made him an ideal candidate for the confined quarters of a ball turret, which is where he ended up.

Another factor of gunnery school that changed was the rank awarded to the enlisted men. In 1943 those, like Hall, who had already completed a technical training course were graduated as sergeants. If they had not been to a technical school, they were made privates first class and then promoted to sergeant at the completion of a technical course, if they were so assigned. By the time Hall and Penn graduated, the rank structure had been lowered. Radio-school-graduate Hall says, "The thing that disturbed the radio men most was that we were going to graduate from two technical schools with the rank of corporal." Penn went directly to gunnery school, serving as a private, with advancement to private first class upon graduation.

In the earlier days, attending gunnery school was a voluntary matter. Later, men were selected to become gunners, which some resented. Many of the involuntary trainees were unable to take the training satisfactorily, while a good number of others were eliminated from the program because of a professed fear of flying.

The standard gunnery course length was six weeks. "We started with three weeks of ground school, then three more of flying and shooting," says Penn. While earlier students had studied several types of machine guns and sights, by 1944 the .50-caliber machine gun, which had become standard on all AAF bombers, was concentrated on. Penn says, "We learned every detail of that gun and, as in the movies, were able, at the end of school, to take them apart into the seven major groups and reassemble

26

Sgt. Duane L. Hall at Avon Park, Florida - 1945 (Duane Hall collection)

Corp. John H. Penn is standing, fourth from the left. White marks indicate crew members who were later killed on a night training flight Alexandria, Louisiana, Sept. 1944 (John Penn collection)

them while blindfolded." Hall adds that they also received "lots of theory about sighting, deflection shooting, range estimation and aircraft recognition of both friendly and enemy aircraft." "Intermixed with the technical aspects of the job, such items as military law, military courtesy, safeguarding military information and property were also taught." adds Penn. Students were also indoctrinated in high altitude flying and taken for a "flight" in an altitude chamber to the equivalent of 38,000 feet.

In the early time period the qualifications of gunnery instructors was spotty. Instructors were usually taken from a graduating class, at first involuntarily but later the wishes of gunners were taken into account and some attention was paid to ability. Morale was often low among instructors because of their low rank. During 1942 most instructors were privates first class and corporals. In later years most instructors were sergeants.

By 1944 the instructor situation had changed. Penn says, "We were given the best training possible by instructors most of whom had been in combat as aerial gunners. I remember how very dedicated they were to make the job easier for us kids." Hall agrees, saying, "We had excellent instructors and equipment, because by this time in the war the guys before us had learned the hard way and many of our instructors were combat veterans."

Synthetic trainers were used in some cases to teach turret control and to practice tracking and sighting. One simple trainer employed a large concave screen upon which the instructor would move the beam of flashlight while the student practiced tracking, framing and triggering his machine-gun. The "Jam-Handy" was a more elaborate trainer which employed two movie projectors. One of the machines projected combat film on the wall of enemy fighter aircraft making attacks against a bomber. The student tracked the fighter and opened fire when the enemy was within range. If the range was closer than 600 yards, the sound of a machine gun could be heard. If the range was beyond 600 yards a bell rang. The second projector could be turned on by the student and it would cast a spot of light on the picture showing where the correct aiming spot was, and the student would be able to check whether his aim was proper or not.

By the time gunners were being trained for B-29s, synthetic trainers had become highly sophisticated. Penn recalls, "At the gunnery school at Harlingen, Texas an entire flight hangar was converted into a theater of sorts, with a wide, curved screen utilizing three to five synchronized projectors with sound, giving the B-29 student gunner, who was positioned high on a platform and equipped with a gunsight, an entire 180 degree view. Large fighter groups "attacked" the plane from all angles ranging from nine o'clock to three o'clock and from the top of the screen to the bottom, with appropriate sounds of combat."

Following the familiarization period in ground school, gunnery students progressed to live firing practice on the ground. "Earlier generations of students," says Penn, "were taught 'up' from the B-B gun, through the .22 rifle, but it was determined as the war progressed that these basics were not necessary for heavy machine gunners and that the whole series took up much valuable training time."

Safety around weapons was stressed heavily by the instructors. Both Hall and Penn were introduced to the hazards of the weapons early. Says Hall, "The point was brought to us very quickly before ever firing the .50s that they could be very dangerous. Before we reached Yuma a machine gun had been taken off the practice firing line and removed to the cleaning tables without being inspected. There was a round left in the chamber and it, 'cooked off', or fired. The round went through several of the metal tables throwing metal splinters into about 10 or 12 students, who had to be taken to the hospital. The round went on down the road about 1¼ miles and went through a small wooden shed. Needless to say, we always checked our guns before removing them to be cleaned."

At the Las Vegas sub-base, Indian Springs, where all the weapons firing took place, Penn's instructors also impressed the students with weapons safety. He says, "When we finally graduated to use of the machine guns we found that the conservative range masters first had us shoot several rounds in a chained-down .50 MG from a bench that was fixed in place so that the gun could not be raised or swung from side-to-side. When we first tried the chained-down MGs, one of them 'ran away' and fired all 20 rounds in the belt, scaring us all. We later found that the gun was 'rigged' on purpose by the teaching staff to demonstrate the possibility of such an event and to teach students how to stop a runaway gun."

Gunnery students were also trained in skeet shooting using .12-gauge shotguns. Penn says, "The shotguns were used to teach us deflection shooting, the Air Corps term for lead required to hit a moving target." At Indian Springs they used their shotguns firing from the back of a pickup truck. Penn says, "It was fitted with a circle of steel to keep us from falling out. As the truck raced around a random curving road we would be presented with clay pigeons popping out from all levels and angles so we could practice deflection shooting. We took turns shooting and hiding in the 'hot boxes' where we loaded and fired the clay traps. Later, the hand-held shotguns were supplanted by a shotgun in a real upper turret that was operated hydroelectrically."

Then it was time to move to shooting at moving ground targets with a proper machine gun. This was done, Penn says, "by firing from the bench at a large moving target mounted on a driverless jeep, which rolled on a circular track hooked to a rail. This was good practice since as the jeep traveled around the track it went in various directions and distances from the gunner. The large, square target sticking up from the jeep (which was hidden behind a revetment) had concentric ring targets painted on large sheets of paper. Each gunner fired ball ammunition whose points had been dipped in paint, actually lithographic ink, of a variety of colors. When the bullets hit the paper target a smear of color would be left on it. Since each gunner's bullet colors were known, it was possible to tell who did what." Gunners were given some 65 hours of this type of ground live firing.

Finally, gunners were to put into practice in the air what they had learned on the ground. In the earlier days a variety of aircraft were used as gunnery trainers. But, only the Lockheed AT-18, equipped with Martin turrets, proved satisfactory until B-17s and B-24s became available to gunnery schools. A variety of aircraft also were used to tow the aerial targets, which were of the sleeve or flag type. By the time Hall and Penn arrived for training, they both flew B-17s and tow target airplanes were Martin B-26s. By 1944 students were scheduled for 12 two-hour training missions, but could be awarded their wings if they had as few as six. High altitude missions were part of this flying training.

A criticism of the earlier aerial gunnery training was that the tow target plane would fly a parallel course to the aircraft carrying the student gunners. The students then had to merely aim at the target, which hardly gave them practice in deflection shooting and which were conditions that would hardly have been encountered in actual combat. In shooting at sleeve targets, each student's ammunition was again colored to enable his marksmanship to be scored when the target was dropped at the base following the mission.

An improvement on the sleeve targets were gun cameras, special movie cameras mounted in turrets. Actual fighter aircraft would then make attacks using normal pursuit curves as the students tracked the attacker. Later, on the ground, the student's performance could be assessed when the film had been developed. While this was an excellent method of training

Shotgun-mounted turret at the Indian Springs auxiliary of Las Vegas Army Air Field (John Penn collection)

Firing a machine gun turret at a moving ground target at Indian Springs (John Penn collection)

students, there were problems in procuring, processing and assessing the film in time to be useful.

Later, in 1945, still trying for realism in training gunners, the frangible-bullet system was introduced. This method employed bullets that were made of lead and plastic which would turn to powder when they hit a target. Targets were modified Bell P-63 Kingcobra fighters that were equipped with armor plate to protect critical areas of the aircraft as students fired frangible-bullets at them. The RP-63s, as they were designated, had radiosonic equipment which would register the hits of the frangible ammunition. A meter in the pilot's cockpit counted the hits and lights on the wingtip flashed whenever the RP-63 took a hit so that the gunners could tell when they were scoring. Like the gun camera, there were problems that prevented the frangible-bullet program from becoming widespread. The bullets themselves were lighter, had less powder and less speed than normal ammunition, so gunsights had to be adjusted especially for the ammo. Too, the bullets caused excessive carbon in the gun barrels leading to frequent gun malfunctions. Then there was the problem of the fighter itself, which often took hits in critical areas such as coolant radiators and lightly armored areas.

Most gunners who went through gunnery school have stories to tell about student gunners hitting the tow plane. Hall and Penn both have theirs, too. When Hall first arrived at Yuma, he says, "I went down to the flight line to look at a B-17. I noticed that on one B-17 there was an American flag painted on the fuselage near one of the gunners' positions. I asked one of the instructors what it meant. He said that one of the students had been trying to get out of the AAF, but had no luck. On a training mission he had deliberately shot at the B-26 tow target plane and had knocked out an engine. In trying to make it back to the base on one engine, the B-26 crashed just short of the runway. Luckily, no one was killed. The student gunner got his wish— out of the service and into prison. A short time later the flag was removed from the B-17."

Penn's encounter with someone hitting the tow plane involved a pilot of the Womens Airforce Service Pilots (WASPS) who was flying the B-26 assigned to tow for the B-17 flight Penn was training in. Penn says, "One day, while practicing position firing, one of the student gunners drew his lead from the wrong side of his sighting ring and instead of hitting the tube-shaped target, plowed about four or five rounds of .50-caliber ammo into the empennage of the B-26. The WASP cut off and dropped the tow target, banking away from the B-17. She was heard on the radio getting the identification of the B-17 from whose waist gun the hits had come. By the time we landed she had traced the code color of the ammo fired into her aircraft tail and was waiting for the errant student gunner. We stood around in a circle and listened to the best chewing out we had thus far ever heard in our lives. We couldn't have blamed her if she had taken a swing at him."

After six weeks of what Hall recalls as, "one of the most enjoyable times of my life, as I look back on it," it came time to graduate; time to receive those sought-after silver wings and time to get a first stripe or an additional stripe. For Penn, the graduation ceremony was a pleasant memory — Hall's experience at the graduation ceremony was quite different.

Penn remembers the occasion clearly, recalling, "The day we graduated we went to the Post Theater and heard some speeches — I finally got to see the Commanding Officer, the first time I had ever seen a colonel's insignia. While we would only be awarded Private First Class rank, at least we were going to get our wings; the real sterling silver wings with the flying bullet that pointed down and that looked very much like bombardier wings. Even though my last name did not begin with an end-of-the-alphabet letter, I somehow or other was placed about third or fourth from the end. When my name was called I marched smartly up the side steps to the stage and saluted the colonel. He reached to his right for my wings but there was none to be handed to him. They had miscounted the number of wings needed! The colonel seemed to turn blue, asked someone whose fault it was, and then turned to me and those few behind me and made a most deep apology. He reached into his pocket and took out some money. He called another officer and told him to run to the Post Exchange and buy some more wings. We all waited patiently, and when we were presented with our wings there was a big round of applause from the rest of the troops. We all sped back to the barracks, sewed on our new PFC stripes (which meant $54 a month), rushed to get our one day passes (our first) and finally rolled into the sin city of Las Vegas."

"The graduation ceremony at Yuma," Hall remembers, "left a lot to be desired. We lined up down at the quartermaster buildings. In single file, we passed by a sergeant who handed us our wings and threw down some corporal stripes at us as we passed by. I asked him if they could spare all the ceremony?"

✫ ✫ ✫ ✫

Although Sgt. Hall and Corporal Penn had received their wings and were full-fledged gunners, like most gunners their training was not over. Now they were to go on to training as a member of a combat crew. Gunners would be flying with the other crew members with whom they would go into combat and they would be flying the type of combat aircraft which they would use in one of the several overseas theaters of operation. The new training would be called, variously, Operational Training Unit (OTU) or Replacement Training Unit (RTU).

When the big expansion of the Air Corps began in 1939, as the U.S. could see that it might become involved in the war in Europe and in Asia as the result of Japanese aggression, there were no provisions for specialized training beyond flying school graduation. This applied mostly to pilots, since bombardiers, navigators and gunners did not attend specialized schools, but were trained in operational units, as were pilots who finished flight school. By 1941, it was apparent that this system would no longer suffice because of the sheer number of combat units being formed.

The concept of the Operational Training Unit was developed, based upon observations by Americans of the RAF operational training system, in which recent graduates were given eight to twelve weeks of training as a team in the aircraft they were to fly in combat. The AAF adopted a modified version of this plan. Since new groups were being formed at a rapid rate, new flyers were assigned to older groups, where they trained as a team of crewmembers. This led to overages in the number of crews assigned to the old group, so when a new group was activated, the overages were transferred to form the nucleus of the new group.

The OTU system worked well, but when replacement crews were needed for overseas, they were drawn from the OTU, which defeated the purpose of training a unit as a team. So the Replacement Training Unit system was developed, which trained combat crews who would go over-seas as individual crews to replace other crews in combat units. By the end of 1943 the RTUs were the major way of training combat crews. In 1944, RTUs were designated as combat crew training schools or stations (CCTS).

John Penn went from Las Vegas to the CCTS at Alexandria AAF, Louisiana, where he was assigned to a newly formed B-17G crew. Duane Hall went from Yuma to Gulfport AAB, Mississippi, and, like Penn, was assigned to fly B-17Gs.

The concentration of training under the OTU-RTU systems was on the heavy bomber groups. The aim of unit training was to develop a closely knit, organized group team that could pass tests in high-altitude flights, precision bomb runs and demonstrate its ability to assemble efficiently after takeoff, fly all types of formations and to do these operations under conditions of radio silence. Bomb units were also required to be able to service and repair their aircraft under field conditions.

The training was normally conducted in three phases , with the first devoted to individual instruction in their specialties. Gunners concentrated on air-to-air-firing and strafing of ground targets. In the second phase, gunners and the rest of the crew developed teamwork as a crew, learning how to work together in performing missions. Then the whole group came together in the third phase, refining the capabilities of the unit. Medium and light bombardment groups followed a similar pattern.

Of his training at Gulfport, Hall says, "The training was very intense, ground school several times a week, when we weren't flying. Ground school consisted of classes devoted to the various crew specialties, as well as classes the entire crew attended. There were debriefings after we flew missions, watching combat films of actual bombing missions, critiquing films of fighter attacks we took during flying, working on guns and radios, taking first aid classes, Link training, tearing apart engines, etc. It never ended, except for an occasional day off.

"The flying end of it was just as intense. Here was the first chance we had to use the various skills we had learned to work together as a crew. We went on bombing and navigation missions of eight to ten hours over much of the southeast part of the United States and the Gulf of Mexico, including Cuba. Some of these flights were at altitudes of 32,000 feet on oxygen. Even with the heavy flying suits, boots and gloves it was constantly freezing. Here was where the pilots, navigators, engineers, radio operators and gunners put all of those ground school hours to one sole purpose; to get a bomber off the ground, to fly it to a target and to get the bombs on that target.

"We went through daytime bombing raids over the Gulf of Mexico and Florida, strafing attacks on ground targets, air-to-air gunnery practice on towed targets, firing with camera guns at attacking fighter planes making simulated attacks, night navigational missions in single and multiple formations, learning how to fly formation, sending out position reports every half hour, learning how to do other crew member jobs such as flying from the right seat, learning how to repair equipment in the air, and learning how to use navigational and radio equipment."

At Alexandria, Penn had experiences similar to Hall's. Penn thought the air-to-air gun camera missions were especially valuable for gunners. P-47 fighters made simulated firing passes against the bombers, while the bomber gunners fired back, using gun cameras. Then, on the ground later, after assessing the film, the fighter and bomber units exchanged gun camera film to enable them to see how the other scored, a valuable learning experience.

Penn says that if ground targets weren't available for strafing practice, they would fly over the Gulf of Mexico until a school of sharks were spotted. One of the gunners, usually the ball turret gunner like Penn, would fire at the sharks first. When he hit a shark, the whole school would churn up the water in a circle, probably attacking the wounded shark. Then the churning, frothing water would become the target for the rest of the gunners for their strafing practice.

Both Hall and Penn comment that within the crews, crew members had to know their own specialties, but also had to cross-train with the others so as to be able to take over in the event of an emergency. In a letter home to his parents, Penn said, "I'm going to be Charlie Jenning's assistant radio man and am learning to send and receive radio." His pilot, seeing that Penn had worked during a summer vacation in high school installing and testing hydraulic systems in new A-20 attack bombers at the Douglas plant in Santa Monica, also assigned him to moniter the B-17 hydraulic system. Like many pilots, both Hall's and Penn's pilots made certain all crew members had a chance to fly the airplane to at least be familiar with some of the controls. In another letter home, Penn told his parents, "Our pilot is teaching us to handle the Fort, so tomorrow is my turn to fly it. One or two of us get about an hour or so of stick time each day." This preparation paid off for many a pilot. Elsewhere in this book are accounts of gunners who saved their ship and crew by being able to fly the aircraft when both pilots were knocked out of action.

Although the B-29 very heavy bombardment operational training program followed along the same lines as the heavy bomb training, there were some unique differences. Instead of accepting crew members directly out of their specialized training, those with considerable experience in their specialty were sought. This included gunners. As an example, in the early B-29 program, pilots with 400 hours of four-engine flying experience were sought. But by 1944 it was found that the minimum four-engine time had to be increased to 1,000 hours. Other differences in B-29 training included long-range missions at high altitudes and navigating and bombing by radar.

Between December 1942 and August 1945 the OTU-RTU system turned out about 27,000 heavy bombardment crews. A little more than half of these were B-24 crews while the remaining were B-17 crews. Medium bombardment crews trained during the same period totaled about 6,000, while the total for light bombardment was 1,600. The B-29 training program, which began in late 1943, produced 2,350 crews.

Ball turret gunner John Penn did not complete B-17 combat crew training. At about the end of his training, his B-17, returning from a night bombing mission, crashed on the approach to the field in a small forest a few miles from the field. He says, "Of the eight crew members that were on board, only three of us came out alive. I was in the hospital for about six months, but kept on flying pay. I was grounded and sent to Ardmore AAB, Oklahoma for clerical duties in that field's 222nd Combat Crew Detachment. After a few months there, and unable to stand the idea of not flying, I signed waivers and was sent to B-29 gunnery training at Harlingen, Texas. I trained as a right blister gunner and completed the training at about the time of VJ Day."

Penn was released from the service, entered the University of Southern California, where he received both a bachelor's and master's degree in psychiatric social work. He served a post-war hitch in the Air Force Reserve. Employed by the California State Department of Corrections for 25 years, Penn retired in 1976 as a Unit Supervisor, Adult Parole Division. His retirement home is in El Toro, California.

Radio operator/gunner Duane Hall completed his OTU training at Gulfport and says, "After our first OTU training was completed we were supposed to go to Savannah, Georgia, pick up a new plane and fly it over to England. When the Nazis quit we went to Avon Park, Florida and proceeded to go through OTU training two more times until the surrender of Japan."

Following VJ Day, Hall, too, became a civilian. Like Penn, he entered college, graduating from Occidental College in Los Angeles. Later he received a master's degree from San Diego State University. He entered public school teaching and retired from the Spring Valley, California school system in 1981. Hall served in both the Air Force and Navy reserves and retired as a Chief Master Sergeant from the 452nd Air Refueling Wing (AFRES) at March AFB, California in 1984. He lives in Chula Vista, California where he works as an insurance investigator.

III

5. Pearl Harbor

The credit for what may have been the first downing of an enemy aircraft by an American aerial gunner in World War II might go to a young radioman-gunner manning the twin .30-caliber machine guns mounted in the rear cockpit of a Navy SBD-3 Douglas Dauntless. 21-year-old W. C. Miller, a tall, dark-haired youngster from Thomasville, North Carolina, was making what was supposed to have been his last flight before returning to the United States when he got his short and violent introduction to aerial combat.

Two weeks earlier, in late November 1941, Miller and his unit, VS-6, Scouting Squadron Six, had left Pearl Harbor on the aircraft carrier *U.S.S. Enterprise*, the "Big E", on a secret mission to deliver a squadron of F4F-3 Wildcat fighters belonging to Marine Fighting Squadron 211 (VMF 211) to Wake Island. They were under war orders to destroy any potential enemy ships or planes if they met any. When about 200 miles from Wake Island, the Marine squadron was launched for the final flight to its new base. On the flight, one pilot thought he saw three warships through the mist, but when search aircraft scouted the area, nothing was found. If the pilot had been right and the ships located, history might have been radically changed.

The voyage of the *Enterprise* back to its home port of Pearl Harbor was somewhat delayed by a storm, which prevented the carrier from refueling its accompanying destroyers. Therefore, instead of arriving on a Saturday in early December, in time for welcoming parties with wives and sweethearts, the *Enterprise* would not reach land until Sunday morning.

When about 210 miles south of Barbers Point, located at the southwest tip of the island of Oahu, the *Enterprise* prepared to launch the squadron of dive bombers in which Miller served. When the aircraft carrier was in port at Pearl Harbor, the squadron flew from the airfield at Ford Island, in the center of the harbor. That was their destination on this Sunday morning.

As Miller prepared to board his SBD, he assisted his pilot, Lt. (later Rear Admiral) Clarence E. Dickinson, in adjusting his straps and radio cords, as he usually did, standing on the wing of the SBD. The two had flown together as a team for nine months.

SBD Dauntless dive bombers head out on a strike (McDonnell Douglas photo)

SBD gunner checks his weapons (McDonnell Douglas photo)

Miller remarked to Lt. Dickinson that his four-year tour of duty at sea would be ending in a few days, and that he hoped he would not get wet on this last flight together. Of the twenty-one members of his radio class, Miller told his pilot that he was the only one who had not experienced a ditching with his aircraft in the sea. Lt. Dickinson assured him that the morning's flight would be just routine.

After the launch, at about six-thirty, the squadron formed into nine two-plane sections, flying at 1,000 feet above the ocean. Their approach to Pearl Harbor had to be made through a corridor which would identify them as friendlies to the air defense units on the island. Miller carefully took radio bearings on a Honolulu commercial radio station to make certain they were in the proper approach zone.

When the two-plane section was within 25 miles of Barbers Point, they climbed to the prescribed altitude of 1,500 feet. The time was five minutes past eight.

The flyers noticed two distinct columns of smoke ahead of them, but thought little about it. Smoke clouds were routine matters in the islands, when it was the custom to set fire to sugar cane fields during the harvest seasons. The leaves of the plants burned away, leaving the stalks for those doing the harvesting.

The crew noticed four ships off the entrance to Pearl Harbor, but quickly identified them as American. They did notice, however, what looked to be artillery shell splashes in the water off the entrance to Pearl Harbor, and dangerously close to the shore. They were certain, since it was Sunday, that target practice was not underway. Maybe some Army Coast Artillery battery commander had gone mad.

As they approached the shoreline, they now saw that the smoke columns were coming from the Pearl Harbor area and that there were smoke balls over the area — those were flak bursts, which were causing the splashes in the sea. Pearl Harbor was under air attack.

Lt. Dickinson signalled his wingman to close up the formation and to charge the guns. The pilot charged his fixed twin .50s in the nose and Miller readied his twin .30s mounted on the circular steel track in the rear cockpit.

When the two dive bombers got within three miles of the shoreline, they spotted a large four-engined patrol plane emerging from the smoke cloud. It did not appear to be an American plane, so the two planes began a climb of 6,000 feet to intercept the large plane. While still at some distance, the patrol plane must have seen the two planes approaching, as it ducked back into the smoke cloud. The Dauntlesses followed, but were unable to locate the huge plane and gave up the chase.

As they emerged from the cloud, so did two Japanese fighters, diving on the scout planes from above. On the first pass, the wingman's plane was hit, at first smoking, then bursting into yellow flame. As the fast moving Zero overshot the two SBDs, Lt. Dickinson got a look at the insignia, confirming that they were indeed Japanese fighters. He thought the red disc on the white wing looked like a fried egg with a red yolk. He fired his nose guns at the enemy but missed.

Below them, the wingman's plane was spinning toward the ground, with one parachute blossoming just before it hit the earth. The pilot had been able to bail out, but the gunner, whose exit was hampered by the machine gun track that encircled him, was unable to get out.

Quickly following the first attack, another five Japanese fighters began attacking the SBD of Dickinson and Miller, this time concentrating on the lone scout plane. Miller fired away as Dickinson used hard turns to attempt to spoil the aim of the attackers. Then Miller called to pilot that he had been hit, but that he thought he had shot down one of the enemy fighters. Dickinson got a glimpse of the flaming enemy plane that his gunner had downed.

Now the Japanese pressed the attack with even more fury, tracers zipping by the SBD. Finally, the left wing of the SBD was hit with the explosive and incendiary rounds of cannon fire, and flames from the wing fuel tank erupted. Dickinson called to Miller to see if he was all right. Miller answered that he had expended all of his six cans of ammunition, and just as he said that he uttered a loud scream. Dickinson could not get a further reply from him.

Then, the controls of the SBD failed, shot away by the enemy planes. As the scout plane went out of control, Dickinson called to his gunner to bail out, but Miller did not reply. Dickinson jumped from under 1,000 feet of altitude and landed safely.

Miller died on the first day of the war. He did, though, get credit for an aerial victory, which was corroborated by a Marine captain near Ewa Field, over which the air battle that began World War II for the United States took place.

6. Tokyo

Corporal David J. Thatcher, a gunner in the first offensive raid of World War II by Army Air Force units, or by any American flying unit, distinguished himself in that attack in a manner far beyond his 19 years. Thatcher was the gunner-engineer in the B-25 piloted by Lieut. Ted W. Lawson on the Doolittle raid of Tokyo. Designed to avenge the attack by the Japanese on Pearl Harbor, 16 Army Air Force B-25s launched from the U.S. Navy carrier *Hornet* struck industrial and military targets in the Tokyo area and in other industrial areas in a surprise attack that reeled the Japanese. While small, that attack sent the message to Japanese authorities that their homeland was not invulnerable to attack, as they had assumed, and changed the way the enemy used his forces in the Pacific. He could no longer assume that his offensive forces could operate as freely as they had in the Pacific, and some of his military effort had to be diverted to homeland defense. Thatcher, whose home town was Bridger, Montana, would do his part during and following the raid.

In the days and weeks after the Pearl Harbor debacle, American civil and military leaders pondered how to strike back at the Japanese. President Franklin D. Roosevelt, himself, badgered his military advisors to come up with a plan to punish the Japanese. There were no bases near enough to Japan from which land-based bombers could strike. And Navy carriers, with their shorter-range fighters and bombers, would have to approach the islands so closely that there would be grave risk of losing them.

According to some accounts it was a Navy captain, and not even a flyer, who came up with the idea of launching longer range AAF bombers from a Navy carrier to do the job. Another Navy captain, a flyer, roughed out the details and decided it was feasible. Chief of Naval Operations, Admiral Ernest J. King, on whose staff the two officers worked, sent the two to AAF chief, Lt. Gen. H. H. Arnold, to discuss the possibilities. Arnold was immediately enthusiastic over the project and he and King agreed that their services would work together to bring it about.

General Arnold picked for his project officer a flyer of some renown on his staff whom he used as a trouble shooter for special projects. His name was James H. Doolittle and his credentials for a job that required both superb flying abilities as well as technical know-how were first-rate. Lt. Col. Doolittle had entered the Air Service in World War I, but too late to see combat in France. Following the war he participated in all sorts of daring flying endeavors, setting speed records, winning trophies for air races and acrobatics, pioneering navigational routes and developing blind flying techniques and equipment. He also received one of the first Doctor of Science in Aeronautics degrees ever awarded by the Massachusetts Institute of Technology. In the years between 1930 and 1940, as a civilian, he managed the aviation department of the Shell Oil Company. Recalled to duty as the war clouds gathered, one of his special projects as a trouble shooter for General Arnold was to evaluate the performance of the Martin B-26 Marauder, which had the reputation as a "widow-maker." He proved that the airplane was a solid performer if pilots were properly trained, and the B-26 went on to a distinguished combat record in World War II. Obviously, here was the man to work out how to fly a medium bomber from the deck of an aircraft carrier.

Doolittle was charged by General Arnold to select an AAF bomber that could fly 2,000 miles yet be able to take off in 500 feet with a bomb load of 2,000 pounds. In addition, it had to be able to take off in a narrow area not more than 75 feet wide. This narrowed the choices to one aircraft, the B-25 Mitchell, one of two proposed by Doolittle. Only then was Doolittle told that the 75 foot-wide restriction was to enable the bombers to clear the superstructure of an aircraft carrier.

The aircraft being modified for the raid were 24 new B-25B models. When the members of the 17th Bomb Group picked up the planes at the modification center they thought the extra fuel tanks installed in the bomb bay and in the crawlway were to give them more endurance for their mission of sub-patrol at their new base in Columbia, South Carolina.

The B-25B was the first Mitchell to come equipped with power turrets. Previous models used three flexible .30-caliber guns and one .50-caliber mounted in the tail. The B-25B had one .30-caliber in the nose and two .50-caliber turrets in the waist, each with two guns. There was no tail gun because the upper and lower waist turrets could cover the rear. The upper turret was a direct fire unit with a Plexiglass dome. The ventral turret was sighted with a periscope with the gunner firing from a kneeling position. The lower turret was fully retractable, the guns slipping into notches in the fuselage.

Corporal Thatcher was among those of the 17th Bomb Group and 89th Recce Squadron who were approached to see if they would volunteer for a hazardous combat mission. They were told no other details. Thatcher volunteered, as did all other members of the 24 crews that were selected. Crewmembers were not hand-picked for their skills, but rather because they were among the most experienced in the B-25 bomber, which in

January 1942 was relatively new to the AAF. They were average AAF flight crews.

At Columbia the volunteers were formed into crews, and Thatcher was assigned to Lieut. Lawson's. Other members of the crew were Lieut. Dean Davenport, of Portland, Oregon, co-pilot; Lieut. Charles L. McClure, of University City, Missouri, navigator; and Lieut. Bob Clever, of Portland, Oregon, bombardier. Pilot Ted Lawson, in his book, *Thirty Seconds Over Tokyo*, described gunner Thatcher as, "only nineteen, but very quiet and industrious." Lawson and the rest of his crew would owe their lives to this quiet and industrious teenager not many weeks in the future.

The crews in Thatcher's squadron left Columbia, flying to Eglin Field, in the panhandle of Florida not far from Pensacola. There they met volunteer crews from the other squadrons of the 17th Bomb Group. There were 24 crews and aircraft in all. On the 3rd of March, 1942, their leader, Lt. Col. Doolittle arrived. He gathered the crews together and told them that what they would be training for would be the most dangerous thing they had ever done, and that if they wanted to drop out it would be all right. None of the crew members did. Doolittle told the men that he could not at that time tell them what their mission would be and that it was highly secret and they were not to discuss it with anyone, even among themselves. He said that the crews would get the idea of what they were in for as soon as they began training.

The first inkling came when the training officer turned out to be a naval officer, Lt. Henry L. Miller, a flight instructor at Pensacola Naval Air Station. His pupose was to instruct the pilots in the techniques of making short field takeoffs. The training was done at a remote auxiliary field far from curious eyes. White lines and flags were placed at intervals of 200, 300 and 500 feet along the runway for the pilots to gauge their distances. The goal was to have each pilot be able to take off at least two times in 700-750 feet with a plane loaded to 31,000 pounds gross weight. This weight included 1,141 gallons of fuel and 2,000 pounds of bombs.

While they were training, further modifications were made to the B-25s. The lower turrets, which continually malfunctioned and jammed, were removed. This saved 600 pounds and allowed the space to be replaced with a 40-gallon fuel tank. The upper turrets gave a lot of trouble as well, but were retained.

Then the Norden bombsights were removed, Doolittle telling the crews that it was inevitable that some of the ships would fall into enemy hands

12th Air Force B-25Js in action over Italy in 1945

and the super-secret bombsight could be compromised. Besides, at the bombing altitude at which the mission would be flown, 1,500 feet, Norden sights would be of little value.

To replace the Norden sights, the mission's bombing and gunnery officer, Capt. Charles R. Greening, designed a simple, low-level sight, called by some the "twenty-cent bomb sight," but which Greening called the "Mark Twain." Greening also installed in the tail of each bomber two dummy .50-caliber machine gun barrels made of wood to give "protection" from the rear. Each airplane was also equipped with a strike camera, either a still or a movie version.

The crew training was intensive, flying from seven in the morning until ten at night. Most of the training had to do with the short takeoffs and low level bombing both in the daytime and after dark. Thatcher and the other gunners got almost no chance to practice live gunnery with the turrets, which were new to them. What little "dry" training they could do showed them that the turrets malfunctioned often. Some pilots could make a takeoff in less than 400 feet at airspeeds of between 55 and 60 mph, instead of the usual 80 to 90. Toward the end of March after about three weeks of training, their final test came on a practice mission from Eglin to Fort Myers, Florida, then across the Gulf of Mexico at low level to Houston, then returning to Eglin.

If any of the B-25 crew members doubted what sort of a mission they would be on, it was dispelled by lectures they received from their Navy instructor, Lt. Miller. He talked to them about shipboard courtesy and etiquette, and even explained how to take a shower bath without wasting precious water. He gave the AAF flyers a complete glossary of nautical terms as well.

With no previous warning, Lawson, Thatcher and the rest of the crew were awakened one morning in late March at about three o'clock and were told they would be leaving Eglin at 11 a.m. Together with four other aircraft, the *Ruptured Duck*, as Lawson's crew had christened it, headed west. They were ordered to fly at low level all the way and to keep a close check on their fuel consumption. After stops at San Antonio, Phoenix and March Field in California, the planes arrived at the AAF servicing depot, McClellan Field, near Sacramento, California. There the planes were further modified, receiving new propellers and giving up much of their radio equipment. Doolittle explained to the crews that where they were going radios would not be needed. Lawson correctly guessed, after hearing his leader, that their mission would involve the Japanese.

For the few days they were at McClellan they continued practicing full-flap takeoffs from small, deserted airports. Then came the order to fly to Alameda Naval Air Station on San Francisco Bay. As the *Ruptured Duck* approached the field, the navigator, Lt. McClure, asked the pilots to fly under the San Francisco Bay Bridge, so that he could film it with his movie camera. Co-pilot Davenport said that the Pan American pilots did it all the time in their clippers, so Lawson obliged. Then, as they approached Alameda, they could see an aircraft carrier at its dock, with three B-25s already loaded on the deck. Someone remarked on the intercom how small the carrier looked.

At Alameda, 16 of the 24 B-25s were loaded on the aircraft carrier *Hornet*. Those crews whose planes were not loaded were very disappointed, but some of them got to go aboard the vessel as spare crews. The next morning the ship departed Alameda, and flyers still did not know what their destination would be.

Then, in the afternoon of the first day out, April 2, 1942, Doolittle called all the crews together. They were finally going to know their destiny. It was Japan itself, Doolittle told them. They were going to bomb targets in Tokyo and four other Japanese cities: Yokohama, Osaka, Kobe and

Nagoya. They would take off from the *Hornet*, hit their targets, then fly on to small airfields in the part of China that was not occupied by the Japanese. There they would be refueled and fly on to Chungking, where the planes would be based to take part in the war in the far east.

During the next two weeks the crews studied their charts and maps, memorized their targets, computed fuel consumption and worked on their airplanes. White lines were painted down the left side of the deck, one for the nose wheel and one for the left main wheel, to guide the pilots on the takeoff roll to insure that the right wing would not strike the carrier's superstructure.

At long last, the B-25 gunners got to practice shooting their turret guns. Kites which were flown from the stern to allow the carrier's anti-aircraft crews to get some practice also served as targets for Thatcher and his fellow gunners.

In one ceremony, duly recorded by Navy photographers, Doolittle fastened some medals the Japanese had awarded American military men during peacetime to one of the 500-pound bombs that would drop on targets in Japan. Admiral Halsey also took part in the media event.

The bomb load for most of the planes consisted of three 500-pound general purpose bombs and one 500-pound bomb of incendiary clusters. Also carried aboard would be ten five-gallon cans of fuel to give the planes an extra 50 gallons to extend their range.

As the day neared for the mission, Doolittle called the crews together for one last chance to back out of the mission. No one did. Then the first pilots were asked if they wanted to make any changes in their crews. One pilot asked that his co-pilot be replaced by one of the spare pilots aboard.

On the day before the launch, the upper turret on the *Ruptured Duck* went sour. The crew worked feverishly to get it operational, but were out of luck. They would find themselves flying the mission with a defective turret, their main defensive protection against what they felt would be certain attacks from Japanese fighters.

The plan for the raid had been to try to get within 450 miles of Japan, launch the planes at dusk, bomb at night, then recover the aircraft at Chinese bases after sunrise. Meanwhile the *Hornet* and the other ships could escape under the cover of darkness. Doolittle felt that they could launch at 550 miles from their targets, but that anything beyond 650 miles was considered to be too far to have a reasonable chance of mission success.

Their plan was spoiled by a Japanese picket ship which spotted the carrier task force on the morning of the planned launch day, April 18, 1942. They were still 800 miles from their targets and ten hours from the planned launch time. But, the safety of the task force had been compromised, so Admiral Halsey gave the signal to launch the B-25s anyway. Within about 30 minutes, Doolittle, the first to launch, rolled down the 467 feet of tossing wet carrier deck and took off without a hitch. Lawson's plane was seventh to go, and he and the crew made it all right in spite of the fact that Lawson made the takeoff with his flaps up!

For the next two or three hours, the planes droned just above the wavetops at a sluggish, but fuel-conserving speed. The profile of the flight was to stay low, then as the target neared, to climb to 1,500 feet, drop the bombs in trail, the incendiary last, then dive down to the deck once more to escape.

Lawson asked Thatcher to test his turret, which was electrically powered, to see if it was operational. It wasn't, but the guns fired, aimed straight back to the rear. There was an emergency power system, controlled by the pilot, but it was not operational either, the first time they tested it. Later, Thatcher was able to get some power to the turret by the emergency system, but they needed to conserve the system and agreed not to turn it on unless they were being attacked.

When they finally arrived over land Lawson and his crew expected to be intercepted. But, for a while, they saw no other aircraft. Then, suddenly, directly ahead and coming right at them were six Zeros, in two Vs of three each. The fighters were flying at about 1,500 feet. On they came, and passed directly over the bomber. Then as the second V passed over the B-25 one of the fighters broke from the formation and started to dive at the Americans. Thatcher watched him — Lawson asked Thatcher if he wanted the emergency power turned on. Thatcher replied to wait a little longer. Then, just as suddenly, the fighter disappeared and Thatcher could no longer see it.

As they approached their target in Tokyo, there were no enemy planes in sight, but as they climbed to their bombing altitude they received some flak bursts. The gunners were leading the bomber too much and the shells exploded harmlessly ahead of them. Then it was time to drop the bombs on the target, a steel-smelter. After letting the bombs go, it was back down of the deck, still expecting a cloud of Zeros at any minute. None came. As they pulled away from the target they could see smoke starting to rise from it.

Then they spotted six Japanese biplane pursuits, flying in a tight formation and well above the bomber. Thatcher waited for them to dive on the bomber, but the pursuits just maintained formation and ignored the B-25.

Now over the water, Thatcher got a chance to use his gun. A large, armed yacht loomed ahead and Lawson told Thatcher to give it a burst after they passed over it. Lawson pulled the nose up to give Thatcher a clear shot, and the young gunner raked the deck with his .50-calibers.

As they turned west over the China Sea, the weather began to deteriorate, with showers and squalls. Lawson had to fly the bomber at less than 50 feet to stay out of the clouds. As they drew close to the Chinese coast the weather grew thicker and Lawson was kept busy dodging the outer islands hilltops. Darkness, too, was approaching. When they reached what they thought was the mainland, they could find no identifying landmarks along the coast. Finally, Lawson had to climb to get over the weather when suddenly there appeared a wide beach that looked as if it could support a landing. Lawson felt they could land there, spend the night, then continue on the next day with the 100 gallons that remained in the plane's tanks.

He dropped the bomber down and dragged the beach — it was clear and smooth. As Lawson made his landing approach to the beach, the engines, for a reason he could not explain, both quit suddenly. The plane hit the water with such a jolt that both pilots were catapulted through the windshield and the bombardier was thrown through the nose Plexiglass. Thatcher, in the tail, was bounced around considerably and was unconscious for a short while, but his heavy flying clothing protected him from all but a bump on the head.

The plane went down about a quarter of a mile from the beach and in about ten to fifteen feet of water. Somehow, all the crew members made it to the beach, shivering in the cold and rain, and bleeding from their various wounds. Lawson was in the worst shape and would lose a leg. Thatcher was in the best physical shape.

As they lay on the beach, suddenly Thatcher, the only crew member to have retained his .45-caliber pistol, stood and pointed the gun over Lawson's head and asked if he should shoot them. Lawson rolled over and saw two men standing on a small cliff staring down at them. Lawson told Thatcher not to shoot, but wasn't certain why he said that. They turned out to be Chinese, two of a number who would help the crew back to safety.

The crew was taken by the Chinese to a house for the night, a primitive shelter that did little to ease the miseries of the flyers. All except Thatcher were seriously injured, and it was he who helped with first aid. He also went back to the plane to see if he could find the first aid kit, but high tide had submerged the craft. In the morning he made another trip to the plane, but could salvage only a carton of cigarettes and a lifebelt. He went to the plane even at the risk of being captured, for the Japanese had outposts in the area within three miles of the house where the crew stayed. It was Thatcher who talked the Chinese into carrying his four injured crewmates to safety, avoiding the Japanese outposts and once hiding in a junk from a Japanese gunboat.

In the official War Department communique issued a year after the raid, Corporal Thatcher was cited for his initiative and courage in tending to the injured crew and for arranging their movement to safety. It credits Thatcher for saving the crew from capture or death and selflessly administering to their needs day and night until proper care could be gotten for them. Thatcher eventually joined another crew in returning to the U.S., because his crewmates could not travel for months after their crash. He received the Silver Star medal, the third ranking decoration for action in combat, as well as the Distinguished Flying Cross and the Air Medal.

Tech. Sgt. Eldred V. Scott was one of three gunners on the raid who may have shot down a Japanese plane, although none could be confirmed. Scott, from Atlanta, Georgia, attended high school in Phoenix, Arizona. He enlisted in the Army (Infantry) and later transferred to the Air Corps and graduated from Mechanics School.

Scott was a crew member on the B-25 *The Whirling Dervish*, piloted by Lt. Harold F. Watson. He was busy right after takeoff from the *Hornet* because the extra fuel tank that had been installed in place of the lower turret began leaking. This caused him to transfer fuel from that tank to the main as soon as possible. Then he checked the guns in his upper turret and found that the hydraulic charger was out of commission. he removed the charger and charged the guns by hand.

Then he began opening the five gallon cans of fuel and poured the contents into the turret tank and transferred the fuel to the wing tanks. When this was completed he cut holes in the cans and threw them overboard. Col. Doolittle had warned the crews not to dump the cans one at a time because the trail of floating cans could lead the Japanese back to the *Hornet* and the other ships.

When *The Whirling Dervish* reached the coast, Scott was impressed with the beauty of the countryside. It looked to him just like the pictures in his school geography book.

The bomber passed over an airfield where rows of bombers were lined up and the propellers of some fighters were turning as if they were standing alert. Then Scott spotted five biplanes in the air. But they appeared to be trainers, so he did not fire at them. When they were on the outskirts of Tokyo the flak started. It was intense but not very accurate. The pilot dropped the bomber to low level to escape it. Then it was time for the bomb run and they pulled up to the 1,500 foot bombing altitude for bombs away.

Scott watched where their bombs hit and they were right on target. As he was looking back he saw tracers arcing toward the B-25. Then he saw that the tracers were coming from a fighter which was below and behind them, about 100 yards away. He opened fire, but his sight was fogged up, so he had to rely on his own tracers to tell him whether he was getting the range of the fighter. Evidently he was, becuase after a long burst the fighter fell off on its left wing and he never saw it again. Scott believes he downed the plane, but he could not be absolutely certain.

Outbound from the target the plane flew near some cruisers and battle-ships, which opened fire on the bomber. Later, Scott fired at some fishing boats but did not think he hit them.

Like the B-25 of Thatcher, Scott's plane ran into bad weather as it approached the coast of China. After 15½ hours in the air, Scott's crew bailed out in fog and darkness. Before jumping Scott stuffed some cigarettes and a pint of whiskey in his jacket. His parachute opened all right and caught in the top of a tree. Because of the fog and darkness he could not see how high he was off the ground. So he lit a cigarette and dropped it, watching the glow of it as it fell. It disappeared into the murk. He decided to remain in his harness until daylight. He sipped on the bottle of whiskey for awhile, then fell asleep.

In the morning he could see that the tree he was in overhung a high cliff, so his prudence had paid off. He easily climbed down, found shelter with some Chinese, was reunited with his crew and they eventually made their way to safety.

Tech. Sgt. Scott was commissioned a first lieutenant in April, 1943 and became an aircraft maintenance officer. He made a career of the Air Force and retired as a Lieut. Colonel in 1959.

☆　　☆　　☆　　☆

Sgt. Melvin J. Gardner of Mesa, Arizona was credited in the official communique with downing two enemy fighters, but there is some doubt about whether they actually were downed.

Like Scott, Gardner attended Airplane Mechanic's School at Chanute Field, Illinois. He was assigned to the 34th Bomb Squadron at March Field, California before joining the Doolittle force.

On the *Hornet*, Gardner was a crew member of the B-25 *Hari Carrier*. Their primary target was a refinery at Yokohama, but as they approached it they were jumped by four fighters. one of them made a pass at them but missed. When the second made a pass, Gardner gave it a few short bursts from his turret and the fighter left. By now the pilot had full throttles on the B-25 and they ran away from the other fighters. Then they saw that a great number of airplanes were converging on them, so the decision was made to go to the alternate target, another oil refinery and tank farm. They stayed low and hit the refinery with incendiary clusters from 600 feet rather than 1,500 feet. They were rewarded with the sight of flames and smoke when the bombs hit the target.

As they headed out over Tokyo Bay another enemy fighter made a firing pass at the B-25 and this time Gardner's rounds found the mark, as the fighter pulled up into a steep climb and began smoking heavily.

Like most of the other crews, Gardner's bailed out over the China mainland. Gardner sprained both ankles upon landing, but soon linked up with the rest of the crew and they made their way to safety.

Sgt. Gardner elected to stay in the China-Burma-India theater to fly more combat. He was killed in action in June 1942 returning from a bombing mission to Lashio, Burma.

☆　　☆　　☆　　☆

Staff Sgt. Edwin W. Horton was another gunner/mechanic who is believed to have downed two enemy fighters on the raid. Horton, from North Eastham, Massachusetts, first served in the field artillery at Schofield Barracks, Hawaii. On his second enlistment he joined the 95th Bomb Squadron at March Field, California before joining the Tokyo Raiders. He was a graduate of the Gun Turret Maintenance School, the Aircraft Armorer Course as well as the Aircraft Mechanic's School.

Horton was a last-minute substitution on the crew of Lt. Richard O. Joyce. Because of the considerable trouble the turrets were giving the Raiders, Horton, because of his training and extensive experience, was pressed into service.

Horton was the first in his bomber to spot an enemy aircraft. Just one-and-one-half hours after taking off from the *Hornet*, he sighted a large patrol plane directly ahead and high. The pilot just added some power and they were soon out of range of any trouble. Horton did not fire at it because the range was not close enough.

The target of Horton's B-25 was the Japan Special Steel Company, which they hit with their first two 500 pounders. The other bomb and the incendiary cluster were dropped in the industrial section in the Shiba Ward. Then the flak became intense and accurate. Horton's plane was one of the few that sustained flak damage.

Leaving the target they were jumped by nine Zeros. The pilot gave the Mitchell full power and dove away from the attack, skimming the water. Then, three Kates joined in the chase, but at 330 mph, the B-25 easily out-ran them. The Zeros did not give up, although they did not seem to want to press the attack. Horton fired at them at intervals to keep them away. Crossing some mountains, they lost the nine Zeros.

Then, suddenly, a single fighter appeared alongside them and a bit high. Horton opened up on it as did the bombardier in the nose. Horton believes he knocked the Japanese plane down, but cannot be certain.

Just when they thought they had seen the last of fighters three more fighters jumped the bomber. This time the pilot quickly pulled up into some clouds and they eluded any attack.

Horton's crew bailed out over China, linked up and all made it to safety. Like Gardner, Horton remained in the China-Burma-India theater, serving there until July, 1943. Horton remained in the Air Force and retired as a master sergeant in 1960.

☆   ☆   ☆   ☆

In all, nine of the 16 Tokyo Raiders were intercepted by Japanese fighters. None was shot down by the enemy, either by fighters or by flak. Only one, however, made a safe, wheels-down landing. That one landed in Russia, after experiencing excessive fuel consumption. The crew and the airplane were both interned because Russia was not at war with Japan. About a year later the crew managed to escape into Iran by arranging bribes.

Eleven crews, including that of Doolittle, bailed out while four attempted crash landings. Only one crewman, gunner Corporal Leland

D. Faktor, Plymouth, Iowa, died in the bailouts. Eight men were captured, and three of these were executed by the Japanese after a "trial." One of those executed, Sgt. Harold A. Spatz of Lebo, Kansas, was a gunner. Sixty-four men made it to safety.

The raid, while small, did cause the Japanese to think again about their defenses and to shift some of their strategy. It caused them to withhold four army fighter groups for home defense when they were urgently needed in the Solomons. It could be said that the success of the allies in that area may have been partly because of the Tokyo raid. Most of all the raid raised morale in the United States at a time when U.S. forces had suffered devastating setbacks in Hawaii, the Philippines and other areas of the Pacific.

7. Midway

Six months before, the Japanese had dealt the military might of the United States a serious blow, decimating the aerial strength of the Army Air Forces in the Pacific theater and crippling the surface fleet of the Navy at Pearl Harbor. Now, the Japanese hoped to finish off what was left of the American forces by drawing them into a battle for the island of Midway.

Fortunately for the United States, the Navy's aircraft carrier force had escaped untouched, as none of the carriers assigned to the Pacific Fleet happened to be in port on December 7th, 1941. But now, an inferior force of American craft and aircraft was to face a superior Japanese force as it was spotted on June 3, 1942 by a Navy PBY Catalina within 500 miles of Midway.

Three Japanese forces, under the command of Admiral Isoroku Yamamoto, approached the island from three directions. From the northwest came a task force that consisted of four large aircraft carriers, two battleships, ten cruisers and 12 destroyers. From the southwest approached the landing forces aboard 12 troop transports, escorted by two battleships, ten cruisers, one aircraft carrier and 20 destroyers. Admiral Yamamoto was in a third task force consisting of three battleships, one aircraft carrier, three cruisers and 13 destroyers. Excluding the troop transports, the entire fleet consisted of 74 combat vessels.

The smaller American fleet included but three aircraft carriers, to be pitted against the aircraft on alert aboard six Japanese carriers.

The air defenses on Midway itself were of dubious value. A small fighter force of Marine F4F Wildcats would be the main challenge to the crack Zeros of the Japanese fleet. Another larger force of Marine Brewster F2A Buffalo fighters would prove no obstacle to the Japanese. Another group of completely obsolescent Vought SB2U Vindicator dive bombers would be no threat to the Japanese. There was potential for destructive power in the presence of 17 B-17E Flying Fortresses of the Army Air Forces, but the crews were inexperienced and had not completed their training when they were thrown into the fray.

Much of the strike potential on the island was placed on a small force of ten torpedo bombers. Six were Navy Grumman TBF Avengers, which would get their first taste of combat. The other four were Army Air Force Martin B-26 Marauder medium bombers which had been modified to carry torpedos suspended from their bellies, with crews trained by the

Navy in torpedo launching tactics. Two of the B-26s were from the 38th Bomb Group and two were from the 22nd Bomb Group.

On June 3rd, first into the battle were the B-17s, whose crews reported they inflicted substantial damage on the Japanese fleet. In fact, only one bomb hit one ship, a troop transport, starting a fire which was quickly put out.

In the dark early morning hours, four PBY Catalinas, carrying torpedoes, found the invasion fleet, using radar, and slammed a torpedo into a tanker. After also strafing the decks of some transport ships, the awkward amphibians managed to withdraw to safety, unscathed.

As June 4, 1942 dawned, the American strike force from the island rushed into battle. B-17s went aloft, Marine fighters and dive bombers took to the air, and the torpedo bombers hurried into action. The targets assigned to the six TBF torpedo bombers and the four modified B-26 Marauders were the aircraft carriers of the Japanese task forces.

The Marauders flew in a diamond formation, about 800 feet above the water. In the slot position was the B-26 of First Lieutenant James P. Muri of the 22nd Bomb Group. Shortly after leaving the runway at Midway, crews of the torpedo strike force sighted the enemy fleet in the distance. But between the attacking force and their targets were swarms of Zero fighters that had set up a defensive shield for their task force. The Marauder gunners called out a force of about 18 Zeros that could be seen orbiting at 12,000 to 15,000 feet ready to pounce on the speeding bombers.

But, before the enemy fighters could attack, the depressed guns of the battleships began to find the range of the approaching B-26s. When the four bombers dropped down close to the water to dodge the flak, the big 16-inch guns of the capital ships sent of towers of water in front of the bombers, requiring the pilots to make turns to avoid them.

Now six Zeros joined the fray, attacking with fury and ignoring the defensive fire being returned by the gunners in the B-26s. The bomber pilots now had to jink and slam their aircraft around to try to spoil the aim of the Japanese fighter pilots. The gunners aboard Lt. Muri's plane were slammed around in their positions, but stuck to their weapons.

Staff Sergeant John J. Gogoj, in the upper turret of Muri's plane, was first to feel the wrath of the savage Japanese attack. A Zero found the range of his turret and the Plexiglas cover over the turret exploded in a shower of plastic shards that gouged into Gogoj's face. He fell to the floor of the bomber from the impact of the hit on his position. Stunned, he

Martin B-26s of the 322nd Bomb Group (449th Bomb Squadron) on a mission over Europe. At the time (August 9, 1943) the 322nd was still part of the 8th Air Force, but two months later the unit was transferred to the 9th Air Force

gathered his senses and, struggling against the careening maneuvering of the airplane, climbed back into his turret.

As he swung his twin .50-calibers to meet the attack of a Zero, once more the turret was hit by cannon fire from the fighters. This attack put the turret out of commission, with hits on the guns themselves and on the wiring for the power unit. Sergeant Gogoj, though, remained at his position thinking to bluff the attackers that the manned turret still had defensive capabilities.

Then, yet another attack by the fighters found the range, and a machine-gun slug struck Gogoj in the forehead and stayed there. Again he fell to the floor, writhing in pain.

He plucked the slug from his forehead, opened his first-aid kit, stuffed sulfa powder into the bleeding wound and fashioned a patch to halt the bleeding. Now, thoroughly battered from his wounds and from being slammed around in the careening bomber, Gogoj nevertheless managed to crawl back into his turret to continue his bluff against the Zeros, and there he stayed!

Gogoj was not the only gunner in trouble. The tail gunner, PFC Earl D. Ashley caught five bullets in his leg and hip from a determined Japanese fighter pilot who streamed a long burst directly into the tail. Ashley, out of commission, wanted to let someone else man the critical tailgun position and take over his single .50-caliber weapon. As he lurched forward from his tail position, Sergeant F. Melo, who operated the two .30-caliber machine guns on each side of the lower aft fuselage, attempted to assist him before taking up the tail gun position. At that moment a slug ripped through the fuselage and grazed Melo's forehead, so he too was wounded.

Nevertheless, Melo started toward the tail gun position, when he was again hit in the right arm. Two other spent slugs broke his glasses in his pocket.

Again Melo struggled toward the tail gun, but when he was finally in position the gun jammed after the first round was fired at an oncoming Zero. He managed to clear the jam, and began pouring lead at the attackers.

Suddenly, though, he became aware of flame behind him. Tracers from the Japanese rounds had set a cushion on fire. As it blazed, Melo attempted to throw it out a hatch in the tail, only to see it sucked back into the fuselage. As it came back in, it caught his flying clothing on fire as well as another cushion. He had to beat the flames of both out with his bare hands.

Melo tried to call his pilot to tell him about the fire, and another which had started up, but the interphone system had been shot out by the enemy fighters. Although badly wounded, Melo made his way forward through the bomb bay to tell his pilot, Lt. Muri, about the fire and that everyone in the rear was wounded. Just after he did so he collapsed.

Realizing how vulnerable the bomber was without manned defensive guns, the copilot, Lieutenant Pren L. Moore left his seat and rushed to the rear of the bomber, first giving the wounded men sulfanilamide tablets, then throwing the blazing seat cushions overboard before manning the tail gun himself. Just as he did, he saw another Marauder flame and hit the water.

Muri spotted an aircraft carrier and began his torpedo run. The carrier maneuvered to give the oncoming bomber the least exposed approach to a run. At the signal, Second Lieutenant Russell H. Johnson, the bombardier, pulled the release on the torpedo and the weapon headed for the starboard bow of the carrier. Now, the carrier loomed large in Muri's windshield, and he pulled back on the controls as he struggled to get above the huge vessel. As they zoomed over the mast of the carrier, the crew could see the flag of the rising sun. Bombardier Russell, now manning the single .30-caliber machine gun in the nose, hosed a long burst at the carrier's island scattering some 50 to 75 men standing on the island.

Lightened of its load, the B-26 began to pick up speed and put some distance between itself and its attackers. But, vibrations caused by holes in the plane's propellers made Muri throttle back. Landing would be a problem because hydraulic fluid had been lost, and Muri expected he would have no brakes. The landing was successful, although not pretty. After receiving medical aid, the crew went back to their plane, #1391, to assess the damage. They quit counting after they had tallied up more than 500 bullet and shrapnel holes.

Muri and his crew were one of two B-26 crews that survived of the four that attacked the Japanese fleet. Of the six TBF Avenger torpedo planes that went out, only one made it back to Midway. None of the ten scored a hit on the Japanese vessel.

Damage to the Japanese by the B-26s consisted of two downed Zeros by tail gunner T/Sgt. Raynard S. White, flying in the crew of the Marauder leader, Capt. James F. Collins, Jr., of the 38th Bomb Group, whose plane also made it back to Midway. Gunners manning the B-17s accounted for eight more Zeros downed.

The torpedo planes form the U.S. aircraft carrier *Hornet*, going in low against the Japanese fleet as did those from Midway, fared no better. Fifteen Douglas TBD-1 Devastators went in low and slow and none came back. They scored no hits. It was the same story for 26 other torpedo bombers — no hits and 20 of them didn't make it back to their carriers.

While the Zeros were engaging the low flying American attackers just above the waves, the air above the enemy fleet was free for any who wanted it. Who wanted it were the Douglas SBD-3 Dauntless dive bombers from the U.S. carriers *Enterprise* and *Yorktown*. Diving at near-vertical angles from 17,000 feet the SBDs concentrated on the four aircraft carriers of the enemy.

Manning the twin .30-caliber guns in the rear seat of one of these attackers was a young radioman/gunner named Adkins. He flew with his pilot, Ensign W. R. Pittman; both were assigned to VS-6, Scouting Squadron Six, operating from the *Enterprise*.

Adkins was a good example of what feats can be performed by mere mortals when engaged in combat. Combat sometimes brings out in people the ability to do things they would not ordinarily feel they were capable of. Sometimes this manifests itself in a super-human exhibition of physical strength; other times it surfaces in actions that are pure reflex rather than reasoned behavior.

Adkins' twin .30-caliber guns that protected the rear of his SBD were mounted on a circular steel track inside of which he rode. To install or remove the gun assembly required the strength of three men of a plane crew, as the guns weighed 175 pounds and were awkward to handle.

Adkins was of average size and strength, but evidently when his crew mounted his guns they were incorrectly installed. Adkins found this out when his pilot rolled into his dive to attack the Japanese carrier *Kaga*. The gun assembly came loose from the track, and Adkins, who was now on his back in the steep dive, quickly grabbed the guns and hung on to them. After the bomb was released and the SBD pulled out of its vertical dive, the plane of Pittman and Adkins was jumped by a Japanese fighter. Adkins stood up in the rear cockpit holding the assembly and fired one of the guns as if it had been a shotgun, one hand clutching the barrel which rapidly became blistering hot. Adkins, whose actions were witnessed by several of the pilots of his squadron, kept firing until the enemy plane was downed.

When his SBD returned to the *Enterprise*, several men helped remove the gun assembly from the cockpit. Then they dared Adkins to try to pick it up. Much as he tried, he was unable to lift the guns from the deck.

While gunners in the torpedo planes were dueling with the Japanese Zeros at wave height, the dive bombers manned by gunner Adkins, pilot Pittman and their shipmates were relatively free to plant their bombs on the flight decks of the Japanese carriers. Two carriers were sunk in the early afternoon of June 4th, one with the help of a torpedo from an American submarine. Another two survived the night but sank early on June 5th, one after having been strafed by the gunners of six B-17s which were enroute from Oahu to Midway. The torpedo planes and their crews may not have sunk any enemy ships, but the diversion they provided in drawing fire from flak batteries and Zeros allowed the dive bombers to deliver their ordnance.

The defeat of the Japanese invasion force at Midway was of monumental importance to the naval war in the Pacific. Never again were the Japanese able to mount such an attack. Lost were the cream of the crop of Japanese pilots and aircrews as well as four capital aircraft carriers, the most powerful of the Japanese fleet. Losses in numbers were significant. Upwards of 3,500 men died, 20 ships went down and 275 aircraft were lost to the Japanese. On the American side, one aircraft carrier, the

Yorktown, went down, along with one destroyer. 150 U.S. airplanes were downed.

Military historians call the Battle of Midway the most important single engagement in the naval war in the Pacific. And it was primarily an air-surface action, except for help of some submarines. But, it was the air power of the two services that foretold the future of the ultimate defeat of the Japanese war machine.

8. Ploesti

The Ploesti raid, which bore the code name TIDAL WAVE, was the first major assault by bombers of a strongly defended strategic target in World War II. It was executed by five groups of B-24D Liberators flying out of North Africa which attacked the German oil production facilities in Romania, a distance of some 1,100 miles from base to target.

Ploesti supplied the German war machine with about 60 percent of her crude oil, and had been a target considered worthy of attack since shortly after Pearl Harbor. Since much of the production of the Ploesti fields was destined for the Eastern Front, its destruction would also help the embattled Russians. The Russians themselves had bombed the facilities several times, but with little effect. A previous raid in June 1942 by 12 B-24Ds of the HALPRO group likewise was ineffectual.

The force assembled consisted of five bombardment groups totalling 177 B-24Ds. Two groups, the 376th and the 98th, were from the Mediterranean area, two were brought from the Eighth Air Force in England, the 44th and 93rd, and the 389th was diverted from a scheduled move to the United Kingdom. The mission commander was Brig. Gen. Uzal G. Ent and the leading group commander was Col. K. K. Compton of the 376th Group.

Benghazi in Libya was selected as the training and launch site, and five bases were built in the desert. Dummy targets representing Ploesti targets were laid out on the desert so that the formations could practice attacking them at low level, which was the tactic selected for the mission. In addition, drawings made with a low altitude perspective of the approaches to the targets were studied by the crews, as were defenses and routes.

The bombers were equipped with new low-level bombsights and the range of the planes was extended by installing two auxiliary bomb bay tanks, for a fuel capacity of 3,100 gallons. 1,000 and 500 pound demolition bombs and incendiaries were all equipped with delayed fuzes, from 45 seconds to six hours.

On the morning of August 1st, 1943, 1,725 Americans and one Briton took off. Unexpected weather over Bulgarian mountains separated the groups somewhat, but all continued toward the target. A couple of enemy airplanes spotted the formation, so the German and Romanian defenses were alerted. As the bombers approached the Initial Points (there were three of them), they dropped down to low level.

At the second of the three IPs, Col. K. K. Compton gave the lead airplane pilot the order to turn on course for Ploesti for the final bomb run. This was 20 miles short of the final IP, and instead of heading for Ploesti, the two leading groups, the 376th and the 93rd were heading for Bucharest, the capitol of Romania. The Germans, seeing this, assembled their alerted fighters over the city rather than over the oil refineries. Leaders of second group, the 93rd, seeing they were taking the wrong course, broke radio silence and called out the error, but to no avail. Finally, Col. Addison Baker, the 93rd commander, broke off from the lead group and headed for the oil refineries striking them before the lead group, which never got over the target.

In spite of the fact that only four groups attacked targets, some of which belonged to other groups, the mission was considered a success. About 42 percent of Ploesti's total refining capabilities were destroyed and as much as 40 percent of the cracking capacity was cut off for from four to six months.

A few weeks before Ploesti raid, a rather unique personality showed up at the American bases near Benghazi. He was a short, blond Royal Air Force officer, Squadron Leader George C. Barwell. On his tunic he wore the half-wings of an aerial gunner above his British Distinguished Flying Cross ribbon. Barwell, an accomplished mathematician, was acknowledged to be the world's leading theoretician in aerial gunnery. He followed in the footsteps of his machine-gunner father, who died in World War I while serving as an officer in the London Machine Gun Regiment.

Barwell had originally entered the RAF pilot training program. But his probing mind and voice challenged his flight instructors' methods of teaching flying. The RAF was in a hurry to turn out pilots and had little patience with the questionings of a know-it-all that could slow down the training. So, Barwell found himself washed-out of the pilot program and assigned to gunnery training and later to bombers.

After he had flown a number of night missions, Barwell let it be known that the training gunners had received had not prepared them for the realistic problem of defending against enemy fighters. He announced that firing at towed targets in training was in no way the same as firing at fast enemy fighters in a three-dimensional aerial situation. He proved his own theories by shooting down several opponents during fifty night missions over Germany.

But, once more, Barwell's challenges got him in trouble. On a night mission, his pilot turned back from the target without dropping his bombs because of intense concentration of flak in the area. Barwell let his pilot know over the interphone that his job was to fly over the target no matter what, but the pilot returned the bomber to its base in England. Once on the ground the pilot made his report appear that he had accomplished a great feat, and ultimately received a decoration for the mission. This was more than Barwell could take so he publicly denounced the pilot in the officers' mess. This got him banished to the wasteland of the Benghazi desert teaching gunnery at an RAF base called Berka Two. Surrounding Berka Two were the five B-24 bases where the build-up for TIDAL WAVE was going on. The Liberators with their multiple gun stations were an attraction to the British officer and he soon became friends with the American flyers.

Brigadier General Ent, mission commander for the Ploesti raid, knew that his gunners could use additional training, and what better way that to have the world's leading expert do the job. So, he borrowed the British officer to conduct the training.

In his typical blunt fashion, Barwell told the American gunners that what they were doing was all wrong. This got the expected reaction: they were qualified gunners, and who was this Limey to tell them they didn't know what they were doing? But, gradually his theories began to make sense to the more perceptive American gunners, while others held that Barwell didn't know what he was talking about.

Barwell's theory was that leading a fighter was wrong, and even the fancy American computing gunsights were not solving the very complicated problem of resolving relative air speeds, altitudes, angles, temperatures, and a myriad of other variables that comprise aerial gunnery. Barwell maintained that his system, position firing, had proven itself in combat. In position firing, the idea was to fire at a fighter in the same way the fighter was firing at the bomber. As the fighter made his pursuit curve, at some point he would be firing directly at the bomber. The gunner in the bomber, then, should fire directly at the fighter, rather than drawing lead on the enemy. Finally, the skeptics challenged the challenger. They told him that if he knew so much about it, he should fly with them and show them how it is done.

Now, Barwell had been made a ground instructor, and was not supposed to fly even in RAF aircraft; moreover, special permission was required for non-Americans to fly in U.S. aircraft. So, Barwell said nothing. But at a briefing for an attack on a German Air Force airfield on the island of Crete, Barwell showed up. He volunteered to man the top turret on the Liberator that was to fly Tailend Charlie, thought to be the most vulnerable position for fighter attacks. He was assigned to fly with Colonel Jack Wood's Sky Skorpions, the 389th Bomb Group.

What the group did not know was that British forces the night before had staged a fake commando raid and had simulated an invasion of Crete by dropping thousands of plastic doll parachutists complete with toy guns that sparked as they dropped. The Germans were on full alert and hopping mad at having been kept awake all night. So, what was supposed to have been a "training" combat mission for the green Sky Skorpions turned into a blazing air battle, with more than thirty of the latest model Me-109s scrambling to take out their anger out on the hapless Liberators.

American gunners sprayed the air with their weapons, often hitting their wingmates in the raging battle. Barwell's twin-fifties remained silent — he was taking notes on the various attacks to use in instruction later on the ground. Then, a German fighter began an attack on the airplane in which he was flying. He calmly asked the tail gunner not to lead the fighter, but to fire directly into it. As the undamaged fighter began to pass the B-24, Barwell gave it a short squirt and the Messerschmitt broke up. Barwell asked the navigator to give credit to the tail gunner for the kill. When another fighter made a pass, Barwell's guns jammed, so he continued making his notes.

Barwell continued to fly missions, day after day, and sometimes twice a day, demonstrating his techniques. Soon, skepticism among the gunners turned to praise. While the Americans counted his victories in the dozens, he claimed that he probably shot down seven or eight Germans while flying in the Liberators. He began getting letters from parents of gunners and even some homemade cookies and biscuits. The gunners tagged him Lucky Barwell. He said that while he was trying to be scientific about the business of aerial gunnery, he admitted that one did need luck as well.

When the time came for the mission on Ploesti, Squadron Leader George Barwell had become a fixture with the Americans. Still without permission of his own service, he was designated to man the top turret in the B-24 of Major Norman C. Appold, of Detroit, Michigan, who was to lead the third squadron of the first wave of Liberators. This was the leading formation of the five waves of attackers, and the one that made the wrong turn at an Initial Point.

After turning short of the proper IP, the force began picking up flak. Appold and Barwell flying about a mile behind the leaders would see that the 88s were fusing point blank to get the low-flying bombers. Barwell told the gunners to fire at the gun positions but aim at the gunners, not the guns themselves. Appold recalls looking out the window and seeing dozens of Germans scattered by Barwell's short, accurate bursts and credits him with silencing much of the flak in their flight path.

While they were receiving heavy ground fire, Barwell asked Appold where the fighters were. Why were there no Messerschmitts, since the anti-aircraft units certainly had been alerted? The Messerschmitts were airborne all right but were patrolling the city of Bucharest, 40 miles away, which lay in the path of the bombers because of the wrong turn. The error had given some luck to the Americans — it kept the German fighters away from them for the first part of the battle, at least.

Barwell did sight some low-wing fighters, although they did not look like any he had seen before. They were Romanian IAR-80's and were to beat the Germans into the fray. As the formation of bombers drove blindly on toward Bucharest, American gunners began seeing all sorts of unusual aircraft that had been scrambled by the Germans to keep them safe from the bombers. There were Heinkel 111 bombers, Junkers 52 transports, Storch liaison planes and even a British-made Gloster Gladiator that had been sold to Romania before the war.

The IAR-80 fighters, though, were getting into position to attack the B-24s. Rear gunner S/Sgt. Leycester D. Havens of Rusk, Texas in the Liberator *Jersey Bounce* was the first to call out bandits at six o'clock. His pilot, Lt. Worthy A. Long of Texon, Texas, felt a thump, which was a direct hit on the tail turret. Havens told his pilot in a weak, surprised voice that he had had it, and became the first American to die in combat in the big raid.

It was not until those in the lead aircraft could see the spires of the city of Bucharest that the leaders realized they had made a wrong turn. The formation wheeled to the north toward their targets, but by this time other formations of bombers were already hitting the targets and a wild array of bombers, explosions, towering columns of smoke and intense flak could be seen over Ploesti. Seeing this melee, the mission commander, General Ent, radioed to his formation that they had missed their target and bombers should strike targets of their choice. As the formation broke up, some dropped on a power station, some on pumping plants, while others just got rid of their bombs.

Appold, however, told his section to hold their bombs. Instead of scattering around the outskirts of the Ploesti complex with the rest, he made a

8th Air Force B-24H of the 445th Bomb Group (703rd Bomb Squadron) heads out on a bombing mission over Europe

tight turn and flew directly at a refining plant. His five ship formation got direct hits on the plant, destroying 40 percent of it.

Meanwhile, Barwell, in the top turret, continued to suppress flak with short, economical bursts. As Appold withdrew from the target area he flew along a stream bed with his formation. Directly ahead appeared a large stone bridge with what looked to be a flak tower on top of it. Sure enough, large orange tracers began arcing toward the five B-24s. Barwell asked his pilot to drop the nose a bit and with one five second burst disintegrated the tower. Flying down the stream bed probably shielded the small formation from the German fighters that had now entered the fray. So while the master gunner scored lots of punishment of the enemy, Barwell did not get a chance to get a shot at an enemy plane during the big raid at Ploesti.

A gunner who was successful in getting in his licks with enemy fighters was S/Sgt. Charles P. Decreval of San Francisco, California. Decreval was the left waist gunner of the B-24 *Sad Sack II* and had previously served with the Royal Air Force. His plane was part of the fourth wave across the Ploesti refineries, the 44th Bomb Group led by Col. Leon Johnson.

Johnson's group turned at the proper initial point and flew precisely the correct bomb run to their assigned target, which paralleled a railroad leading to the refineries. They were met with a surprise from a train speeding along the tracks at nearly the same altitude as the low flying bombers. Magically, the sides of the box cars in the train collapsed so that the dozens of anti-aircraft guns that had been concealed could surprise attacking aircraft.

In the same manner as the Q-ships of World War I, innocent-looking objects could be instantly transformed into avenging destroyers. The Q-train was self-contained, with ordinary box cars transformed into bunk cars, a kitchen, a recreation room, but above all, dozens of anti-aircraft guns with ammunition magazines ready to speed to any suspected target area, which the train was now doing.

Johnson's gunners gave the train their best return fire and succeeded in blowing up the locomotive, but not before a number of Liberators were badly hit.

As Decreval's bomber approached the target it was hit by a hail of small arms fire and he was wounded in the thigh. He strafed gun crews on a roof top, but about that time he noted that equipment inside the plane was being shattered. He put on his parachute, a seat pack, and looked out of his window. Seeing that the plane was at tree-top level, he said he "heroically" decided to stay with his Liberator.

Sad Sack II plunged into the inferno of smoke and flame after dumping its bombs on its assigned target. By now the tail gunner was dead, four other crew members had been hit and the number two engine was out but the prop could not be feathered. The ship vibrated badly. Decreval wondered if those on the flight deck were still alive. His part of the plane was shattered.

Then the Me-109s showed up! Decreval estimated that between seven and nine Messerschmitts began making stern passes at the wounded Liberator. As the first fighter broke off the attack, Decreval's .50-caliber caught it in the belly with a long burst, and the fighter just came apart in pieces. The other waist gunner hit the second fighter with a burst. Another broke off on Decreval's side and he knocked some pieces off its tail. By now ammunition in boxes inside the bomber was going off and Decreval received several shrapnel wounds from that. One round from the fighters struck his seat pack parachute, which probably saved his life.

The fighter attacks then fell off, except for one persistent German who flew directly behind the bomber at about 60 yards with the flaps of his fighter down to allow him to hang behind the bomber with all his guns blazing. Decreval's pilot had decided to belly-land the badly wounded Liberator in a cornfield and as they were going down Decreval vowed to shoot it out with the enemy on his tail. He leaned out his window and swiveled his machine gun parallel with the fuselage, firing inside the vertical fin and below the horizontal stabilizer until the bomber hit the ground. That was his last aerial combat of the war as he and his crew became prisoners of the Romanians. He had become a casualty of the raid, but had made his presence felt hitting both aerial and ground targets and had been part of a force that put the Colombia Aquila refinery out of commission for eleven months.

Another ex-RAF member who dueled with the 125 German fighters that battled the bombers after they had hit their targets was S/Sgt. Charles T. Bridges of Anderson, Indiana. Like Decreval, Bridges was a part of the 44th Bomb Group, led by Col. Johnson. Bridges, a veteran of 53 missions as an RAF gunner, flew as a waist gunner in a Liberator named *Porky II*, piloted by Capt. Rowland Gentry of Miami, Florida. *Porky II* was mortally wounded over the target by explosions from the refineries and storage tanks. Two gunners were killed and two of the bomber's engines were set afire by the blast. When three enemy fighters jumped the Liberator as it was leaving the target area, only the top turret gunner and Bridges were left to attempt to fight them off. Bridges gave them his best, but the fighters prevailed and finished off the Liberator, becoming one of the nine out of sixteen bombers in Col. Johnson's formation to go down. Bridges, who survived the crash to become a prisoner in Romania, managed to stagger from the wreck just before it exploded.

Another Ploesti raider who scored against the Germans in aerial combat with fighters was not a gunner at all, but a radioman. T/Sgt. David L. Rosenthal of Newark, New Jersey was a crewmember aboard *Scheherazade*, part of the 389th Bomb Group force led by Colonel Jack Wood. As pilot Lt. John T. Blackis of New Kensington, Pennsylvania was approaching his target, a boiler house, the bombardier called him over the interphone to say that the bomb bay doors were jammed and would not open. The Tokyo tanks, auxiliary fuel tanks placed in the bomb bay for additional range, were stuck against the doors, which would not roll up. Blackis ordered flight engineer T/Sgt. Joseph A. Landry, of Manchester, New Hampshire, to clear the bomb doors.

Landry's combat position was operating the top turret, so he had to leave his guns to work on the bomb bay doors. As he did, radioman

Rosenthal climbed into the top turret and, although he had no training in operating the turret, began to duel with the flak positions that had now opened up on the bombers. Landry was not successful in freeing the jammed doors, so Blackis ordered the bombs to be dropped through them. This meant that Landry had to manually disengage the bombs from their racks and they tore through the doors as they flew over their target.

Leaving the target, *Scheherazade* was jumped by German fighters, but Rosenthal kept his place in the turret, fighting back. He was credited with downing one Messerschmitt in his first acquaintance with machine guns. *Scheherazade* made it all the way back home, all alone, with Rosenthal in full possession of the top turret.

A tail-gunner who chalked up a victory over a Romanian IAR-80 fighter was S/Sgt. Clarence J. Ducote of Cottonport, Louisiana. Flying in a Liberator named *K for King* as part of Col. Johnson's 44th Bomb Group, Ducote and the other gunners worked over the flak batteries as they approached the target. The command pilot on board *K for King*, Major Dexter L. Hodge of Pledger, Texas, convinced that the Liberator's gunners were the best who ever fired a weapon, had high praise for the way they worked over the flak installations.

Over the target, though, *K for King* paid for its bombing and machine-gunning accuracy. One gunner suffered a severe leg wound. The bomber was even more severely wounded with a two-foot gap in the fuselage, part of a vertical stabilizer missing, the top ripped open, a shattered super-charger and induction system, and oil spewing from the number four engine. Ducote and his crew faced a 1,100-mile flight back to Benghazi.

Hedgehopping away from the target, *K for King* underwent twenty separate fighter attacks. Continuing on three engines, the Liberator hugged the ground. Finally only one fighter remained, an IAR-80, who was determined to down the faltering Liberator. As the Romanian closed in for the kill Ducote got ready to defend his crippled bomber. When the fighter closed to within a hundred yards, Ducote poured fifty rounds into it. The fighter broke off the attack with a rolling dive away — but, since they were at low altitude there was no place to dive and the fighter hit the ground in a huge ball of fire. At last *K for King* was home free.

In one bizarre encounter at Ploesti, American gunners and a German fighter pilot shot each other down. The German involved was Hauptmann (Captain) Wilhelm Steinmann of Nuremberg, who was commander of the Luftwaffe's First Fighter Wing, I-JG4. Because at the age of 30 Stein-mann was considerably older than his fighter pilots he was called "Uncle

Willie." He was the only Luftwaffe pilot to down two B-24s on August 1, 1943 in the TIDAL WAVE action.

Steinmann had not always been a fighter pilot. During the Blitz of industrial centers in England and Scotland, Steinmann had flown bombers on numerous missions. When the Blitz failed to stop British production, the Germans became more defense oriented and many bomber pilots were posted to fighters, Steinmann among them. Before being assigned to Romania, Steinmann had been credited with downing two Russian aircraft on the Eastern Front.

Steinmann's first encounter was with the Liberator *Brewery Wagon*, piloted by Lt. John D. Palm of Lower Valley, Texas, flying in the first wave with the 376th Bomb Group. In the drawing for ships, Palm had drawn *Brewery Wagon*, a bomber noted for its bad luck. Before takeoff, Palm had thrown stones at its fuselage.

When Col. K. K. Compton and General Ent turned at the wrong Initial Point, Palm continued straight ahead to the proper IP. His tail gunner shouted over the interphone that the rest of the formation was turning right, so Palm swung to follow the lead. His navigator, Lt. William M. Wright of Melrose, Massachusetts recognized that the turn was made at the wrong IP, so Palm swung back to a course that would take *Brewery Wagon* to the targets at Ploesti — all alone. After ducking through a brief rain shower, the stacks of the refineries were plainly visible, so Palm headed for the closest one flying at about twenty feet ducking between trees and power poles as they were called out by Wright in the nose of the Liberator.

When *Brewery Wagon* entered the inner ring of defenses around the refineries, the alerted German gunners could concentrate on the lone B-24 churning toward the valuable targets. The ship took a direct 88-millimeter hit in the nose, killing both Wright and the bombardier, Lt. Robert W. Merrell of Los Angeles, California. The blast also knocked one engine out and two others were on fire. Palm struggled to control the plane, but one leg, which he ultimately lost, was so torn he could not control the aircraft, even with his co-pilot's help. Palm salvoed his bombs and turned toward the south, away from Ploesti.

Uncle Willie Steinmann's Messerschmitts had now picked up the bombers and were starting to attack. Steinmann decided to go hunting for aircraft flying alone and readily spotted Palm's luckless ship struggling at low speed with smoke coming from two engines. On his first pass he raked the dying bomber, which immediately crashed. Palm and those of his crew who were still alive survived the crash. Palm even challenged the Germans who captured him with his .45, but his engineer/turret gunner, TSgt. Alexander P. Rockinson of Canal Fulton, Ohio, who was using his web belt to put a tourniquet on his pilot's leg stump, convinced him to put the gun away.

Looking for other easy victories, Steinmann soon picked up the Liberator of Captain Rowland B. Houston of Long Beach, California. Houston had tagged on to the tail end of his unit, the 44th Bomb Group after coming off the target. Steinmann saw the lagging bomber, which was flying at about 150 feet above the ground. Attacking from the rear, he cut back on his power and lowered flaps to slow to the bomber's speed, raking it with fire from wingtip to wingtip. Flames shot out from all across the bomber.

But, this time Steinmann was not going to get off easy, Tail gunner S/Sgt. Milford L. Spears of Springfield, Missouri and top turret gunner and engineer S/Sgt. Walter B. Schoer of Holstein, Iowa were giving the fighter the same sort of concentrated fire as it closed to within seventy feet of the bomber. The engine of the Messerschmitt caught fire and the fighter began to vibrate and shake. The fighter's speed carried it alongside the bomber, which was beginning to fall out of control. Steinmann was also having control problems and was sandwiched between the bomber and the ground. He loosened his harnesses and unlocked and opened the canopy of the Me-109 just before hitting the ground. The next thing he knew he was sitting on the ground with minor injuries, while the fighter and the bomber that had shot each other down burned nearby. He got up and walked away.

No one survived the crash of Houston's plane. Steinmann, who says he admired the tactics of the American bombers on the raid, later commanded a squadron of 30 German pilots in the defense of Anzio beachhead in Italy. At the end of the war he was officially credited with the destruction of 44 allied aircraft.

Even out of the target area, the Ploesti raiders were not safe from enemy fighters, which continued to attack them until after the B-24s were over the Adriatic. Gunners of the 98th group claimed 33 of the enemy fighters downed, but that group lost 21 bombers over the target. The 44th gunners claimed 13 victories but lost 11 planes. The TIDAL WAVE force claimed a total of 51 Germans had been downed.

Because of the mixup over the target, many of the bombers did not return in an organized group, although the 44th and 98th maintained unit integrity. 92 of the 177 attackers made it back to Benghazi. Many of the others, mostly the damaged, landed elsewhere. 19 landed at other Allied fields on Malta, Sicily or Cyprus. Seven landed in Turkey, where the crews were interned. Three crashed at sea.

Fifty-four Liberators were lost on the raid, 41 of them in the target area. 532 crewmen were lost, either dead, missing or interned.

No followup attack was made and it wasn't until mid-1944 that Ploesti was bombed again, this time from high altitude.

9. Schweinfurt

The Eighth Air Force raid against the ball-bearing plants at Schweinfurt, Germany on October 14, 1943 ranks among the most momentous aerial battles of World War II. It was also the battle that tested aerial gunners to the limit of their skills.

The importance of ball-bearings to the Nazi war effort was immense. They were employed in nearly every weapons system used by the Germans, including tanks, armored vehicles, submarines, warships and in a multitude of precision instruments and machinery. They were critical to the operation of combat aircraft was well. In one month the German war industry consumed nearly two and one-half million ball bearings in the construction of aircraft alone. And Schweinfurt was the major producer of ball bearings. If its plants could be destroyed, the German war machine would suffer severely.

Two months earlier, on August 17th, 1943, Schweinfurt had been struck by Eighth Air Force bombers in a dual raid which saw one-half its force strike the Messerschmitt aircraft plants in Regensburg. In that raid, which was the deepest penetration into Germany up to that time, a total of 60 B-17s were lost, 36 to the Regensburg force and 24 to the Schweinfurt force. Allied fighters did not have the range to accompany the bombers all the way to the targets, and most of the losses were from attack by German fighters.

In the October raid, the conditions would be similar. Allied fighters could protect the bombers only as far as the German border before they had to return to their bases. Two wings of B-17 Flying Fortress bombers were sent against Schweinfurt with a total of 291 Forts dispatched. Another wing of 60 B-24 Liberator bombers was also scheduled to be on the mission, but problems with forming the formation resulted in only 29 B-24s assembling. The B-24 mission commander made the decision that the force was too small to put up proper defensive fire against the German fighters, so the B-24s flew a diversion mission over the North Sea to the Frisian Islands before returning to their bases in England.

The model B-17Fs that were used on the raid normally had 12 .50-caliber guns for defense against enemy fighters. In the nose were three flexible guns, one in the center of the nose manned by the bombardier, and two others guns mounted at the sides of the nose, for the navigator. Later model B-17s would sport a chin turret with two .50-caliber guns and provide

8th Air Force B-17G of the 91st Bomb Group (323rd Bomb Squadron) on its bomb run over Germany, August 26, 1944

much better defenses against the head-on fighter attacks which became a standard German tactic.

Immediately behind the pilot stations in the cockpit was a power top turret with twin machine guns manned by the flight engineer. Aft of the bomb bay in the ceiling of the radio room was a single flexible gun that was the radio operator's weapon. In later model B-17s, this gun was deleted, partly because gunners were prone to hit the tall tail of their own aircraft. In the belly of the aft section was another power turret, called the ball turret, which also mounted two guns. At the waist windows were two flexible single guns, one on each side of the bomber. In the tail, beneath the vertical stabilizer were two more machine guns to protect from rear attacks. The defensive firepower of the B-17 was impressive, and on October 14, 1943, Eighth Air Force gunners were going to need every bit of it.

The B-17 wings assembled and headed nearly directly for Schweinfurt, since the targets were at the extreme limit of the bombers' radius of action, even though auxiliary fuel tanks had been installed. The P-47 Thunderbolt fighters which accompanied the bombers joined the formation and the strike force proceeded across the English Channel, into Holland and across Belgium with no interference from the Germans. Then, when the P-47 escort was forced to turn back over Aachen, an epic battle suddenly erupted. The American flyers had been briefed that as many as 300 German fighters were within range of their flight path, and it was apparent that that number was not an underestimate.

In a well coordinated attack, wave after wave of fighters swarmed at the bombers, with as many as 50 or 60 firing attacks occurring simultaneously. First the single-engine fighters made head-on attacks on the bomber formation, pressing in close as they fired their cannons and machine guns. Then the twin-engine fighters, approaching from the rear, lobbed rockets at the bombers, then closed, firing their cannons and machine guns. Then it was time for the single-engine fighters once more. The battle raged from the German border to the target and continued for the return route as far as the French border. It lasted three hours and 14 minutes. Fighters landed for rearming and refueling, taking off to once more join the fray. Even before the target was reached, 21 bombers had been downed, and only 228 of the original force were able to place their bombs on the target.

The number and types of German craft employed in the battle was the most numerous and diverse that the Americans had seen. The mainstay of the single-engine force were the Me-109s and FW-190s, but also seen for the first time in daylight fighting were the small Heinkel He-113s. German twin-engine fighters included Me-110s and Me-210s. The Germans also used Ju-88 twin-engine bombers as platforms for launching rockets, along with FW-189s, which were normally employed only in ground support roles. The twin-engine He-111 bomber was also used to launch rockets, and even some Ju-87 Stuka dive bombers were sighted by some American crews as they struggled to get into the battle at far above their normal ceiling. Waves of Dornier Do-217 twin-engine bombers also showed up, firing rockets and cannons.

Even four-engine bombers joined the fray. Heinkel 177s made rocket and cannon attacks, while the huge FW-220K Kuriers, usually employed against allied merchant convoys in the Atlantic, cruised behind the Forts to relay to anti-aircraft and fighter controllers the route, speed and altitude of the U.S. formation.

The Germans, of course, weren't the only ones firing, American gunners, navigators and bombardiers were delivering punishment to the attackers as they strove to fight off the waves of attacking fighters. Tail gunners and ball turret gunners called out the "bandits" that approached from the rear. The top turret gunner was in the best position to keep track of the battle from above, to the rear, to the front and from the sides. Navigators and bombardiers called out head-on attacks, while waist gunners tracked attacks from the side. All crew members used the clock system for calling out attackers, with 12 o'clock being directly ahead, six o'clock from the rear and nine and three o'clock from the sides. Placement of the attackers also used the relative altitude relationship as well, such as one o'clock level, four o'clock low and eight o'clock high.

In getting their licks in, gunners of the Eighth Air Force could claim victories under the guidelines of some rather rigid rules. To qualify for a claim of *destroyed,* the plane had to be completely engulfed in flame, and confirmed by a witness. If flames were sighted coming out of the engine or a wing, that was not sufficient for a *destroyed* claim. A *destroyed* claim could also be granted if the airplane was seen to explode and disintegrate completely in midair, or if a wing or tail assembly were seen shot completely away. If the fighter was a single-cockpit machine, a *destroyed* claim could be awarded if the pilot were seen to bail out. Of course, if the aircraft were witnessed to crash into the ground after being hit, a *destroyed* claim could be awarded.

A claim of *probably destroyed,* or *probable,* could be awarded if the plane were so badly shot up or completely on fire that it seemed unlikely it would have survived. A claim of *damaged* could be earned if parts of the aircraft were seen to fly off, but not if bullets struck the fighter without visible parts being shot away.

The ferocity of the attacks by the German fighters and other combat craft can be told by the records of the gunners statements made following the mission. Gunners on B-17 number 301 assigned to the 332nd Bomb Squadron of the 94th Group fought fiercely for a one hour period, giving a good account of themselves. Flying at 22,500 feet near Wurzburg, Germany, three Me-109s attacked the plane from the rear. Sgt. E.E. Hunt, the tailgunner, spotted the leader directly at six o'clock and opened fire at 500 yards. The lead Me-109 kept closing as Hunt fired until he was within yards of the bomber. Then it passed directly under the bomber, showing no visible damage from Hunt's defensive fire. However, the ball turret gunner saw the pilot suddenly bail out and a few seconds later the fighter exploded. Chalk up a *destroyed* claim for Sgt. Hunt.

Less than 10 minutes later, the bomber's formation was approaching the Initial Point when eight Me-109s jumped the B-17. Again it was Hunt in the tail who got the action. One Me-109 dove at the bomber from five o'clock high and Hunt opened up, hitting the fighter with his first burst. First flames spurted from the fighter, then the canopy flew off, but the pilot was not seen to bail out. Hunt had to give up watching the crippled plane because other fighters were attacking and Hunt was kept busy fending them off. Two fighters were later seen to hit the ground but neither could be confirmed as the one Hunt had hit, so he received a *damaged* claim for his efforts.

Then it was the top turret gunner's time to see some action. A Ju-88 was spotted diving steeply at the bomber from the four o'clock position. Sgt. F.C. Mancuso in the top turret opened fire and got hits in both engines of the twin-engined attacker. He may have hit the pilot was well, because the plane steepened its dive even more and never pulled out. Tailgunner Hunt watched the German plane hit the ground and explode. Mancuso was credited with a *destroyed.*

Hunt in the tail got back in the action, firing at a fighter making an attack from the side. as he was engaging the enemy plane, he failed to notice a Ju-88 that had slipped in behind the bomber. When Hunt spotted the plane it was just 150 yards away, closing slowly with its nose lit up with blazing cannons. The slow closing speed made for an easy target, and Hunt poured ammo into the cockpit. The canopy was jettisoned and flames poured from the cockpit as the Ju-88 dove down and away, never pulling out. Hunt had his second *destroyed* of the day.

Ten minutes later, another Ju-88 attacked from the side at eight o'clock level, firing rockets and cannons at B-17 number 301. Left waist gunner Sgt. S.J. Maciolek shot steadily at the attacking plane, which suddenly flipped on its back and began an inverted dive. Flames came from both engines and completely enveloped the plane, which was seen to crash and explode. Sgt. Maciolek added the fourth *destroyed* (plus one *damaged*) to the score of the gunners of B-17 number 301 for a little less than a one hour period of the Schweinfurt mission.

Another 94th Group B-17, number 439, had experiences similar to those of number 301. Flying in the low squadron at 21,000 feet, the plane was attacked by an Me-109 coming in from four-thirty low. In the right waist gunner's position, Sgt. McCabe fired a short burst at the fighter. The Me-109 rolled out of its attack in time to give McCabe an excellent shot at it. He gave the fighter a long burst, getting hits all along the fuselage. Quickly, the Me-109 rolled over on its back and began a vertical dive, while Sgt. C.L. Burkhardt in the ball turret watched it hit the ground and explode. McCabe was awarded a *destroyed* for his marksmanship.

Across from him, Sgt. L. Rand in the left waist position spotted another Me-109 attacking from seven o'clock low. When the fighter closed to within 1,000 yards Rand opened up with three short bursts of about 25 rounds each. His tracers were seen to hit the engine of the fighter, and the pilot of the Me-109 promptly bailed out, his parachute opening quickly. The tailgunner, Sgt. W.P. Brown, confirmed the chute and Rand received credit for a *destroyed*.

Tailgunner Brown was the next to get some action when a twin-engine fighter approached from five o'clock high. It closed slowly on the B-17 making short, repeated bursts from its nose cannons. Brown fired several short bursts at the attacker, then a longer burst which hit home. Pieces of the fighter flew off, it began smoking and then sheets of flame spewed from the plane. It began tumbling in a dive and never recovered, striking the ground and exploding. Sgt. Brown has a *destroyed*.

The battle was not over for B-17 number 439, as Me-109s returned, one of them diving at the bomber from the ten o'clock position. Top turret gunner Sgt. C.T. Troott tracked the bandit but held his fire. As the fighter moved to the seven o'clock position in its pursuit curve, Troott opened up, pouring some 50 rounds into the area of the cockpit. Flames burst from the fighter and seconds later it exploded with a roar. Confirmed by the B-17's bombardier, Troott added a fourth *destroyed* to the B-17's score.

Another B-17 from the same squadron bearing the number 248 went one confirmed victory better, downing five of the attackers in just over an hour of savage fighting. Its first attack was near the IP while the bomber was flying at 22,000 feet. Sgt. A.A. Ulrich in the top turret spotted two FW-190 fighters diving at two o'clock high. When they were 800 yards out he opened fire, pouring about 100 rounds of ammo into the leader. He kept firing as the FW-190 came within 50 yards of the bomber and as the fighter passed over the top of the B-17, just barely missing it, flames could be seen spouting from the plane. After it had passed the bomber, the fighter became engulfed in flames, then it exploded, pieces flying in all directions. The pilot made no effort to get out of his craft, and Sgt. Ulrich, who received a confirmed *destroyed* for the kill, said it appeared that the pilot was dead before the explosion.

Ten minutes later, a twin-engine Me-210 fighter fired four rockets at the bomber from six o'clock low. Sgt. C.T. Noulles, the ball turret gunner, got off short bursts as the 210 closed to within 400 yards. The fighter broke off the attack, then came in again, this time firing its cannons. This time Noulles' armor-piercing rounds found their mark, and flames erupted. Shortly after the entire plane disappeared in a fireball, parts flying in all directions. Chalk up a *destroyed* for the ball turret gunner.

Sgt. Ulrich in the top turret got another chance to score after the bomber formation turned for home. An Me-109 dove at his ship from seven o'clock high, and when it had closed to 700 yards, Ulrich squeezed the triggers of his twin .50-calibers in a long continuous burst of about 200 rounds. By the time the fighter closed to within 300 yards, Ulrich knew he had scored, and stopped firing. The Me-109 tried to pull up and escape, but then flames burst out, the plane pitched up, then down, and went into a spin. Shortly after, the fighter began shedding parts and then it appeared to disintegrate in the air. Ulrich had his second *destroyed* of the day.

The tail gunner, Sgt. B. Lewis scored two quick kills in succession, to add to the score of B-17 number 248. The first was another Me-109 which approached at six o'clock level. At 600 yards, Lewis began firing short bursts until the fighter was about 200 yards out. After just 75 rounds from Lewis' guns, the Me-109 began smoking, then flamed. Shortly after, it went into a steep dive and exploded, entering a spin and losing parts as it fell. Kill number one for Lewis.

Five minutes later Lewis was engaged again with a fighter, this time an FW-190 who came in at six o'clock high. Lewis waited until the fighter was within 600 yards, then gave it a steady burst. The fighter kept coming until it passed about 20 feet above the tail of the bomber, and Lewis could see flames coming from the belly drop tank the FW-190 carried. Sgt. Ulrich, in the top turret, watched as the fighter fell off on one wing, burning fiercely and finally exploding. Lewis had his second victory for the day, and B-17 248 had accounted for five of the enemy ships on the mission.

The highest scoring crew on the Schweinfurt mission flew B-17 number 351Z, which was assigned to the 407th squadron of the 92nd Bomb Group. The unit may have been the subject of more attacks by fighters than any other on the Schweinfurt raid. Their first encounter was with about 30 Ju-88s that flew through the American formation firing steadily at all in their path. Then, a lone Ju-88 closed in on the tail of 351Z. Sgt. D.M. Radney fired his twin tail guns in short bursts, while the nose of the Ju-88 sparkled with return fire. When the attacking plane was about 500 yards out the left engine of the German aircraft began spouting flames. The 88 kept coming though, until at 200 yards it broke away from Radney's return fire. Flame streamed back from the engine along the fuselage as it went down. But no one saw it crash nor did the crew bail out, so Radney had to settle for a *damaged* claim.

A second mass attack involved FW-190s coming up from six o'clock low. Sgt. J.W. Disher in the ball turret called out the attacking force and began firing at the closest fighter. But, the German was getting his licks in as rounds came crashing through the belly of the Flying Fortress and Disher was hit with cannon fragments. He kept firing until he saw smoke trail from the Focke-Wulf. It then began to dive and thick smoke engulfed the plane. The pilot was able to jump out of the doomed ship, so Disher had a confirmed *destroyed.*

Now the Ju-88s were back in a mass attack, firing their cannon as they swarmed through the bomber formation. In the top turret, Sgt. B.L. Boutwell fired at one that had singled out his ship and was closing to 300 yards at 2 o'clock. Suddenly, the Ju-88 broke downwards and passed beneath the bomber. Sgt. Disher in the ball turret reported that both engines of the Ju-88 were on fire. Then the copilot shouted that the entire German plane was a ball of fire. When two parachutes were seen to depart the shattered plane, Sgt. Boutwell had his *destroyed.*

At the same time, another Ju-88 was attacking from five o'clock low. Sgt. Radney in the tail again took on an attacker sending out a stream of .50-caliber rounds as the Ju-88 closed from 500 yards to 350 yards. The B-17 was again taking hits from the attacker, but Radney was also scoring as the right wing of the Ju-88 burst into flame. Then the left engine caught fire and the plane went into a dive. No one saw it crash and the crew was too busy fighting off other attacks to look for parachutes. Once again, a disappointed Radney had to settle for less than a *destroyed* and was awarded a *probable.*

Now the crew had to face a new threat. A large Dornier Do-217 bomber climbed up at them from the four o'clock low position, lacing out large cannon shells into the Fort. Sgt. Disher in the ball turret took on the engagement firing three long bursts, each of which scored. The big

German airplane faltered and Sgt. Radney in the tail said that both engines were on fire. The Do-217 fell out of control and eventually exploded in the air. Sgt. Disher had his second *destroyed* of the mission.

Then the Ju-88s were back again and Radney in the tail swung his guns, snapping out bursts at the attackers. Suddenly, an FW-190 appeared directly astern closing to point blank range, its guns blazing. Radney poured lead into the fighter, which seemed to be on a collision path with the bomber. At the last minute the fighter broke to the left, smoking heavily. Then at about 150 yards, the FW-190 suddenly exploded, falling in pieces. There was no mistake for Radney this time and he finally received a *destroyed*.

The next claim belonged not to a gunner, but to the bombardier, Lt. K.A. Pfleger, in the nose. Two FW-190s made a head-on attack coming from one-thirty o'clock. Pfleger fired at the lead fighter until it passed beyond the limit of travel of his gun and out of his sight. Sgt. C.T. Hultquist, at the right waist gun position, saw the FW going by out of control. Then it crashed into another FW-190 who was attacking the bomber from 5 o'clock high, both planes exploding in flames. Lt Pfleger was credited with two *destroyed*.

Sgt. Hultquist, himself, scored shortly thereafter. Several Me-109s came from below at two o'clock. From his right waist position, Hultquist blasted away at the second plane, and almost immediately saw smoke come from beneath the engine. As the Me-109 passed beneath the B-17, Sgt. Radney in the tail saw it smoking heavily and then explode in little pieces. Hultquist had his *destroyed*.

Now it was the turn of the other waist gunner, on the left. A Ju-88 came in firing from the seven o'clock high position and Sgt. N.J. Barbato opened up on it. At 600 yards the right engine flamed and as it passed under the bomber, Hulquist at the other waist position was able to sight it until it hit the ground and exploded. Score one *destroyed* for Sgt. Barbato.

In the final attack by the Germans on number 351Z, it was the navigator's turn to claim a victory. A Ju-88 came at the bomber from the one-thirty level direction, its guns blazing. Lt. P.L. Stebbins returned the fire with a long continuous burst and as the Ju-88 passed the B-17 Sgt. Boutwell in the top turret reported both engines were smoking heavily. The attacker went into a dive and Sgt. Disher in the ball turret was able to watch it crash and explode. Lt. Stebbins had a confirmed *destroyed*.

It was a busy day for the crew of B-17 number 351 Z, who accounted for nine enemy planes *destroyed,* one *probably destroyed,* and one *damaged.*

A B-17 named *Brennan's Circus,* assigned to the 332nd Bomb Squadron, 94th Bomb Group, gave its crew their wildest ride on the Schweinfurt mission. The crew members, led by 21-year-old 1st Lt. Joseph Brennan, the pilot, had a lot to tell debriefing officers when they eventually got home from the mission.

The action started over Luxembourg at 22,000 feet shortly after the escorting P-47s had to turn back to their bases. The tail gunner, Sgt. R.E. King, spotted an Me-109 behind the bomber and high. Then the fighter began a dive, picking up speed. When well below the bomber and closing, the fighter pulled up to make its attack from below. As King opened fire with short bursts the B-17 began taking hits from the Messerschmitt, but King's fire was having an effect, too. At 400 yards the fighter slowly rolled on its back, then appeared to go out of control, spiraling downward out of sight. King received a *damaged* for his claim.

Ten minutes later, another Me-109 was spotted diving on the bomber from six o'clock high, firing as it came. Sgt. W.P. Wetzel, the radio operator, who was on his 25th and final mission, returned the fire with his single gun in the dorsal position. At 300 yards he could see he was getting hits on the fighter in the nose, the engine and the wing roots. Suddenly the fighter exploded and completely disintegrated, pieces going in all directions, and some of them hitting the bomber. Wetzel's claim of a *destroyed* was later approved, but this attack and the previous one had done serious damage to *Brennan's Circus.*

The number four engine was dead and the bomber began to drop back from the formation. As with any wounded bomber, it would receive special attention from the German fighter force. Sure enough, an FW-190 quickly took the opportunity for an easy kill and sped to its target. Sgt. N.P. Loupe in the ball turret had sighted the fighter, though, and when it was 600 yards out he began to fire his twin .50-calibers. Suddenly heavy smoke trailed the fighter and as it passed beneath the B-17 the cockpit erupted in fire. Then the whole plane became a fireball as it spiraled down to its doom. Loupe got a *destroyed* for his marksmanship.

But, just three minutes later four more FW-190s attacked the hapless bomber. Sgt. S.H. Rodeschin, the left waist gunner, fired at the leader Focke-Wulf when it was far out. He had barely begun to fire when the fighter suddenly exploded and the left wing came off. Evidently he had hit a rocket mounted beneath the wing of the FW-190. But still he had his *destroyed,* and had fired only four rounds from his machine gun.

Pilot Brennan was determined to try to stay with the formation for self-protection, but felt he needed to salvo the bombs to be able to do it. Brennan told the bombardier, 2nd Lt. Joseph E. Genone, to jettison their load. But the bomb release mechanism had been badly damaged by the fighter attacks and Genone was unable to get rid of them. Now far behind the formation and under attack by Me-109s who had joined the three remaining FW-190s, Brennan made the decision to drop the bomber down to the deck and head for home. With co-pilot 2nd Lt. Gordon E. White helping him with the sluggish controls, Brennan put the bomber into a diving spiral to keep the fighters from getting a straight shot at it.

One Me-109, however, came at the bomber from the eight o'clock low position and was seen by Sgt. D.A. Nowlin in the left waist gun station. Nowlin opened fire at 400 yards range and it appeared he was getting hits with his tracers in the fighter's fuel tank area. Suddenly the Messerschmidt exploded and became completely engulfed with flame, spiraling out of sight. Nowlin had a confirmed *destroyed,* the fourth for the crew that day.

Still in the spiral, *Brennan's Circus* became the target of another four FW-190s who joined the other German planes. These fired rockets at the bomber, but all missed the whirling plane. Finally, the bombardier was able to jettison the bomb load, and now the B-17 was easier for Brennan and White to control. But the fighters had taken their toll and a second engine was now on fire. As they neared the ground, Brennan pulled the bomber out of the spiral and headed for England on the deck, with just two engines to get them there. The fighters stuck with them as they buzzed over the landscape until eventually they ceased their attacks and turned back.

But now *Brennan's Circus* began to take ground fire from the Germans as the plane limped across occupied Belgium and Holland. Most of the ground fire was from machine guns, but the crew could also see soldiers firing their rifles at them and officers shooting their pistols. Gaping holes appeared in the fuselage and the metal skin of the wings peeled back in several places.

Civilians on the ground, when they heard the bomber coming at such low altitude, rushed from their homes and shops and waved at the crew. Many gave the V for Victory sign with raised arms.

But the Germans were determined to down the crippled plane. As it neared the English Channel, one final barrage delivered the mortal blow, as a third engine was shot out. Continuing on one engine was thought to be impossible, but *Brennan's Circus* struggled along until they were over the water. Sgt. King, in the tail gun station, happily reported that the ground fire was now splashing in the water behind them.

Pilot Brennan, certain they could not reach land, told radioman Sgt. Wetzel to send a *Mayday* distress call that would alert air-sea-rescue that the bomber would be ditching. While only five miles from the British coast, *Brennan's Circus* could not longer maintain altitude. Most of the crew took their ditching positions in the radio room, while Brennan and White put the wounded plane into the water. It was a good ditching and the plane slowly began to settle after it stopped. The dinghies were deployed, and the crew stepped into them without a single person getting his feet wet. An hour later a British rescue boat picked them up and the crewmen of *Brennan's Circus* were on their way back to their base at Bury Saint Edmunds, shaken by their wild ride but joyous at having survived.

Those Flying Fortresses that got through to the target did an excellent job of striking their main objective. The weather was good and the first wave had no trouble identifying the target and placing a high percentage of their bombs in the target area. The second wave, dropping just six minutes following the last of the first wave's releases, had more difficulty finding the aiming point because of the smoke from the previous wave. However, their hits were still acceptable. That was good news. The bad news was that in spite of claims that the Schweinfurt ball bearing plant was almost totally destroyed by the raid, it became apparent after the war that very little damage had been done to the heavy machinery that turned out the ball bearings, and the German ball bearing industry went on with almost no loss of production. Schweinfurt was hit a total of 16 times during the war, but following the October 14th raid the Germans dispersed the industry into smaller factories and plants and were never in trouble over a lack of ball bearings. By the time later raids were flown, fighters had increased range and could accompany the bombers all the way to the target and back, so the tremendous losses of October 14th were not repeated. A total of 60 B-17s did not return from the mission, which meant the loss of 600 crewmen, either dead, missing or taken prisoner.

The losses were such a blow that, temporarily, the Army Air Forces lost air superiority over the continent.

Aerial gunners in the Fortresses on the October 14th Schweinfurt raid claimed to have *destroyed* 186 fighters, with 27 *probables* and 89 *damaged*. Undoubtedly, there were many duplications in claims from two or more gunners, and the feeling is the Germans probably lost about 100 fighters. The exact number will never be known. German records for the day show that just 38 fighters were victims of American gunners, with another 20 damaged. Five other fighters were lost for reasons other than combat, and 11 others damaged. But, the Germans were known to not count an airplane as destroyed if the pilot or crew survived the downing. So their claim for the low figure is probably no more accurate than the high claims of the Americans.

In any event, the aerial battle was of epic proportions, with the Germans fighting a massive, coordinated effort, and the American gunners giving them back just as determined an effort.

10. The Med

The Fifteenth Air Force was a rather latecomer to World War II, not having been activated until nearly two years after Pearl Harbor. It was formed in Tunisia, North Africa in November 1943 with Jimmy Doolittle as its first Commanding General. A month later the headquarters moved to Bari, Italy, where it would remain for the rest of the war.

Its first units came from the Twelfth Air Force, which had been fighting the war in the Mediterranean Theater of Operations. The heavy bomber units of the 12th went to the 15th, making it the strategic command, while the 12th assumed the role of the tactical command in the area. At the beginning six heavy bomber groups (four B-17 and two B-24) moved from the 12th to the 15th along with three P-38 fighter groups and one P-47 fighter group. One Reconnaisance Group also joined the 15th.

As the 15th built up, ten more B-24 and two more B-17 heavy bomber groups were added. More fighter units were added, and the final count of fighter groups was three P-38 and four P-51.

The 15th became the counterpart of the 8th Air Force, both operating against European targets. While the 8th Air Force received more recognition for its combat, the 15th flew against no less important targets. Two of its frequent targets, Vienna and Ploesti, were considered the second and third most heavily defended targets in Europe. In the officer and NCO clubs in the area around Foggia could often be heard the parody of the song made famous by the movie *Casablanca:* "It's still the same old story/the Eighth gets all the glory/while we go out to die/The fundamental things apply/as flak goes by."

So hot were some of the 15th's targets, that some were considered as two missions for 15th crews. Double credits were given for missions to Munich, Bucharest, Ploesti, Brux, Vienna, Craz and others.

Memorable missions participated in by the 15th were those in support of the beachhead at Anzio, Italy and the assault against Monte Cassino. These missions were more of a tactical nature, since they were in direct support of allied ground forces trying to inch their way up the Italian boot.

Probably the biggest single series of raids were in support of Operation ARGUMENT, which came to be known as the Big Week. This was in February 1944 when a combined attack by both the 15th and the 8th was launched to try to deal the German aircraft industry a crushing blow.

For four straight days heavy bombers of both strategic air forces struck at aircraft and ball bearing plants. Targets for the 15th Air Force were at Regensburg and Steyr, Austria on the 22nd through the 25th of February, then bad weather prevented further attacks. It was thought at the time that the German aircraft industry had been dealt a nearly fatal blow. That was overly optimistic, but the raids did disorganize the production for awhile. Sixty-eight percent of the factory buildings attacked were destroyed or damaged and the raids resulted in the dispersement of the German industries. Within a short time, however, the Germans were turning out more fighter planes than ever.

What the Germans could not replace were the hundreds of experienced fighter pilots who became the victims of the heavy bomber gunners, which would prove of high importance as the war went on.

The Flying Quartet began as a trio. Three gunners from the Mediterranean Theater teamed up with another from England to form a formidable force when they volunteered to return to combat with *The Fighting 463rd Bomb Group* in Italy in September, 1944.

All four had completed more than their minimum tours in each theater, and when they joined the 463rd they had among them an accumulated 264 missions against the Axis opposition.

Three of the gunners, Charles Fallon, Eugene Young and Arley Russell, had served together in the 99th Bomb Group. Flying from North Africa, they finished their tour of combat and volunteered to go to England to join the Eighth Air Force. There they met Albert Davis who was well beyond his first tour of combat in Europe. The four decided to take a well-earned rest in the U.S., but after a few weeks of laying about, decided it was time to return to combat. That is when they joined the 463rd in the final stages of knocking out the Axis forces.

Charles Fallon, when he joined the unit in Italy, already had 14 oak leaf clusters to his Air Medal. At 31 years of age, he was the senior in age and had accumulated 71 missions. Targets he had attacked included Bizerti, Tunis, Sardinia and Palermo. Then it was on to Rome, Pisa, Leghorn, Bologna, Foggia, Messina and Naples. Marseilles in Southern France was also among those German-occupied targets he had attacked. He had racked up three confirmed victories against Axis fighters, including two Me-109s and a Reggiane 2001, along with some probables against FW-190s.

Eugene Young's combat record closely paralleled that of Fallon's. Young had just one fewer missions, with 70 in his log book. Targets he had attacked included those in North Africa, Sicily, Sardinia, Italy and Southern France. He had a number of claims against Axis fighters.

Topping the mission count was Arley Russell, who had a total of 78 sorties. He had flown part of his previous tours as a gunner and part of them as an enlisted bombardier. His early missions included such targets as Pantelleria, Sicily and Sardinia. Then it was on to Salerno, Naples, Rome and Southern France. Getting into the big leagues, Russell had been on missions to Vienna, Blechhammer and Regensburg. He flew as a bombardier on four missions against Foggia when it was still in Axis hands. As a gunner, he had four confirmed victories: One FW-190, two Me-109s, and one Reggiane 2001.

The youngest of the quartet, and the last to join the trio to make it a four-some, was Albert Davis. He had been flying with the Eighth Air Force in England when the trio showed up from the Mediterranean. When he joined them to form the Flying Quartet, he had 45 missions in Europe. He had taken part in the early attack against Regensburg when just three air-craft out of his group had returned from that disastrous raid. Among other targets he had attacked were, Kiel, Kassel, Schweinfurt, Bremen, Wilhelmshaven, St. Nazaire, Paris and Bordeaux. Davis, at the time he joined the 463rd in Italy, had two confirmed victories against the Germans, both FW-190s.

The Flying Quartet went on to help finish off the Axis Powers in Europe, but their contribution up to the point of joining the B-17s of the 463rd had already been beyond the call of duty.

Daylight bombing was the trademark of the American Army Air Forces in Europe, and the nighttime attack activities were left to the Royal Air Force. But the poor bombing weather of the 1943-44 winter had led to the development of the "Mickey" radar bombing system, which was used on pathfinders to lead daylight raids on Germany.

The approaching winter of 1944-45 promised to be no better for attacking German targets during daylight than had the previous one, so Mickey was to be employed on even a larger scale. The 15th Air Force in Italy made the decision to keep the pressure on the Germans by mounting nighttime attacks using the radar system, employing heavy bombers singly or in pairs, around the clock. Targets were to be railroad marshalling yards, oil refineries, ordnance depots and aircraft factories.

Sgt. Joseph LaPlace, B-17 engineer/gunner of the 463rd Bomb Group in Italy, was to take part in one of the first of these nighttime raids. He would survive an adventurous mission.

The briefing for this pioneer mission was quite different from the mass briefings that Sgt. LaPlace and his crew had experienced before in preparing for daylight formation raids on German targets. Just ten crewman sat in a semicircle in a tent as they were instructed in what their single Fortress was to do.

The operations officer briefed them on their route, takeoff time, time over target, and return information. Then the intelligence officer flashed pictures on a screen showing what appeared to be X-ray films, but which were projections of what the radar, or Mickey, operator would see on his screen as the target was reached.

Next the intelligence officer pointed out on a map the expected flak positions they would encounter on the mission. He cautioned that while the mission was to be flown at night, there could be interceptions by German night fighters. Escape and evasion information followed in the event the crew was forced to bail out.

The communications officer instructed the crew on call signs, emergency procedures and the importance of radio discipline. His final words were to not break radio silence except in an extreme emergency.

The weather officer was in his usual pessimistic mood. Heavy clouds strong winds and icing conditions would be encountered. While the crew considered these to be hazards, it would also deter enemy night fighters.

The operations officer concluded the briefing with a time hack, and the takeoff was set for 0100.

The crew rode to their ship over muddy roads and gathered beneath the black-painted Fortress for the final instructions from the pilot, Lt. John Pfarr. They climbed in and checked their equipment — flak suits, helmets, oxygen masks and guns. When Pfarr called for the checkin, they all responded.

Then it was time to go. Pfarr called the tower through his throat mike: "*Seasick tower,* this is *Stiffneck, B for Baker,* ready for takeoff." The answer came, "*Stiffneck, B for Baker,* cleared for takeoff." That was the last call to a ground control for a number of hours. The crew was on its own.

The heavily-laden Fortress bumped along the uneven steel mat runway and finally urged itself into the air. Clouds of muddy water spewed in the churning wash of the four propellers.

Then it was up into the swirling clouds, torrents of rain and heavy headwinds. At 10,000 feet Pfarr called for oxygen masks to be donned, and there would be an oxygen check several times each hour.

It grew colder as the Fortress climbed. The outside air temperature gauge showed a minus 20 degrees centigrade, but would drop to a minus 60 degrees by the time the bomber reached bombing altitude. The pilot noted crusts of rime ice forming on the wings, even though the deicing boots were flicking some of the ice off. The navigator reported that they were now over the Alps.

The navigator, Lt. Robert Devine, and the "Mickey" navigator, Lt. William Knechel, had the task of finding the target on this stormy night.

In the top turret, Sgt. LaPlace scanned the night for German night fighters. Other gunners did likewise. Suddenly LaPlace got a call from his pilot, Pfarr, to check the number three engine, as oil pressure was being lost. LaPlace slipped out of his turret and with a flashlight saw that the engine was throwing oil. Taking no chances on a fire breaking out in an overheated engine, Pfarr feathered the prop on the number three engine and they continued on to the target flying on just three engines.

They were approaching the target and the crew concentrated on the bomb run. They were expecting flak and were not disappointed. The erie display of exploding shells in the clouds and darkness was a different

91

experience from daylight flak attacks. The bombs were dropped and their explosions could be seen reflected through the misty air. Then, the tailgunner, Sgt. Lawrence Pottebaum, shouted that there were secondary explosions of a great magnitude, indicating that something certainly worthwhile had been hit.

But, the flak over the target had taken its toll. The oil pressure on the number two engine was dropping fast. Again, LaPlace was called from his top turret station to check it out. Sure enough, an oil line in the engine had been severed and the engine had to be feathered.

With just two engines left, and the 16,000 foot Alps to surmount, Pfarr gave the order to jettison all unnecessary equipment. Their rapid rate of descent slowed as the gear was tossed overboard. They would possibly clear the Alps by a few hundred feet. The alternative was to bail out, but the crew voted to stay with the plane.

Pfarr ordered the radio operator/gunner, Sgt. William Bonaker, to break radio silence and call Air/Sea Rescue service. His call, "*Stiffneck, B for Baker* calling *Bigfence,* requesting a fix," got the reply, "*Stiffneck B for Baker,* this is *Bigfence,* we have your fix. The ceiling is zero at Vis. Give us a call if you are going to ditch."

Pfarr took up the new heading. It began to grow light and they could see a heavy undercast and fog below their flight path. Soon the navigator reported that they had cleared the Alps. All aboard breathed easier. But over the Adriatic Sea, still ten miles from the nearest friendly landing strip, the number four engine suddenly began smoking heavily. Pfarr feathered number four and ordered the crew to the radio room to prepare for a crash landing.

Now, with only one engine operating, the rate of descent was a good 500 feet per minute. Pfarr headed for a small fighter airstrip along the beach and requested a straight-in approach. The control tower had already been alerted by Air/Sea Rescue and was ready to receive the ailing bomber. All other traffic had been cleared.

Pfarr urged his faltering bomber over the sea toward the small strip, and set the plane down precisely on the end of the runway, rolling out to a safe landing. Greeting the Fortress crew as they dropped out of their hatches, thankful to be on the ground, were not only the crash/rescue and ambulance crews, but scores of fighter pilots who had been watching the drama and who offered their congratulations to Pfarr and his crewmates on a fine recovery from an eventful mission.

It was August 1944 and the 15th Air Force was well into its campaign to shut down German oil production, hitting targets from its bases in Italy.

Sgt. Leonard Little was a part of this campaign. A tail turret gunner in the B-24 *Flak Shak III,* he would fly with his unit, the 485th Bomb Group, on the fourth consecutive day that the group had gone after oil targets.

It was 2:45 a.m. on August 24th that Little and his crew mates were awakened to begin the mission. He washed from a helmet, dressed, grabbed his mess kit and left for the mess hall. Crew members ate quietly.

Returning to his tent, Little gathered up his dog tags, pocket compass, watch, a photograph of his wife, a ring and a copy of the New Testament. His money and his wallet were stowed in a metal ammunition box, along with a letter in case he did not make it back.

In the briefing room the gunners sat on bomb fin cases, while the briefing officer drew back the curtain that covered a large map of Europe. The gunners could see a long red line marking the route they were to take stretching to Pardubice on the Elbe River in Czechoslovakia. Then came the briefings on the weather, the route, the target, and enemy defenses. Then trucks took them to their aircraft.

Little and the other gunners performed their preflight inspections of their weapons on *Flak Shak III* while waiting for the officers on the crew to arrive. When they did, escape and evasion kits were passed out and everyone suited up in their heavy flying clothing. Usually when Little boarded the plane, the crew chief rubbed his burr haircut for good luck, but today that routine was forgotten. When Little remembered it, he jumped through the camera hatch and found the crew chief standing fire guard. He had him rub his greasy hands through his hair. Little scrambled back into the plane as it began to move out for takeoff.

Once airborne, Little settled in the waist, lit a cigarette and relaxed. Next to him was the ball turret gunner, Sgt. Leo Gagne, who was listening to the interphone system through his headset. Gagne signaled to Little to look out the waist window and below them they could see a Liberator burning in a ball in a field below. *Flak Shak III,* which had been assigned as a spare aircraft on the mission, would now go all the way to the target.

As the formation climbed over the Adriatic, gunners fired test rounds and checked out their turrets. Then it was time to go on oxygen.

The sun beat through the glass and Little was comfortable in his tail turret. As the formation approached the IP, Little put on his flak helmet and began to watch for flak. He saw none. Then, the bomb bay doors came open and soon the bombs were falling toward the target. Still there was no action from the enemy, but smoke could be seen rising from the target. As they turned for home, all on board *Flak Shak III* began to relax. P-51 Mustangs crisscrossed the formation and all seemed serene.

One Liberator, though, slipped out of formation and began cruising behind and below the other bombers. Little could see that all four engines on the lagging plane seemed to be operating and he could not understand what was wrong. Suddenly, Little saw two Me-109s on the tail of the faltering plane. He got a quick shot at one of them as the fighter passed beneath the tail of *Flak Shak III*. Little yelled into his mike that there were fighters in the area, but no more were sighted just then. Then the lagging plane suddenly went down. Two other Liberators fell out of formation, but still no one called out any fighters.

Off on the horizon, though, a group of 12 to 15 FW-190s could be seen closing on the formation. Little trained his optical sight on them and waited for them to get in range. Still out of range the fighters split into three-plane flights and each flight came after a bomber. Three headed straight for Little's turret.

Little aimed at the fighter in the center and at 800 yards range fired several short bursts. At 500 yards range, Little fired long, continuous bursts. At 300 yards pieces of the cowling of the fighter came off, as well as the canopy. The FW-190 slowed suddenly, stopped firing, then began a roll that took it just beneath the fuselage of the Liberator.

Little now shifted to the fighter on the left, but he could hear shells exploding as they thudded into the bomber's fuselage.

But those shells could not have been coming from the two remaining fighters because they were aiming for the engines and wing fuel tanks. Little looked up and saw a fourth fighter at four o'clock high that was causing the damage to the fuselage. He swung his guns toward the new attacker, but it was too late. Shells blasted into the tail turret knocking Little completely out of it back into the fuselage.

Flak Shak III was now in trouble. Both left engines were on fire and there was a fire over the bomb bay from mangled fuel lines and punctured oxygen bottles. There was a large hole in the fuselage below the right waist gunners position. Hydraulic fluid burned in Little's tail turret.

The six men in the forward part of the plane were not injured, and the top turret gunner, Sgt. Sam Nenadich, had flamed the fighter that Little had not had time to shoot at. But the men in the rear were in bad shape. Little was unconscious, but came to and tried to put out the fire in his turret. When he looked around he saw that the left waist and ball turret gunners had their parachutes on. Both had shrapnel wounds in their legs. The right waist gunner was only shocked by a machine-gun bullet that had passed through the metal eyeglass case he carried in a leg pocket of his flying suit.

Then Little and the right waist gunner cleared the area around the camera door in the bottom of the fuselage. When Little tried to stand and turn the lever to release the camera door, he immediately dropped to the floor in pain. Then he saw that one shin bone was bare and that a foot was twisted out of line. Back on his knees, he took off his oxygen mask and looked through the camera door, now open. It was clear and Little dived head-first through the opening.

Falling through the clear sky he looked back at the *Flak Shak III,* as it trailed smoke and flame, and watched as the other crew members tumbled out of the wounded bomber. After the last man left, the bomber did a partial climbing turn, then spun to the ground.

Sgt. William E. Roberts, Jr., of the 774th Bomb Squadron, 463rd Bomb Group, had the bad luck to be shot down and taken prisoner when he was at the end of his combat tour. He was on his 45th mission as a gunner when his B-17 went down in Hungary in July 1944.

He was taken to Germany and together with some other prisoners traveled around Europe for about a week. He remembered passing through Vienna before arriving at Frankfurt, which was a mass of rubble and where citizens spat at the captured airmen. At Frankfurt, he spent six days in solitary confinement while being interrogated. His meals consisted of a cup of ersatz coffee and a thin slice of black bread for breakfast, and half a cup of warm slop in the evening.

He resisted the interrogations, giving only his name, rank and serial number. At his second interrogation, though, the interrogating officer brought out a folder of the 463rd group. In it was a record of Roberts' past duty stations, the dates he had graduated from various technical schools, the name of the group commander and even where he had been employed before he went into the Army Air Forces.

After a month, Roberts and 43 other men were packed into a railroad box car and spent several days riding to their POW camp at Stettin in East Prussia, now Poland. There he met several men he had known from the 463rd. One of them was smoking a pipe which Roberts had received from home a few days before he was shot down. The other gunner returned the pipe. At first he was billeted in a tent, but after two months he was able to move into a barracks. There the prisoners slept on paper mattresses stuffed with wood shavings.

The main problem was the lack of food. As time wore on they were given less and less. The prisoners spent as much as 17 hours a day lying on their mattresses because they had little strength to do anything else. Eventually they organized classes in Spanish, English and the Bible to try to combat their listlessness. Roberts tells of the one fight he saw among the allied prisoners. The two combatants, who had argued over a card game, were given boxing gloves. The two tried a couple of swings apiece without landing a blow — they were too fatigued to continue, and just stood panting and blowing. Finally the two began laughing at their predicament and made up to each other.

In early February, someone suddenly burst into the barracks shouting that the Russian army was just 15 miles away. The prisoners debated whether to attempt a mass breakout to try to get to the Russian forces. They decided against it, figuring that even if the Germans marched them away, the Russians would soon catch up.

On February 6, 1944, Roberts and his fellow POWs began what became known as the Black March: A full three months of foot travel nearly 1,000 miles westwards across Germany.

During those three months there were no provisions for them to have meals. They were given a couple of potatoes a day and anything else they found to eat was a result of theft or bartering. Roberts and two others traded a gold watch one day for four loaves of bread, six eggs and a small piece of ham. Once in a while they would be lucky enough to steal a chicken. Once, after five days with no food at all, Roberts approached a POW who was cooking something over a small fire. Roberts wanted to get a light for his pipe, but the man thought he was going to take his food from him and warded him off. When Roberts explained what he wanted, the man showed him what he was preparing. It was a tiny piece of a pig's tail, all that the emaciated man had the strength to get when the pig ran away.

All through February, March and April the weary prisoners trudged west. It was on May 2, 1945 when they were finally liberated. Roberts climbed up on a haystack and in the distance saw a British Army tank approaching. When the tank arrived, out came the tank commander and told the prisoners they were free. The tanker received a rousing ovation that he was not likely ever to forget.

But, the prisoners were still on their own. The tank was just part of a spearhead and they had to make their way to the front lines. They walked two miles when they came to a small German village. In it they found a deserted creamery filled with food. Each man carted off 20 pound chunks of cheese that were as big as cartwheels. Others sat licking chunks of pure butter. One man found a wheelbarrow and loaded three of the huge cheeses in it, chewing on a piece of cheese as he went.

Roberts will never forget the sight of those bearded, emaciated Americans, happily staggering down the road toward freedom, burdened beneath loads of German cheeses.

IV
11. Ace-ing The Aces

American aerial gunners could not be expected to know whether the enemy fighters coming at their bombers were greenhorns or veteran pilots, some of whom were fighter aces. But they did score against German and Japanese fighter aces, just as enemy gunners scored against a number of American aces.

A German ace who felt the fury of the American aerial gunners was Major Georg-Peter Eder. U.S. gunners on the heavy bombers in Europe shot down Eder on nine different occasions. These nine downings were just a portion of the 17 times Eder was shot down during the war. He was wounded 14 times.

Major Eder's score against the heavy bomber formations was even higher, however, and he is credited with downing 36 B-17s and B-24s. He was one of the German fighter pilots who developed the head-on tactic of engaging bomber formations. Between the Battle of Britain, when he first began flying combat, and the end of the war Eder racked up a total of 78 victories.

Eder is thought to have tangled with one of the top American aces, fighting to a draw. The American ace was Capt. Robert S. Johnson who is credited with 27 victories over German planes. In the battle, Eder scored heavily on Johnson's P-47 Thunderbolt. His plane was filled with numerous holes, and the only thing that saved Johnson's life was the heavy armor plate behind the pilot's seat. The other factor that accounted for Johnson's survival was that Eder ran out of ammunition. When that happened Eder pulled alongside the limping Thunderbolt and gave a friendly wave to Johnson before he peeled off for home. Feeling that Johnson's badly wounded P-47 would never make it home, Eder claimed a victory when he landed. Johnson's rugged Thunderbolt got him back to England in spite of its sad condition, but once on the ground it never flew again.

A German ace who is ranked as the 13th leading ace of the world felt the ferocity of American aerial gunners many times. He was shot down 15 times during the war, undoubtedly more than once by bomber gunners, but was never injured. In turn, he is credited with downing 203 allied planes during his service, mostly on the Eastern Front. Captain Helmut

Lipfert logged 700 combat missions in a little more than two years of flying and following the war became a reclusive schoolteacher in West Germany.

One day in June 1944, Lipfert led an interception of American bombers, and while he managed on that day to avoid being shot down himself, his formation of Me-109s was decimated by U.S. aerial gunners.

The day was clear, and warning of 300 U.S. bombers approaching targets in Romania was flashed to Lipfert's unit, JG-52. Lipfert gathered the eight pilots he was leading and briefed them on the mission. The nine Me-109 fighters took off and landed at another field for refueling. Then they launched again as the formations of B-17 Fortresses and B-24 Liberators approached. They followed the directions of the ground radar controllers and were the first German fighters to engage the bombers. As they climbed they could see above them three formations of 40 bombers each, with accompanying fighters cruising above them. Nine Me-109s against 120 bombers and who knows how many fighters was a tall order.

Lipfert kept his group climbing until it was out in front of the bombers and level with them. Then he called his wingmen to stay close together and make a line-abreast mass attack on the bombers, attacking from the front. As they turned in on one of the lower groups of bombers, a group flying higher and farther out front began firing at the fighters. Lipfert could see tracers all around him, but he kept his course.

As the nine bored in on the bombers, Lipfert called for them to hold their fire until close in. When they were almost on top of the bombers he gave the call to open fire and blasted away at the B-24 he had picked out. He could see pieces flying off the bomber as he closed. As his bullets found their mark, he could see the explosions of the shells on the

Messerschmitt Bf-109F

fuselage and wings. At the last moment, he dove down and away from his target. As he regrouped his formation for another attack, he could see that the gunners in the bombers had done their work — just six other planes joined up.

Lipfert once again led his formation out in front of the bombers and with seven fighters again attacked head-on. This time the American gunners found the range, and when Lipfert regrouped, just three Me-109s were left.

Back once more for another head-on attack went the fighters, and following that attack just Lipfert and one wingman were left. By now several of the B-24s were smoking and Lipfert decided that he had had enough of the head-on attacks, so he and his wingman went after the crippled bombers. The two attacked one of the smoking bombers, whose gunners put up a stout defense. Lipfert started a fire in one of the left engines of the bomber and his wingman got some hits as well on their first pass. In the second attack, Lipfert hit something vital in the Liberator and it literally burst apart. He did not see any parachutes from the doomed plane.

After checking for American fighters, which were nowhere to be seen, the two attacked a second B-24, which, like the first, put out heavy defensive fire. Two attacks were made on this bomber also. On the second pass the bomber exploded. Two crewmen were seen to bail out.

Lipfert's wingman was out of ammunition, so the two returned to their base. Each was credited with a kill and a total of nine American bombers on the raid were downed.

But American gunners had taken a toll, as well. Lipfert and his wingman were the only two to escape without being hit by the gunners. Of the other seven in Lipfert's formation, one was killed outright and one died in his parachute when fired on by a Mustang pilot. Another parachuted, but received serious burns from his flaming fighter and was out of action for a long time. One other pilot had to parachute from his plane but was unhurt. Two other fighters were so badly shot up that they had to make emergency landings. The seventh plane landed at an allied base.

This day the German ace had escaped punishment from the firepower of the bombers, but on 15 other days he would not be so lucky.

A German ace with 100 victories fell to the guns of gunners of the 306th Bomb Group on April 5th, 1943. Flying from their base at Thurleigh, England, the Eighth Air Force B-17 unit had earlier endured heavy losses, but during the previous month their luck had been good. On April 5th, on a mission to Antwerp, their ill experience would return.

All went well on the Antwerp mission until just before reaching the target. Then, the Focke-Wulf 190s of the JG-26 Luftwaffe squadron attacked, concentrating on the 306th. Leading the German fighters was the squadron commander, Hauptmann Fritz Geisshardt, an ace many times over. The five bombers shot down by the head-on attacks of the FW-190s were all from the 306th Group. 306th gunners, on the other hand claimed five enemy fighters downed. One of them was that flown by Hauptmann Geisshardt, who died of the wounds he received in the battle.

The eighth ranking ace of the Luftwaffe, Lieut. Col. Heinz Baer, traded shootdowns with American fighter pilots and gunners. Baer flew combat for the entire war, logging 1,000 missions between 1939 and 1945. He had a total of 220 confirmed victories, 16 of which were gained in the Me-262 jet fighter. Of these victories, 124 were scored against western allied aircraft.

Baer himself, though, was shot down no less than 18 times by gunners and fighter pilots. He survived the war, only to lose his life in a civilian sport plane accident in 1957.

A Japanese ace who lost his life in a battle with American gunners was Warrant Officer Kinsuke Muto of the Imperial Japanese Navy. Muto was already an ace by the time World War II began, having shot down five planes in the war between Japan and China. Near the war's end Muto was credited with between 28 and 60 victories, depending on whether one believes claims (the higher figure) or the lower figure awarded by postwar Japanese historians.

Toward the end of the war Muto participated in the defense of the main islands of Japan. By that time the Zeros that the Japanese Navy flew were outclassed by the newer U.S. Air Force and Navy fighters. But that didn't stop Muto in his fervor to protect his homeland. In February 1945 a flight of 12 U.S. Navy fighters began a strafing fighter sweep of Tokyo. They were met by a single enemy fighter; it was Muto in his outdated and outmoded Zero. Against the 12-to-one odds, Muto downed four of the fighters, giving the Americans a lesson in flying and gunnery. His aging fighter got him home to fight again.

Of Muto's total victories four of them were downings of the heavy B-29 bomber. Muto was one of a very few Japanese fighter pilots to score against more than one of the big machines. His end came when he was attacking a B-24 Liberator. The date was July 24, 1945, just weeks before the end of World War II.

The only top Japanese ace to survive the war met his match in aerial combat with some U.S. Navy aerial gunners, who put the ace out of action for a year-and-a-half. While the combat action did not technically down an enemy airplane, it might as well have. It was only through desperate measures that the ace and his plane survived.

The Japanese ace was Saburo Sakai, another Japanese Navy Zero pilot. Sakai finished the war with 64 victories, two of which were earned in Manchuria against the Chinese in the 1938-1939 time period. Japanese historians, using the "divide-by-two" rule, credit Sakai with just 32 kills.

It was August 1942 and the American invasion of the Solomon Islands on Guadalcanal was underway. The U.S. invasion fleet was massed offshore and the Japanese intent was to strike both the fleet and the troops already ashore. At Rabaul, on New Britain, 27 Betty bombers were assembled for the mission and they were to be escorted by 18 Zero fighters. The round trip distance from Rabaul to Guadalcanal was 1,100 miles, which would place the Zeros at the limit of their maximum range.

This would be Sakai's first combat against U.S. Navy flyers. Heretofor his battles had been with P-39s, P-40s, B-17s and Hudson bombers. He briefed the other two pilots in his part of the formation to stay close to him.

The Zeros joined up with the Bettys as they climbed to 13,000 feet. Sakai noticed an especially beautiful island, green and lush looking. He located it on his map — he was to be thankful for this later in the mission. It was a hot day and when the formation set course for their target Sakai opened his lunch box and took out a bottle of soda water. Without thinking about the altitude, he opened the bottle and instantly he and the inside of his cockpit were covered with sticky water. And, he could not see! The soda water had covered his goggles and blocked his vision. Disgusted with himself, he spent the next forty minutes wiping his goggles, the windshield and the canopy to enable him to see out.

As the formation neared Guadalcanal it climbed to 20,000 feet. The bombers picked out a large convoy as the target, but still there was no opposition from the Americans. Suddenly, out of the sun, dove six fighter planes and Sakai had his first look at F4F Wildcats. The F4Fs ignored the Zeros and went after the Bettys. Sakai watched as the bombers unloaded on the convoy, but all he saw were geysers in the water, with no ships hit. The Zeros stayed with the bombers until they were out of the area, then turned back toward the invasion site to look for battle.

As they returned, again Wildcats dove out of the sun at the Zeros. Sakai soon found an F4F on the tail of a Zero and dove to attack. The

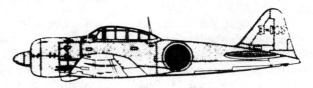

Mitsubishi A6M Zero

F4F broke off its attack and came at Sakai, and for the next several minutes there was a twisting, turning battle until Sakai prevailed and the U.S. pilot bailed out.

Three Zeros reformed with Sakai as they headed back looking for more planes. For a while they did not spot any, and then, suddenly a bullet struck Sakai's canopy just inches from his head. Startled, he looked around to see an SBD Dauntless dive bomber that had the audacity to jump four Zeros all alone. Sakai soon was on the tail of the SBD. His first burst killed the rear gunner and his second caused the Dauntless to go into an uncontrollable dive. The American pilot bailed out. It was Sakai's 60th victory.

Again his group reformed, looking for more action. Sakai spotted a formation far ahead and he and his wingmen closed on it. When he got closer he could see that there were eight planes, headed away from the Zeros. Sakai decided to sneak up from behind on what he thought were Wildcats. But as he and his wingmen closed to within firing range, he could see that they were not F4Fs, but were TBF Avenger torpedo planes. In the rear of the eight torpedo planes were 16 machine guns, eight .50-calibers and

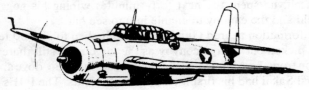

Grumman TBF Avenger

eight .30-calibers, all aimed at Sakai. It was too late to change tactics now and Sakai began firing. Almost at the same time the Avenger gunners opened up on him — he felt tearings at his body, then saw flaming red and passed out.

How long he was out, Sakai didn't know, but he came to when the cold air rushing through his shattered windshield revived him. He pulled back on the stick, instinctively, to come out of his dive. But as he did he realized that he could not see — everything was fuzzy. He was drowsy and had an impelling need to go to sleep. He fought off that desire and took stock of himself.

He headed in what he thought was the general direction of Rabaul. Then he tried to determine what his injuries were. He found that the entire left side of his body was paralyzed and that he was blind in his right eye. A lot of blood was flowing down over his face from his head, and he found that he had a deep crease in his skull. He managed to stuff his scarf up inside his helmet to partially stem the flow of blood from his scalp. He had frequent periods of the desire to sleep, and considered returning to the U.S. invasion fleet to dive into a ship on a suicide strike.

Between periods of falling asleep and rousing himself, he turned back toward Guadalcanal intent on finding a U.S. ship to dive into. Then reason would return and he would once again head for Buka or Rabaul. His fuel was becoming critical. Once, after passing out, he found that he was 90 degrees off course and was headed into the barren Pacific Ocean far from the islands he sought. He turned to the proper course and after an hour of flight sighted the green island he had pinpointed on the way to the target. At last he felt he might make it home.

Shortly thereafter he spotted two Japanese cruisers making full steam in the direction of Guadalcanal. They were on their way to try to inflict damage on the invasion force of the Americans. He considered ditching his Zero beside one of the warships to be picked up and saved. He circled the ships, which were making 33 knots toward the battle, then decided to press on toward Rabaul.

With fuel gauges almost on zero Sakai finally spotted the airfield at Rabaul. But, he doubted his ability to land on the runway and thought about ditching in the water just off the beach. He made his approach to the ditching, and then, when about 50 feet above the water, changed his mind.

After making four separate approaches to the runway at Rabaul, Sakai finally got the Zero on the ground safely. As he rolled to a stop he passed out again.

It wasn't until six months later that Sakai recovered sufficiently to be able to leave the hospital. He was permanently blind in his right eye and was assigned as a flight instructor for a year. He was eventually returned to operational duty in Iwo Jima, again flying Zeros. Then it was back to Japan to serve as a test pilot, flying two newly designed fighters that were to come along too late to stop the final onslaught by the American air forces against the Japanese war machine. They were the Shiden (code name George), designed to outfight the Hellcat and the Mustang, and the Raiden (code name Jack) designed, with its four 20-mm cannons, to combat the B-29 heavy bombers.

Near the war's end, Sakai was back flying Zeros in Japan. After the atomic bomb attacks on Hiroshima and Nagasaki, his commander called the pilots in to tell them that Japan was preparing to accept surrender and they were not to fly combat again. Sakai and his good friend decided that if the B-29s came again that night, they would have one last fight. Their Zeros fueled and armed, they waited until the warning of approaching bombers, then took to the air. They found that eight other Zero pilots had also defied the edict not to fly. Sakai, with his single eye, let his friend lead the night attack on the B-29s. They found a quarry and punished the Superfort until it had to ditch in the ocean, but not before the B-29 gunners had heavily damaged the ace's plane.

The ace might have won his last battle, but he had lost the war.

☆　　☆　　☆　　☆

The first American ace to fall victim to enemy aerial gunners probably was Major John R. Alison. It would be on his first combat mission during which he would get credit for two of his six total kills.

In early 1941, before the U.S. entered the war, Alison was sent to England to help train Royal Air Force pilots in the P-40 Warhawk fighter. Then when the German armies turned eastward toward Russia instead of trying to cross the English Channel to Britain, Russia quickly came in need of assistance. Alison and some P-40s were posted to Russia where he instructed their pilots in flying the fighter.

While he was in Russia, the U.S. entered the war and Alison chaffed to get into combat. After eight month's duty in Moscow and Basra, Alison finally managed to be assigned to the China-Burma-India (CBI) theater of operations.

It was early July 1942 when Alison, leading a flight of four P-40Es, took off from an airfield in India and headed for Kunming, China. He would be assigned to the newly formed 23rd Fighter Group which had as its nucleus pilots and airplanes from the disbanded American Volunteer Group, better known as the Flying Tigers. The total American fighter strength in the CBI in these early stags of the fighting were three squadrons of P-40s plus one flight of four. All four units were based at separate airfields in order to disperse the force for survival against enemy bombers.

At Kunming, he met the leaders of the AAF contingent, including Brig. Gen. Claire Chennault. Alison was told that the airfields that were home to the fighters were high in priority as targets for Japanese bombers. Waves of 40 to 50 bombers, accompanied by a like number of fighters, would strike the airfields. And since only one squadron of P-40s was normally in a location where it could participate in the defense against the raid, just ten to 15 P-40s would be available to intercept upwards of 100 enemy aircraft. The odds against the Americans were long.

After receiving his briefings, Alison was sent to join a squadron (the 75th) which was based at a forward field at Hengyang, about 600 miles east of Kunming. The 2,700 foot dirt runway had been leveled by hand by Chinese coolies.

Not long after he arrived, Alison and the rest of the pilots were awakened one night by the banging of a stick on a tin can, accompanied by shouting of "air raid" in broken English. The Chinese had set up a primitive system of observers on hilltops with field phones to give warning of an impending bomber attack. The Japanese bombers were headed for Hengyang! Would the airfield be their target?

Alison and the other pilots stood out-of-doors listening for the hum of aircraft engines. Then the hum came, gradually building to a roar. The airfield was the target. Many people on the field took shelter, but Alison and some of the other pilots stood outside to watch the raid. The bombs fell, but the accuracy was only fair, yielding light damage. Dummy P-40s attracted some of the attack, leaving the well-camouflaged real fighters intact.

As he stood watching the raid, Alison could pick out the exhaust flame from the Japanese bombers. Even though the P-40 was not equipped for night combat he wondered if the P-40s would be able to make a night interception of the bombers using the Chinese warning system plus the telltale light coming from engine exhaust stacks.

He told his squadron commander, Major David L. "Tex" Hill, who had become an ace while flying with the Flying Tigers and who would add six more kills to his score for a total of 17.25 enemy planes downed in the war, that if the bombers came again the next night, he was going after them. He was joined by Capt. Albert J. "Ajax" Baumler, a pilot who had become an ace in the Spanish Civil War by downing eight Fascist planes and would add another five while flying with the 23rd Fighter Group for a total of 13. Baumler was the first American pilot to become an ace in two wars.

The next night the attack came at two o'clock in the morning. Alison and Baumler dashed to their planes, which had been placed in an alert condition near the runway. With Alison leading, they took off from the unlit runway using moonlight to guide them. Several other pilots who had decided to join them also took off. The pilots had estimated that the bombers that had attacked on the previous night had been flying at about 8,000 feet. So, the plan was to climb to 10,000 or 12,000 feet while circling to the left and then make a diving attack on the unaware bomber crews.

Soon the control tower, whose radio was being intermittently jammed by the Japanese, reported that the formation was over the field. Alison, also over the field, could not spot the formation of bombers below him. A second time the bombers circled over the field, but had yet to drop any bombs. Still, Alison, flying at 12,000 feet could not see the Japanese planes. Then, he decided to look above him and suddenly he saw a blueish light. As he looked closer, he could see six lights — the flame from the twin-engines of three bombers — they were Type 97s, or Sallys. He radioed to Baumler and the other pilots that the bombers were at 15,000 feet instead of 8,000 and Alison began to climb for the attack.

As Alison closed on the V-formation of three bombers, he lined up on the one to the left to keep from being silhouetted against the moon, which was on the right. Then, the formation suddenly wheeled to make a third run on the field. When the turn was complete Alison pressed forward for the attack. Just before he fired, he saw bright flashes from the right and felt thumps on the fuselage of his fighter. The gunner in the plane on the right spotted the P-40 because after the last turn, the fighter was now outlined by the moon. The gunner's fire was accurate and Alison could feel hits in the engine, and into the instrument panel in the cockpit.

He closed even more on the bomber on the left and soon was pouring rounds into it. It began smoking and oil was streaming from an engine, but the bomber would not go down. Suddenly it veered away from the formation.

Alison, whose plane was still taking hits from the bomber on the right, quickly crossed to the right and set up to take on his tormentor. The bomber on the right held its course as Alison approached and the rear gunner again began to pour lead at the P-40. Alison ignored the fire and began returning it with a vengeance. After a long burst, a wing tank exploded in an orange fireball and the bomber plunged toward the ground, out of control. Alison saw no parachutes.

Now Alison would concentrate on the lead bomber and as he closed he could see that the bomber was releasing its bombs. He pressed forward, his own engine beginning to smoke. In range, he concentrated on hitting the fuel tanks in the wings. The bomber gunner opened up on him. With ammunition running low, Alison concentrated his fire and was rewarded with another wing fuel tank explosion and the lead craft plunged to the ground.

But, now his own engine was knocking and missing and he reduced the throttle. As each second went by the engine ran more and more roughly and Alison knew he had to get on the ground fast. He circled over the field as he dove down toward it. Then, at 3,000 feet, the engine quit. He would have to try a dead-stick landing — and at night!

On his approach to the short runway his airspeed was too high and it soon became apparent that he would overshoot the runway. Automatically, from habit, he jammed the throttle forward — the engine tried to respond with a coughing. Then came a fireball as the engine exploded. He would have to crashland his ailing fighter.

He turned away from the city ahead and saw he was approaching the Siang River. He decided that was the place to put down, but then a bridge loomed ahead. He barely mushed over the bridge and the airplane was through flying. It hit the water hard and Alison's head was thrown against the gunsight.

Alison did not lose consciousness, however. He scrambled over the side of the sinking fighter and swam to shore, where some Chinese took him to the airfield. When the other pilots, who had seen Alison's plane go past the field and crash, saw him, they were overjoyed. They thought he had been killed.

All in all, it had been a good night. Alison had two victories and Baumler had finished off the first bomber Alison had fired at and had downed another. Four bombers against the loss of one fighter. But the Americans, who had written off Alison's plane as unrecoverable, hadn't counted on the resourcefulness of the Chinese, who somehow managed to bring it up and return it to the base.

But even more significant than night victories over four out of six bombers, was the fact that it was a very long time before the Japanese returned to Hengyang at night.

Within weeks of Alison's downing another American who would become an ace fell to the guns of an enemy gunner. This time the American wore the uniform of the Royal Air Force and flew an Eagle Squadron Spitfire fighter.

Squadron Leader Chesley G. Peterson, of Santaguin, Utah, had entered pilot training of the Army Air Forces before Pearl Harbor. He completed primary flight school in good fashion but when he got to basic flight school at Randolph Field, Texas, he was washed out. At first he thought the authorities had discovered that he was underage for the training program, but his records read he was eliminated for a "lack of flying ability." He vowed to give up flying because if the AAF was correct, he would be a danger to himself.

After returning to civilian life, he was again bitten by the flying bug and went to Canada to seek RAF pilot training. He duly got his wings and joined a squadron in England, flying Hurricane fighters. When the Eagle Squadrons (composed mostly of Americans flying for the RAF) were formed, Peterson became commander of the No. 71 squadron. He was now flying Spitfires. He soon began making a name for himself and was awarded the British Distinguished Flying Cross. A bit later he was given the DSO, an even higher medal, which was pinned on by King George VI himself. Peterson was racking up scores over the Luftwaffe and downed six enemy aircraft while flying for the British.

Then came the day the ace was downed himself. It was by a JU-88 bomber aerial gunner, whose excellent shooting Peterson praised. It was the day of the Dieppe landing, which Peterson's squadron was covering. He got into the battle with the JU-88 bomber over the coastline. Both he and the German rear gunner fired simultaneously and both scored telling blows. The JU-88 turned over on its back, then plunged into the sea. Peterson was not in much better shape — his Spit was burning. He headed for the English Channel and stepped smartly over the side and parachuted to the water. Twenty minutes later an RAF Walrus rescue plane picked him up.

This was not the last time Peterson would find himself in the water. After the U.S. entered the war the Eagle Squadrons were disbanded and the Americans were transferred to the AAF, most of them going to the 4th Fighter Group. At first they flew their Spitfires which were transferred with them, then they flew P-47 Thunderbolts, and ended the war flying P-51 Mustangs.

Peterson became, at 23, the youngest full colonel in the AAF and was given command of the 4th. In a dogfight with a Focke-Wulf 190 over Holland, Peterson's P-47 took hits in the engine. The rugged Thunderbolt did its best to get Peterson home, but about halfway across the Channel Peterson's fighter was down to 1,000 feet of altitude and dropping. He took to his parachute, but it streamed and he hit the water in nearly a free-fall attitude. By all rights he should have been killed, but he had the luck to survive. He was picked up by another British Walrus rescue plane. This time he spent four days in the hospital suffering from shock, temporary blindness and assorted bruises. He downed one more enemy plane while flying for the AAF making seven victories his total score for the war. Peterson stayed in the Air Force and upon retirement had become a Major General.

Another American ace who fell victim to the marksmanship of a German aerial gunner was Captain Walker M. "Bud" Mahurin, Ft. Wayne, Indiana, who was one of the leading aces in the Eighth Air Force.

Mahurin joined the 56th Fighter Group at Mitchel Field, NY and went with the group when it moved to England. The 56th Group would become the leading fighter group in the Eighth Air Force for aerial victories over the Germans, scoring 665.5 kills. The group also produced more aces than any other fighter group in the Army Air Forces. Known as "Zemke's Wolf Pack", the group was led by Col. Hubert A. Zemke and its squadrons contained such names as Gabreski, Schilling, Johnson as well as Mahurin. Zemke, Gabreski and Mahurin were all downed in combat but all survived the war. The group flew P-47 Thunderbolts for its entire wartime service, the only Eighth Air Force group to do so.

Mahurin had a colorful career with 56th Group. In addition to downing 19.75 Germans while flying with the group, he was involved in a couple of incidents which got him in trouble with his superiors. The first occurred when he was on a training flight in the U.K. He spotted a B-24 Liberator bomber which was new to the European theater at the time. One account says the incident happened as Mahurin was making practice fighter attacks against the bomber, while another account says that he was trying to fly close formation with it. Whatever the situation, Mahurin misjudged his position and came up under the bomber's propellers, which promptly chewed the tail off of Mahurin's fighter. Mahurin parachuted safely and the bomber, though damaged, made a safe landing. At the time, P-47s were in short supply and those in charge were not happy.

Another incident that got him into trouble with his bosses happened in combat. There was fierce competition among fighter pilots in the 56th Group in the racking up of kills. Mahurin was one of the leaders in the race to accumulate victories. On one mission he was assigned to fly as wingman with one of the flyers whose score Mahurin was trying to beat. Mahurin spotted a bandit, but instead of calling it out immediately, he dove toward the German plane. When he got almost to within firing range, he made the radio call he should have made earlier. If he had done that his leader, of course, would probably have scored a kill. Mahurin did instead. When he got back to his base, his C.O. told him he was going to discipline him for violating the teamwork concept. The next day, however, Mahurin and his C.O. were called before a general, who congratulated Mahurin on his performance in combat. When the C.O. said that he was going to have to discipline Mahurin, the general replied that the C.O. could go ahead, but he would look silly because the general had just recommended Mahurin for the Distinguished Service Cross.

Mahurin met his match in combat at the hands of a rear gunner of a Dornier Do 217. The Do 217 was a twin-engine bomber that was used

111

heavily by the Germans in the war. It, like most German bombers, clustered the entire crew in the forward part of the ship. It was armed with two flexible guns in the nose and two more in a top turret. To protect from the rear and from below, there were two more guns installed in the belly of the crew compartment, facing aft. It was the gunner at this station that downed Mahurin's P-47.

Mahurin parachuted from his plane in enemy territory, escaped from capture and with the aid of the French underground made it back to his unit in England.

In July 1944 he returned to the States and was assigned as squadron commander of the 3rd Fighter Squadron of the 3rd Air Commando Group at Lakeland, Florida. His group, which he later commanded, went to the Pacific where he added another kill to his score, for a total of 20.75 victories in World War II.

During the Korean conflict Mahurin returned to combat, this time flying F-86 Sabre jet fighters with the 51st Fighter Group, which he later commanded. He added 3.5 more enemy airplanes to his record of kills, becoming the only American ace to have victories over German, Japanese and North Koreans (or Chinese).

He was shot down again and captured, spending the entire 16 months of his imprisonment in solitary confinement.

Navy and Marine Corps aces were not immune from being downed by enemy planes. In fact, the Marine Corps' highest scoring ace, Captain Joseph J. Foss (26 victories), fell victim to a gunner's deadly aim. (There are those who say that "Pappy" Boyington, of Black Sheep fame, with 28 victories, is the highest scoring Marine. Just 22 of them, however, were scored while flying as a Marine pilot while the other six were downed when he flew as a Flying Tiger.

"Pappy" Boyington had a checkered career as a civilian following the war, but Foss went on to even more fame. Foss switched from the Marine Corps to the Air National Guard when he returned to South Dakota as a civilian. He rose to become chief of the South Dakota Air National Guard and attained the rank of an Air Force Major General. He entered politics, and as a returning war hero, could not lose an election. He eventually became governor of his home state. Later, he was made commissioner of the now-defunct American Football League.

In his boyhood in South Dakota Foss participated in outdoor activities such as hunting and fishing. He became an excellent marksman which undoubtedly contributed to his ability to down enemy planes.

Foss arrived in Guadalcanal during a desperate time in the fighting for control of the island and the seas around it. It was October 1942 and the Japanese were landing troops and supplies in an effort to retake the island. Because of losses of American surface ships and aircraft carriers, the Japanese Navy's battleships could stand offshore uncontested and shell the U.S. aircraft on Henderson Field.

Then in November a U.S. Navy scout plane spotted an 11-ship Japanese naval task force headed for the island. The Americans knew that the ships contained reinforcements for the Japanese forces that had already been landed. These additional troops could prove to be a factor leading to the defeat of U.S. forces on the island.

Word was flashed to the auxiliary field where Foss' squadron, VMF-121, was based, alerting the squadron for an immediate strike. Twenty-three F4F Wildcat fighters would escort seven SBD Dauntless dive bombers and three TBF Avenger torpedo bombers. Eight AAF P-39 Aircobra fighters also participated. The F4Fs would each carry 200 pound bombs. The small bombs would not do much damage to the warships, but the job of the fighters would be to provide a diversion for flak gunners so that the bombers, with their heavier ordnance, could effectively strike the task force. Foss led a flight of eight of the fighters.

The formation of planes was climbing through 15,000 feet when Foss spotted some specks to the right, at two o'clock. He called out the bandits — six float-type Zero fighters. Leaving the rest of the Wildcats with the bombers, Foss took his flight out after the Zeros, jettisoning the bombs on the way.

The formation of Zeros was headed away from the Wildcats and descending. Foss swung his fighters in behind them and closed the distance. As the two formations converged, the Japanese planes made no effort to defend themselves. The Wildcats were not spotted until they were in close firing range. Foss opened up on the Zero he had chosen and pounded it with bullets. After a long burst the Zero exploded in a fireball. Foss was surprised to see a parachute blossom shortly after — the pilot had escaped the explosion!

Other Wildcat pilots also scored on the Zeros, but one F4F did not rejoin the formation when Foss gave the call to form up.

Grumman F4F-3 Wildcat

Then they could see the invasion force and they prepared to make their simulated attacks. Because of the way the fighters were approaching the fleet, Foss gave the order to attack in reverse order: the seventh aircraft first, with Foss diving last. As the plane in front of Foss was making his dive, Foss spotted what he thought was an enemy plane approaching. Sure enough, it was another float plane, this time a two-seater.

Foss and the enemy plane approached head-on. Suddenly Foss realized that the float-plane was trying to ram him. He banked steeply to the right to esscape and as he made the turn the enemy pilot chopped his throttle in such a way that the rear seat gunner had nearly a straight shot at Foss. Foss' fighter began taking hits in the cowl and the wings. One round burst through the canopy. The Wildcat absorbed many hits before Foss could jam the stick forward and dive beneath the Japanese plane.

He knew his plane was hurt badly, but the engine was still running smoothly. He decided to attack from below and pulled up into a steep climb at the float plane. He poured many rounds into the belly of the Japanese plane before it, too, exploded. Both the pilot and gunner were able to parachute to the sea. Number two for the day!

Almost immediately Foss spotted another two-seat float plane, this time below him. He checked his engine instruments and everything seemed to be working so he dove to the attack. This time the gunner in the rear cockpit did not see the Wildcat and after a long burst the Japanese plane began to smoke, then burst into flames as it headed for the sea. Number three!

Foss spotted F4Fs below him circling. They had completed their mock attacks, so Foss called for a joinup and headed for home. Soon he was joined by another F4F that was shot up even worse than Foss' fighter was. The two wounded ducks would go home together.

Then Foss spotted some airplanes behind them that were approaching quickly. Zeros! Almost at the same time, the engine of his Wildcat began to sputter and cough. The accurate shooting of the enemy gunner was finally taking its toll. Knowing that he could not take on the Zeros to protect himself and his battered wingman, Foss began a dive toward a cloud deck below. It was their only chance. Then, suddenly, his engine cut out altogether. After a short silence, it cut back in again — then out and in again. Now his engine instruments were giving him erratic readings, but he finally made it to the cloud deck. Foss did not know until later that the Zeros shot down the other Wildcat.

Foss continued descending in the cloud deck with his engine becoming rougher and rougher. He broke out of the cloud at 3,500 feet and spotted no more Zeros. But it was raining heavily as he continued above the sea. Then, he made out the coastline of an island. It had to be Malaita, north of the Solomons. He spotted a small village and considered that if he was going down it might as well be near civilization. He could not remember, however, whether this part of the island was in American or Japanese hands.

Then, the engine began knocking heavily, vibrating the entire airframe. He made his decision — he would ditch near the village. He opened the canopy and pulled back on the throttle. That did it — the engine quit for good. He lined up with the swells as he had been taught by the Navy and Marines and the Wildcat hit the sea with a crunch. The canopy slammed forward and the Wildcat began to sink almost immediately after it stopped. Water was soon over the railing and gushing into the cockpit, but Foss could not get the canopy open. He strained and heaved and finally it slid back. But now he was underwater and could not get out of the cockpit because his leg straps to his parachute were still fastened. Then as the cockpit filled with water, the parachute started floating to the surface but pushing Foss' head down in the water. The chute pulled him to the surface, but his head was still down in the water. He was drowning! Then, out of instinct, he pulled the inflation cords of his life jacket and as it inflated his body became upright and his head popped to the surface. He sputtered and disgorged water and after awhile regained his senses.

Taking stock of his situation, he estimated that he was about two miles from shore. The weather was so bad that he did not expect rescue airplanes to be able to spot him. It was late afternoon with just a few hours of daylight left. The waters were shark-infested. He decided to swim slowly toward the shore while there was still daylight, although he knew the tides in the area could be strong. After swimming for awhile he saw that he was making little, if any, progress. Then darkness fell and he stopped swimming.

Long after it became totally dark he suddenly spotted a small light, which seemed to be moving. Was it a boat? Then he felt movement near him. Sharks! They were circling around him! He broke another of the shark repellent capsules that he used intermittently throughout the afternoon and hoped they worked as advertised.

Now the light was getting closer, but Foss made no sound. He wanted to determine whether those on board were friendly or not. Then he could make out that it was a native dugout. He could see figures in the boat as it moved closer to him. Now he began hearing voices in a language he could not understand. Then came a loud voice, telling those on board, in English, to look over there. Relieved, Foss yelled that he was a friend, a birdman, an American. The boat approached and he could see the natives pick up clubs. They continued to jabber, but did not use their clubs. Then a pair of arms stretched out toward him. They were the arms of an Australian sawmill operator on the island. Also in the boat was a priest from the Buma Mission, the settlement Foss had seen from the air. He was safe.

A native had seen his crash landing, and several canoes had gone out to search for the birdman. Foss would fly again, no thanks to a Japanese floatplane gunner. And after a number of other exploits he would be given the Medal of Honor by President Franklin D. Roosevelt, himself.

Some months after Capt. Joe Foss was downed by an enemy gunner, another Marine Corps fighter pilot arrived in Guadalcanal. He was First Lieut. James E. Swett of San Mateo, Calif., known to his fellow flyers as

"Zeke". Like Foss, Swett was destined to receive the Medal of Honor for his bravery in combat and, like Foss, he was destined to be shot down by an enemy aerial gunner.

Marine Corps fighter pilots seemed to have had a monopoly on the Medal of Honor during World War II. Nine Marine fighter pilots received the nation's highest decoration for valor, which was more than AAF fighter pilots (5) and Navy fighter pilots (2) combined. (It is interesting to note that of the five AAF fighter pilots receiving the MOH, none was from the Eighth Air Force, which had more fighter aces than any other overseas combat command. MOH winners in the Eighth were gunners, bombardiers, navigators and bomber pilots.)

By the time Swett got to Guadalcanal in early spring, 1943, it was no longer the center of aerial and ground combat. The last of the Japanese ground troops had left the island and Swett had flown ground support missions for several weeks without having seen an enemy airplane. He was beginning to wonder if he would ever see aerial combat.

He would, and he would have Admiral Yamamoto to thank for it. Smarting at the loss of Guadalcanal, the admiral planned revenge air raids against allied forces in the area. He transferred combat planes from four aircraft carriers to augment the land-based planes in the area until he had assembled between three and four hundred bombers, fighters and torpedo planes. Allied intelligence sources noted the buildup, but could not determine the purpose of it.

On the morning of April 7, 1943, Lt. Swett had the duty of leading the dawn patrol for his squadron, VMF 221. His flight of four F4F Wildcats orbited on station for two hours with the usual early morning dullness — nothing was doing. They returned to their Henderson field auxiliary field and landed, through flying for the day, they thought.

But just as Swett and the three other pilots of the dawn patrol were climbing from their cockpits, the word was flashed to command centers that Australian coastwatchers had spotted a huge armada of enemy planes headed for Guadalcanal. The fleet of Japanese planes amounted to a total of 177; 110 of them Zero fighters and 67 Val dive bombers. The Americans would put up 76 Navy and Army Air Forces fighters against them.

The Wildcats of Swett and his division were quickly refueled and they were soon back in the air. Their orders were to defend the ships in the harbor at Tulagi, on Florida Island, obvious targets. He headed north in a climb and arrived over the harbor at about 17,000 feet. Almost immediately he spotted a gaggle of 20 enemy fighters at ten o'clock and he headed for them. Then he picked out a covey of Val dive bombers at a lower altitude which were headed for the ships in Tulagi Harbor.

He decided to go after the Vals to help protect the ships, and dove to the attack. As he approached the Vals he could see Zeros directly overhead diving toward him. He kept on his course toward the dive bombers hoping he could outrun the Zeros and get to the Vals before they got to him. He had outrun his wingmen and was all alone with no one to cover him.

Swett closed on the first Val, glancing around to find that he was indeed outdistancing the Zeros. The Val was in a glide straight ahead and when Swett was in range he fired, hitting the Val squarely with his first burst. Soon black smoke and flames erupted from the dive bomber and as Swett ducked underneath it, the Val went out of control, spinning toward the water. In his first try at aerial combat, Swett had shot down an enemy plane!

Then he shifted his attention to another Val, after checking that no one was on his tail. He closed rapidly on it, and again he scored with a short burst. The Val disintegrated in the air and Swett's Wildcat fought its way through the debris. He had number two!

Now he was down at low altitude and nervous about tangling with Zeros down low. But none were around. Off to his left a third Val was in its dive on a ship. Swett headed for it. He could not catch it before it released its bomb, but he stayed right with it in the dive pullout. He fired a couple of bursts at the bomber, but nothing happened. Then, he felt his plane rock and vibrate. He looked to his left and saw that there was a gaping hole in his wing, that his left flap was badly damaged and that one of his wing guns had been partially knocked from the wing. He looked around and saw no enemy fighters. What had hit him? Then he saw the puffs of black smoke — he had been hit by flak gunners from his own ships.

Swett's engine seemed to be running fine so he pressed the attack against the third Val. They were both down to 500 feet over the island now as Swett fired burst after burst at the enemy. Finally flames erupted from the Val and it turned on its side and crashed into the trees. Swett had his third victory.

He checked his tail and was still alone. Then he looked his plane over and checked the engine instruments. Except for a little control sluggishness from the wing damage everything looked fine. He estimated he still had one-half of his ammunition remaining, so he headed back to Tulagi to look for more Vals.

It was not long before he found them. Seven Vals were forming up after having made their attack. They were flying at 800 feet. Swett headed for the tail-end-charlie and gave it a good burst from his five remaining .50 calibers. Pieces and parts flew off the striken dive bomber, then it began to flame just before it hit the water. Four down.

Just after the attack Swett came to realize that he had been aware of the rear gunner in his fourth victim. He had not noticed them in the first three fights with the Vals. He wondered why he had not been fired at by them. Or had he? Now as he lined up on the next trailing Val, he was aware of the rear gunner. But, the gunner had not noticed Swett's Wildcat. Swett closed and gave the Val a healthy burst. Soon fire arced from the wing roots and the plane went into the water. Five down and he was an ace only minutes after meeting the enemy for the first time!

Swett quickly slid over behind the next Val and saw that the gunner had not seen him. He fired away and this time was rewarded with a large explosion. Again the Wildcat flew through the debris. A sixth victim of Swett's accurate shooting.

There were still plenty of Vals available, so Swett lined up on what would be his seventh score. After the first burst the Val began to smoke but continued flying. Swett hit him again with a long burst. He knew he must be low on ammunition. Finally, the Val nosed over and crashed into the water.

There were more Vals ahead and Swett wondered when the rear gunners would awaken to what was going on behind them. He would find out soon.

For his eighth attack he picked a Val off to his right. He would have to make a deflection shot at this one instead of a stern attack. As he swung into the attack and approached firing range, he felt sudden thumps on his Wildcat. He had been hit! The gunner had opened fire first. The front part of his canopy was shattered and there was blood on his face.

He continued on his firing run, opening fire when in range, but he could tell by more thumps that his plane was being damaged. As he got closer the gunner suddenly slumped and stopped firing. Swett saw the Val begin to smoke, but just then the chattering of his guns stopped. He was out of ammo. He quickly banked away and began looking around. He didn't have time to watch the last Val. He had to watch for Zeros now that he was defenseless.

He headed away from Florida Island southward toward Guadalcanal. Now he checked his engine instruments — the engine temperature was in the red and the oil pressure was on zero. He would never make it to Guadalcanal. He turned back to Florida Island where he would have to ditch the plane. As he approached the water he noticed muzzle flashes from a small island off the coast. He was being fired at again by his own troops!

The Wildcat bounced off the water before finally stopping, nose down. Swett's head had been thrown against the gunsight. He was dazed and in sharp pain with a broken nose. Water began pouring into the cockpit, but he was unable to get out at first. One of his straps was caught. As he sank ten, then twenty feet below the surface he finally pulled the cords to inflate his Mae West life jacket and was pulled to the surface. He inflated his small life raft and was picked up by a rescue boat shortly after.

Naturally there was some skepticism when Swett made his claim for seven kills from his hospital bed. So, an intelligence officer was sent to make a five-day trip to Florida Island to talk to witnesses to see if the claim could be verified. He returned with certain verification for all seven of Swett's claims — the first fighter pilot to down that many in one day (A Navy pilot was later to score nine kills in one day). The eighth Val, and the one whose gunner had downed Swett, may have been the one ground troops found crashed on a small island, but this could never be verified.

Swett's seven kills were not a fluke. He went on to double that amount during the rest of his combat tour, with his accurate shooting and excellent flying accounting for a total of 15.5 enemy planes.

Another Marine Corps ace and Medal of Honor winner who took a swim through the courtesy of a Japanese aerial gunner was Lieut. Robert M. Hanson. Hanson was the third ranking Marine ace with 25 victories. Twenty of these kills were recorded in just six consecutive flying days!

Hanson was born in India, the son of an American missionary. He spent his youth partly in India and partly in Massachusetts. When he completed high school in the U.S. he returned to India where he became a national wrestling champion. He was bicycling through Europe before returning to the U.S. for college and was in Austria when the country was occupied by the Germans. He was in college when the Pearl Harbor raid occurred and shortly entered the Navy pilot training program.

His dunking by a Japanese aerial gunner happened when his squadron,

VMF-215, was covering the allied landings on the island of Bougainville in the Solomons in November 1943. Flying his Vought F4U Corsair, Hanson spotted six Kate torpedo bombers headed for the American invasion fleet. All alone he hurled his fighter at the formation and broke it up.

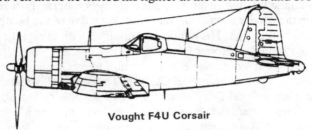

Vought F4U Corsair

Then he returned to the attack, shooting down one of the Kates. He kept at his attacks until finally the five remaining Kates jettisoned their torpedos and fled.

He rejoined his flight which shortly became engaged in combat with between 20 and 30 Zeros and Kates. Again attacking the Kates who were after the U.S. ships, Hanson shot down two more torpedo bombers, for a total of three victories for the mission. A Kate rear gunner scored at least one victory for himself when he damaged Hanson's Corsair so badly that he was forced to ditch the plane in a bay. He made a good landing and was able to get safely into his rubber dinghy. He drifted for six hours and then spotted part of the task force. He paddled toward it and was soon picked up by a destroyer. In a few days he returned to his airfield on Vella Lavella, another island in the Solomons chain, and was soon flying again.

Three months later, while in the last few days of his third combat tour and preparing to return to the States, he was scheduled for a mission to escort bombers and to strafe gun emplacements. The ground targets were on the island of New Ireland, northeast of Rabaul. The Japanese gunners in the gun emplacements met Hanson's flight with withering ground fire, which increased with each succeeding attack by the Corsairs. On one attack Hanson's fighter continued in a shallow dive and eventually hit the ocean in a large splash. Since no effort was made to bail out from the Corsair, it was assumed that the ace had been killed by the ground fire. No trace of Hanson or his plane was ever found.

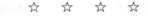

Lt. Commander Edward H. "Butch" O'Hare, first Navy ace of World War II and Medal of Honor winner, lost his life to an aerial gunner. The question is whether it was an enemy gunner or an American gunner.

O'Hare, who had 12 victories before he died, was an early hero when he single-handedly took on nine Japanese Betty bombers who were intent on sinking the carrier *Lexington.* He shot down five of the bombers and scattered the other four. His actions are credited with saving the carrier. He won the Medal of Honor for this feat.

His tragic death would come in an attempt to protect another carrier, the *Enterprise.* It was during the fighting for Tarawa and Kwajalein in late 1943. At night several Betty bombers began shadowing the big carrier dropping flares around the perimeter and generally making a nuisance of themselves. The Americans felt they were preparing for some sort of attack and developed a counterattack.

A TBF Avenger, equipped with radar for aerial interceptions, would be put in the air near the carrier at night. Flying its wing would be the new F6F Hellcat fighter planes who would attack when the TBF located the Bettys. Sure enough, the first night this defense force was put up the Bettys came in for the attack.

The TBF spotted a target and O'Hare, who was flying one of the fighters, and his wingman went after it but were unable to find it. Meanwhile the TBF spotted another target, closed on it, identified it visually as a Betty and the pilot fired at it with his two wing guns, getting good hits. The Japanese gunners returned the fire, but their accuracy was poor. As the TBF pilot peeled off from his attack, the turret gunner also got some good hits on the Betty and it went burning into the sea.

Moments later the TBF pilot and gunner repeated the feat and a second Betty flamed and crashed. Now O'Hare and his wingman wanted to rejoin the TBF. All three planes turned on their position lights to aid in the rendezvous and the fighters joined the torpedo bomber, one on each side. As they joined, the turret gunner of the TBF thought he saw an unlighted plane slice through the formation, and he fired a short burst. Then the lights of O'Hare's Hellcat were seen to dive away to the right. No trace of his plane was ever found. And the question of whether the guns that downed the ace were from an American plane or from the Betty that was thought to have flown through the formation is a question that will probably never be answered.

12. Bringing The Bird Home

There were a number of cases during World War II when gunners in combat flew their airplanes home when their pilots were either wounded, killed of otherwise incapacitated. Many times these gunners were also the flight engineers in the crew, not only because they had experience with engine controls, instruments and cockpit switches and levers, but because most of them could taxi the airplanes, which gave them familiarization with the flight controls, especially the rudder and brakes. In addition, engineer/gunners monitored the takeoffs and landings of big bombers from their engineer position just behind the pilot and copilot and were familiar with the procedures and sequences of takeoffs and landings. Added to this was the fact that the engineer/gunner normally operated the top turret in B-17s and B-24s, which was located immediately behind the flight deck, and thus easily accessible to the pilots.

In other cases the gunner who brought the ship back was one who had some experience as a pilot. Many of these were former aviation cadets who had washed out of pilot training and had at least some experience in flying, even though it may have been only a few hours in small planes.

One of the gunners who brought his ship back early in the war was Sgt. John J. Able, gunner/engineer on a B-17 assigned to the 43rd Bombardment Group flying out of New Guinea in the South Pacific. But the story of John Able does not start with him, but rather with his pilot, Capt. Jay Zeamer, Jr.

Zeamer had originally deployed to the South Pacific with the 22nd Bomb Group where he was assigned as a copilot flying B-26 Marauders. He flew some combat missions in the Marauder, but was not satisfied with his role in the 22nd, so he asked for a transfer. He got his wish and was assigned to the 43rd Bomb Group which was equipped with B-17 Flying Fortresses.

Like the 22nd, the 43rd was based in Australia but deployed forward to New Guinea to fly combat missions. Zeamer took a liking to the big bird right away, but couldn't get himself assigned permanently to a crew — there was no shortage of copilots because everyone wanted to fly B-17s. So, when the 43rd deployed to New Guineas, Zeamer was left behind in Australia.

It happened that a badly damaged B-17 had been dragged to one end of the field to be taken apart bit by bit and used as a source of parts to repair operational aircraft. Zeamer saw that with hard work it could be repaired and made flyable. He somehow got authorization to attempt what many considered was an impossible task and after much effort the junked bomber was ready to fly. The unit in New Guinea was notified and they replied that they would send a crew down to Australia to pick it up.

Zeamer was having none of this — it was his airplane! He went through those flyers who had been left behind, as he had, and recruited a crew. Sgt. John J. Able, gunner/engineer, was one of those who joined Zeamer.

The pickup crew climbed aboard the band-aid B-17, cranked it up and flew to New Guinea. When they arrived, there was an effort to assign the airplane to others, but again Zeamer rebelled. His Fort was for him and his crew. They even slept in the bomber to protect their precious plane. Somehow, they got away with it and were the talk of the group. Even overlooked was the fact that Zeamer had never been checked out to fly B-17s as pilot.

When the missions were handed out, though, Zeamer and his crew got those that no one else wanted: those that were dangerous or that were scheduled in bad weather. They took all that came their way and without exception, even when others did not return in bad weather or other unfavorable conditions, made it through without any problem.

Then one day along came a mission that was exceptionally rough: a lone reconnaissance over the northern Solomon Islands. It was one of those missions that no one would want to order a crew to take. The commander knew it had to be a volunteer mission. Zeamer happened to be the first pilot he ran into, and the commander told him about the mission. Zeamer knew the odds, so he gathered his crew and they were told what was involved, straightforward and without pulling punches. Without hesitation the entire crew volunteered.

The patchwork Fortress and its castoff crew took off on their impossible mission, augmented by a photographer who shared the nose with the bombardier and navigator. They flew over island base after island base, with the photographer recording the intelligence information that was vital to the progress of the fight against the Japanese in those desperate early days of the war. Surprisingly, they encountered no flak or fighters at their flight altitude of nearly 30,000 feet. All was quiet on the interphone as the gunners scanned for enemy fighters. John Able, at his post in the upper turret, had his twin fifties at the ready.

They were coming to the final target: an airstrip on Buka, the northernmost island in the Solomon Islands chain, and a base noted for its aggressive and experienced Zero pilots. The gunners strained to see if they could spot fighters rising to meet them. The ball turret gunner was the first to see the Zeros beginning their climb and called out that at least ten were on the way to intercept the lone B-17. The gunners increased their alertness, the photographer continued shooting pictures, and Zeamer and his copilot kept flying a steady course.

Then, from the nose, Lt. Joseph R. Sarnoski, the bombardier, called out more fighters that were rolling down the runway to join the fray. He estimated that at least 20 were on their way.

It was decision time for Jay Zeamer. He could at this point have broken off his photo run and escaped from the attack. A lone B-17 against twenty enemy fighters was certainly no match and his combat judgement would never have been criticized for avoiding such odds. But Zeamer held his course. He knew how important this photo mission was to the allied forces in the area. The B-17 droned on and the camera shutters kept clicking.

Then it was too late to turn away. The Zeros were upon them and marshalling for what looked to be an easy victory for the fighter pilots. The main attack would come from the nose. John Able, in the top turret, swung his twin fifties to the front of the airplane, and Lt. Sarnoski manned his single fifty in the nose. The other gunners tracked the other Zeros that were taking positions on either side of the bomber.

Then the Zeros came at the Forts, two at a time in a coordinated attack from the front. Bullets and exploding cannon shells raked the bomber — hits were taken in the plexiglass nose, in the cockpit and all over the fuselage. Five of the crew were injured on the first attack, but all stayed at their positions. It was Sarnoski in the nose who scored first against the Japanese, downing the lead fighter, as John Able in the turret watched it flame and then erupt in a ball of fire.

Able, himself, got the next Zero with one short burst into the engine of the attacker. It too flamed into a fireball that just missed striking the bomber.

In the next attack, the Fort was hit again, but again Sarnoski downed one of the attackers, which became a ball of fire. He then downed a third attacker, which went spinning out of control to the sea.

All the while, the photographer, who had not been injured, stayed at his work with his cameras. Then, he called the wounded Zeamer to say that he had his pictures and the mission was over. Zeamer swung the bomber toward home plate.

But they still had to battle through the fighters, which were grouping for another frontal assault. This time the fighters made an even more determined attack and the bomber suffered grievous damage this time to the control and hydraulic systems and to the oxygen system. Since they were then at 28,000 feet, Zeamer had to start a long dive for a lower altitude where the crew could continue to breath. As the attack continued, bombardier Sarnoski in the nose accounted for another Zero downed and one of the gunners knocked a wing off one of the attackers.

The attacks by the fighters came with even more fury. The crew had accounted for at least five Zeros, and the remaining Zero pilots were ferocious in their attempts to exact revenge. Sarnoski was hit again, this time mortally, as he tried to keep firing his gun. The two pilots received more wounds as they struggled to control the wounded bomber. And the attacks continued. After forty continuous minutes, the Zeros, either out of fuel or out of ammunition, turned back to their base at Buka. And, not a moment too soon for the B-17.

In the battered Fortress, the bombardier was dead, the navigator severely wounded, the copilot was unconscious, the pilot seriously wounded with one leg shattered and only one arm usable, John Able, in the top turret, was wounded but able to move, and other gunners were wounded. Except for the tail gunner and the photographer, the entire remainder of the crew was suffering from one kind of injury or other.

Then when Zeamer collapsed beside his unconscious copilot, the Fortress had no pilots. John Able would have to take over. He stood between the two pilots, grasped the controls and began flying the airplane. Knowing the general direction toward the base at Dobodura, New Guinea, Able put his back to the sun and hoped for the best. Others in the crew tried to administer aid to the two pilots. Zeamer, especially was bleeding profusely. The pilot would regain consciousness for short periods, during which he would give instructions to Able on operating the plane and finding the base, then his pain would cause him to lapse into unconsciousness for another period. For almost three hours they continued on until, finally, the navigator and others began recognizing landmarks that led the way home. Able began a letdown and shortly after, both pilots regained consciousness. Able had flown the plane home, but to make a landing in the condition the plane was in was another thing. The pilots decided to see if, between them, they could bring the bomber down safely. The copilot could work the rudder, and Zeamer, with his one useful arm, would control the elevators and ailerons.

They approached the 7,000 foot runway straight in, even though it was downwind, hoping that the pilots would not pass out again before they could get the plane on the runway. Even though the flaps could not be lowered and the brakes had been shot away, the two pilots managed to stop the crippled bomber at the end of the runway. Zeamer, his ragtag crew, and the band-aid bomber had come home from another mission and the intelligence people got their photographs.

Zeamer had lost so much blood that it was several days before he was out of danger. His mangled leg required amputation. 120 pieces of metal were removed from his body. Zeamer and the dead bombardier, Sarnoski were both awarded the Medal of Honor.

The patchwork bomber that gunner John Able flew home stood for several days off the runway. Small groups of men would gather to marvel at the beating the Fortress had taken. One even began to count the number of holes and tears in her fuselage. When he got to 1,000 he gave up. What was the use of going on?

In early 1944, 7th Air Force Liberators found themselves with the task of cleaning up Japanese-held islands in the Central Pacific that had been bypassed in the movement of the allies to the north. A number of these would be key locations in the drive to retake the Philippines. One of the most important of these islands was Truk, in the Carolines. Known as the Japanese Gibralter of the Pacific, Truk was a major supply and support center for the Japanese Navy and was stoutly defended from air attack both by fighters and by flak.

The Liberator *A-Vailable* from the 30th Bomb Group was assigned to make a night attack on Truk, and approached its target at 10,000 feet. As the Lib closed on its target, searchlights, followed by flak found the bomber. *A-Vailable's* pilot, Lt. Woodrow Waterous, took evasive action, then dived toward the target releasing the bombs at 6,000 feet. Still trapped by the searchlights and headed out to sea, they were almost out of range when the tail gunner spotted the shadowy outline of a Zero coming in at 4:30. The right waist gunner missed with a short burst and the ball turret gunner could not see the fighter because his windows were fogged up.

The Zero made another pass and this time the upper turret gunner nailed the fighter with a devastating blast that sent the Zero flaming into the sea.

The Zero got only five cannon hits on the bomber, but those hits did considerable damage. The trim tabs were knocked out, the radios dead, and large chunks were torn out of the nose section. The navigator was wounded in the leg, the copilot was dead, and the pilot, Waterous, was nearly blinded with wounds on his face. When the copilot was hit he slumped over the control wheel, sending the bomber into a dive. Waterous was finally able to regain control, but not until the airplane was down to 3,000 feet above the water.

Sgt. Paul Regusa, the engineer/gunner, took over the copilot duties, calling out instrument readings to Waterous, who could see only blurs. It would be a five hour flight back to their base, with a blind pilot and an unconscious navigator.

Sgt. Regusa gave up the copilot seat to Sgt. Bill Shelton to enable him to see if he could do something about the radios. As Regusa made his way back through the bomb bay he glanced down and saw that a 500-pound bomb dangled from its rack. He called for help and the right waist gunner and Regusa lay on the catwalk an cranked the bomb bay doors open. Suspended above the ocean the two struggled to free the bomb. Suddenly it released, but fell only part way, got hung up on something and now was swinging halfway out of the B-24. Struggling even harder, the gunners finally managed to manhandle the bomb back into the bomb bay and were able to secure it. They cranked the bomb bay doors closed once more.

Now fuel was running low and the pilot ordered the crew to jettison everything they could overboard. Out went guns, ammunition, flak jackets, and the Sperry ball turret.

As daylight came, all they could see ahead was water. Waterous prepared everyone for ditching, because without a navigator, they weren't even certain they were on the proper course for their base on Eniwetok. But just about the time all hope was gone, they sighted their goal. Now sitting in the copilot's seat was the bombardier, Lt. Bob Irizarry. Using the eyes of Irizarry, Waterous was able to bring the wounded B-24 safely back home.

Later in 1944, the 30th Bomb Group was softening up the Japanese-held fortress on the island of Iwo Jima, and gunners again were called upon to aid in the piloting duties.

The B-24 *Chambermaid,* with the crew of Lt. Bill Core departed

Saipan, where the 30th had moved, bound for Iwo. *Chambermaid* was on her 35th mission, having seen one crew through a combat tour and was now providing Core's crew with its sixth.

It was a daylight raid and in spite of some sticky weather, the formation of Liberators was able to stay together. Fifteen minutes from their target they saw a group of eight Japanese fighters below them, which was unusual.

Equally unusual was the fact that the Japanese pilots began making attacks from below. One Zero was hit by the fire from the Liberators and blew up. But, again, the Zeros used unusual tactics in that they did not break off the attack as the target was approached to avoid being hit by their own flak. The bombs were released on the installations and storage areas at the airfield on the island, but the fighters continued to attack.

Then, shortly after bombs away, Sgt. Mil Howard, manning the nose turret, called on interphone that his turret had stopped working. At about the same time, Sgt. George Shahein said that fluid was leaking into his ball turret and he couldn't see a thing out of it. Obviously the bomber had been hit. Bombardier Melvin Harms investigated and found that a flak hit in the nose had broken some hydraulic lines and the fluid had spread throughout the B-24, leaking into the ball turret.

Two fighters continued making passes at the plane, which now had two useless turrets. As one Zero came in from two o'clock cannon fire ripped into the cockpit behind the copilot's head, wounding him in the back of the head and in his back. He was dazed.

The second fighter now attacked from the left as the gunners tried to fight it off. Pilot Core now took stock of the damage the Liberator had sustained. In the cockpit the left outboard engine throttle had become disconnected and could no longer be controlled. The number two throttle was stuck in its position and could not be moved. Both engines were running at high rpm and consuming fuel rapidly. The right outboard engine was spurting oil, and Core knew that it might not last long. He felt the chances of getting the bird home were very remote.

Core called his flight leader and asked for protection, and four Liberators dropped back and surrounded the injured plane, giving protection from the fighters.

But, there was more bad news to come. The top turret gunner, Sgt. Richards, had been blown out of his turret by cannon fire and lay bleeding, while an intelligence officer who was along for the ride, lay beside Richards with 40 pieces of shrapnel in his body. Both men could bleed to death before they reached Saipan.

Those in the crew who were not wounded tended to the severely wounded first. Then it became the copilot's turn and he made his way back to the waist for treatment.

Core called for waist gunner Sgt. Robert Martin to man the copilot's position. Core knew that Martin could fly and was a frustrated pilot. He had washed out of pilot training after 150 flying hours, and Core had always felt that his experience might come in handy some day. The time was now.

Martin settled into the copilot's seat and Core gave him the controls. Core wanted to work on the throttles to see if he could get the engines back under control, because at this time he could control only the right inboard, with the two left engines running at high speed, while the right outboard continued to lose oil, smoke and burst into flames momentarily, then the fire would go out.

By experimenting, Core found he could slow down the number one engine by feeding it air from the turbocharger. He slowed down number two using the feathering button to cycle the rpms.

Martin continued to hand-fly the bomber, struggling against the surges of power from the speeding engines. The airplane wasn't speeding, though. It was making only 140 knots and using fuel at an alarming rate. The plane was also descending at 40 feet a minute. Martin's problems were complicated even more when they ran into turbulence.

Then the order came to lighten the plane, and the crew began dumping overboard guns, ammo, flak jackets and anything else that was loose. While attempting to unbolt and jettison the Sperry ball turret, the special wrench, slippery with hydraulic fluid, dropped overboard.

Core had almost given up reaching Saipan, but as the hours went by it looked more like a possibility. He knew though that he would not have any brakes. The engineer had tried to repair the hydraulic lines in the nose, but had no luck.

Core's flight leader suggested that he try the method used by other Liberators to help stop a brakeless bomber. This was to rig two personal parachutes, one on each side, to the gun mounts in the waist. Then, when on the ground, the parachutes could be deployed to slow the airplane.

Dusk was approaching as *Chambermaid* neared her base. It had been five hours since the cannon shells had slammed into her fuselage.

Sgt. Martin took the controls while Core went to check the airplane in preparation for landing. The crew had to crank the gear down, and while the right wheel went down and locked, the left remained firmly locked in its well. The crew had to kick the nose gear down. Core took the controls again and Martin hand-cranked the flaps down. As they approached the runway for the two-wheeled crash landing, Martin first cut the number one engine. As the big plane touched down at 105 mph Martin chopped the power on the other three engines. The parachutes were popped.

For a few seconds the plane rolled level on the right gear and nose wheel, then the left wing dropped, a propeller came off and the plane began skidding wildly off the runway. It went a hundred yards through gravel and dirt, finally coming up against a revetment with a thud, the left engine burning and the back of the fuselage broken. But, amazingly, none of the crew was killed. Most had been cut and bruised, but none, except the wounded, came out of the mission with serious injuries. *Chambermaid* had taken care of her family.

Tech. Sgt. Doug Labat and the crew of the B-24 *Old 26* knew they were likely to encounter a lot of action as they were briefed the night before for the mission. Their target, which they would strike from their home base in India, was a Japanese fighter airfield in occupied Burma. On the field were many, many Zeros.

As the Liberator climbed to its bombing altitude of 16,000 feet, the pilot and copilot switched seats. Since their bomber was on the left side of the formation, it would be easier for the pilot to fly formation from the right seat. Behind them, performing his flight engineer duties, was Sgt. Labat. When they reached enemy territory he would take his combat station in the top turret.

The bomber formation encountered no opposition until just after bomb release. Then 16 Zeros dove out of the sun and attacked. Labat swung his twin .50s toward the attackers, but another Zero, separate from the other fighters, began a head-on attack. Cannon shells tore through *Old 26* starting a fire in a wing tank and smashing into the nose.

Now a second Zero made a head-on attack and this time Labat was ready for it. Labat gave the fighter a short burst, then as it came closer poured a long burst into it. His guns got so hot that the turret cut out until Labat hit the reset button and continued firing. He wondered why the nose turret was not firing as well, not knowing that the nose gunner had been killed in the firing pass of the first Zero.

Then two things happened at once. Labat's rounds found their mark, exploding the fuel tanks of the Zero as it zoomed over the top of the Liberator. And the Zero's cannon shells found their marks too, sending flying glass and debris against Labat's legs, along with a rush of cold air.

He knew the plane had been hit severely. He could see the wing tank still blazing and the bomber was sliding right wing down in a dive beneath the bomber formation. He tried to get out of the turret to see what other damage had been done, but was pinned in by G-forces. Someone in another aircraft was calling for them to bail out of their wounded plane.

He finally managed to get out of the turret and went forward to see what was happening in the cockpit. What he saw was bad. The copilot in the left seat was slumped forward over the control column, causing the dive, and the pilot in the right seat was dazed and bleeding. There was a large hole in the windscreen in front of the copilot, and when Labat pulled the copilot off the controls, he could see he was dead from an explosive 20-mm cannon shell which had gone off in his face.

Labat unstrapped the copilot and dragged him from the left seat. Then he climbed into the left seat, grabbing the controls and manhandled the diving plane back to level flight. They were now down to 8,000 feet. In the dive two Zeros followed and inflicted more damage on the already stricken bird.

But, now *Old 26* was on its own, far from its formation and still over enemy-occupied territory. The fire in the wing tank had gone out, but the hydraulic system had been cut in several places and the prop governor in the number three engine was frozen at 2,300 rpm. But the plane was still flying and was able to join up with another formation of B-24s for mutual protection.

The pilot had lost some of his dazed condition and told Labat he would take over the piloting. Labat went back to his turret. Then the navigator, who was not getting responses to his intercom calls, came to the flight deck to see what was wrong. He saw the pilot's condition, gave him first aid and then climbed into the left seat to help fly the airplane.

Now another Zero came after *Old 26* in a head-on attack, and Labat answered the enemy fire with short bursts which caused the Japanese fighter to go into a dive. Labat later was given a probable for that attack.

When at last the enemy fighters had given up, Labat left his turret to perform his flight engineer duties, such as checking the fuel remaining for the long flight home. Then he replaced the navigator at the controls to enable the navigator to resume his navigation chores. The pilot was still in a semi-conscious state and continued to make, out of instinct, adjustments to the controls, which Labat corrected with patience. The gunner began to think about the landing at the home base and could picture how he would make the approach.

His musings were interrupted by another call of bandits at five o'clock. Two Zeros were trailing the B-24. Then the navigator called to Labat that there was an emergency landing field nearby and that they should head for it. As Labat pushed the nose over to let down for the landing approach, the Zeros lost interest and turned back.

As Labat flew the downwind leg of the traffic pattern at the emergency strip, the crew reported that one of the main gears would not lock in place. Labat again gave the controls to the navigator and hurried to attempt to work on the emergency gear extension system to get the main gear to lock. He was finally able to do so.

Rushing back to the flight deck, Labat saw that the pilot had recovered sufficiently to attempt the landing. They were now over water on the final approach, but a dike at the end of the runway loomed up. They were too low. Labat called at the pilot to pull up. As the pilot hauled back on the control column the wheels of the bomber glanced off the top of the dike. But then the wounded B-24 settled onto the runway just as if it had been a normal landing.

Labat knew that with the little remaining hydraulic pressure there could be only one application of brakes to stop the speeding plane. He called to the pilot and navigator to keep their feet on the brakes and not let up. They did, and the big bird rolled to a stop. As they stopped, the wounded pilot slipped into complete unconsciousness and Labat and the navigator had to carry him out of the plane to the waiting ambulance.

His copilot was knocked unconscious by a burst from an enemy fighter which found the cockpit, and his pilot suffered from a bullet which had entered his mouth and gone out through his shoulder. The crew of the B-17F *Dangerous Dan* was in a precarious situation, until engineer/top turret gunner Cliff Erikson slipped from his turret, took over the controls, and, with directions from his wounded pilot, flew the Fortress back to

England and landed it successfully — his first landing ever.

The date was June 11, 1943 and the target for the 8 AF bombers was Bremen, Germany. Clouds at the target forced the bombers to divert to Wilhelmshaven. While on the bomb run heavyflak had badly damaged the lead ship, causing it to yaw and slow down. This sudden maneuver caused the other formations to split up, which was just what the Luftwaffe fighters had been waiting for. They came at the bombers concentrating on the high group, the 379th Bomb Group, of which *Dangerous Dan* was a member. And *Dangerous Dan* might have been a casualty of the savage attack, as were eight other Forts, had it not been for new-found talent of gunner/engineer Cliff Erikson.

13. Of Actors, Politicos and Cowboys

World War II attracted many notable personalities into the armed services, and many of them served in flying assignments. A large number of these personalities were from Hollywood but there were some political and sport figures who suited up for flying duties as well.

Flying had proved attractive to many film stars, and a number of these used their pre-war skills to train Army Air Forces, Navy and Marine pilots. These included Richard Arlen, John Payne, Robert Taylor (Navy) and Robert Cummings. Actor James Stewart, after instructing in B-17s in the U.S. went to the Eighth Air Force in England, flying 20 missions in B-24s as squadron commander of the 703rd Bomb Squadron of the 445th Bomb Group. Comedian George Gobel instructed in B-26 Marauders before becoming a Hollywood personality. Actor/director Jack Webb was also an AAF B-26 instructor. Serving as transport pilots were Gene Autry, Dale Robertson and Ernest Gann, flying C-47s, while Tyrone Power flew Marine R5D-3s in the Pacific with VMR-353. Ed McMahon flew F4U Corsair fighters while Wayne Morris became Hollywood's only ace, earning seven victories over Japanese aircraft flying F6F Hellcats from the carrier *USS Essex* with VF-15. Future star Dennis Weaver was a Navy flyer, and William Conrad was reportedly grounded for flying his fighter plane beneath the San Francisco Bay Bridge. Tennessee Ernie Ford and Cameron Mitchell served as bombardiers. Former child star Jackie Coogan flew as a glider pilot in Burma with the First Air Commandos.

Vice President George Bush flew as a TBM Avenger torpedo bomber pilot in the Pacific, while former senator George McGovern flew a combat tour as a B-24 pilot in the 455th Bomb Group of the 15th Air Force. Barry Goldwater was an AAF instructor pilot in the Air Transport Command.

In the world of sports, Tom Landry flew 30 combat missions with the Eighth Air Force in Europe as a B-17 pilot. He survived a crash landing that sheared off both wings of his bomber. Ted Williams was a Marine fighter pilot during World War II and fought in combat during the Korean fracas as well. Tom Harmon flew B-25 bombers for the AAF, at first. But after a crash landing on a ferry flight in the jungle of South America, from which he was the only survivor, he was changed to P-38 fighters. He was shot down by Japanese fighters and spent 30 days making his way back to his base. He is officially credited with downing two enemy aircraft in the 14th Air Force in China while flying with the 449th Fighter Squadron.

A number of entertainment and political personalities also served as aerial gunners. The most prominent was actor Clark Gable.

From 1930 to the time of Pearl Harbor, Clark Gable had made upwards of 45 movies. He made eight in 1931 and another eight in 1932 alone before slackening off to a rate of three films a year. He had firmly established his stardom by playing male leads in *Mutiny on the Bounty* and *Gone With The Wind* and had won an Oscar for best actor in the film *It Happened One Night*. He had been among the top ten stars in Hollywood for more than ten years. Just after Pearl Harbor, in January 1942, his wife, actress Carole Lombard was killed in an airline crash near Las Vegas, Nevada. Gable, who was devoted to her, grieved so that he could not bring himself to resume acting, and he thought more and more about going into the military service. He began to get his affairs in order, such as closing up the ranch that he and Lombard had loved so much.

There are conflicting stories about much of Gable's wartime service. A biography of Gable by Lyn Tornabene gives one rendition of his entry into the service that began with a telegram from the Chief of the Army Air Forces, General H.H. Arnold, inviting him to join the AAF and saying that he had a highly important assignment for him. The telegram was sent to his studio, MGM, where it was sidetracked so that Gable never received it. The biography goes on to say that after Gable got his affairs in order and took a fishing trip, he enlisted in Los Angeles in August 1942.

A biography of General Arnold by Thomas M. Coffey, on the other hand gives a different version. The biography maintains, based upon information from General Arnold's son, H.H. Arnold, Jr., that Gable met with General Arnold to talk about his coming into the AAF, and that an MGM press agent who went with Gable to the meeting tried to talk General Arnold into taking Gable in as a captain. General Arnold is said to have told Gable that he just could not come into a service as a captain when he had no military experience. Gable is said to have telephoned General Arnold that evening agreeing with him and told the general he would start as a private.

In any event, Gable was enlisted as a 41-year-old private, but that would not last long, since his first assignment was to Miami Beach to attend the 13-week Officer Candidate School which would make him a second lieutenant upon graduation. The highly important assignment that General Arnold had for Gable was to make movies of varying activities in the AAF for public relations purposes. It was no coincidence that an MGM camerman, Andrew McIntyre, also became an OCS trainee and was at Gable's side constantly during the training. The academic portion of the training gave Gable little trouble. He said it was like learning a script. Gable duly graduated and received the gold bars of a second lieutenant. Then he received a specific assignment from General Arnold to do a film on aerial gunners since casualties among gunners were high and the AAF was having trouble enticing men to become gunners.

So, Gable and his camerman sidekick Andrew McIntyre went off to aerial gunnery training at Tyndall Field, Florida. Gable was promoted to first lieutenant there one month after he had graduated from OCS. Gable received his gunner's wings on January 7, 1943, as did Andrew McIntyre.

The next assignment for the two movie-makers was to Pueblo, Colorado, where they were assigned to the 508th Bomb Squadron of the 351st Bomb Group, a B-17 unit which was training for overseas combat. Their assignment was to make a film of a typical heavy bomb unit getting ready for combat. While there, Gable assembled a number of other AAF men who had been Hollywood moviemakers. They called themselves "The Little Hollywood Group." While the bomb group trained, Gable's crew traveled to Los Angeles assembling equipment for their task.

The bomb group went overseas in April 1943. Gable, now a captain, just six months out of OCS, went with it. They were assigned to the Eighth Air Force in England based at Polebrook.

There are many conflicting stories about how many combat missions Gable flew as a photographer and aerial gunner. Accounts vary from one, to five, and to "a half-dozen." The one mission we know for certain that he flew was to Antwerp on May 4, 1943. It was in the B-17F *Eight Ball,* assigned to the 359th Bomb Squadron of the 303rd Bomb Group, which was piloted by Capt. William R. Calhoun of Birmingham, Alabama. Targets were the Ford and General Motors works; there were no losses.

He is also said to have flown the first mission of his own group, the 351st, on May 14, 1943. The target, an airfield at Courtrai, Belgium,was supposed to have been a milk run. According to one of his fellow moviemakers, a 20-mm round came up through the bottom of the plane, knocked the heel off Gable's boot and went out the top of the fuselage near Gable's head. Two of 34 Fortresses were lost on the raid.

On another mission, where Gable manned a gun in the nose, he told the press that a German fighter pilot came head on so close that he could see the pilot's features. He fired his gun and said he didn't see how he could have missed the attacker, but he admitted that he did.

On June 6, 1943 in an Associated Press story filed by Leo Branham that appeared in the *Los Angeles Times,* the reporter claimed that "his (Gable's) sole operational mission to date" was the May 4th mission to Antwerp. So, if Gable flew the Belgian mission on May 14th, the Associated Press did not know about it.

Other missions Gable is said to have flown include a raid to the Ruhr Valley in Germany in the lead aircraft of the group that attacked Gelsenkirchen. He filmed gunners at work in a 351st Group B-17 piloted by Major Theodore Milton. Also in August 1943 Gable flew a flight in a 91st Bomb Group B-17F named *Delta Rebel No. 2.* The plane did not return from the first Schweinfurt mission a few days later.

It is said that Hermann Goering, the German Air Minister, placed a bounty on Clark Gable to the fighter pilot who could down him, dead or alive. Goering is said to have placed a $5,000 price on the downing in addition to a furlough and immediate promotion for his capture. Of course similar stories are told about a variety of people Goering is supposed to have wanted to capture. The one about Gable was related by one of "The Little Hollywood Group" who was a screen writer.

The story is told about Gable's identification with the combat crews. One day he went to the base hospital to see a turret gunner he knew who had returned from a mission badly wounded. He found the young gunner wrapped in bandages like a mummy with only his face showing. The chief surgeon, a colonel, told Gable that the boy was loaded with morphine and would not know that Gable was there. Then, the surgeon began to describe the gunner's injuries and said that he had only a few hours left. As Gable listened to the medic, he saw large tears welling out of the gunner's closed eyes. He grabbed the surgeon by the arm and shoved him out of the ward and into the hallway. The senior officer protested, but Gable told him that if he ever did anything like that again he would kill him. Then Gable left. This, too, was reported by one of Gable's screenwriters.

By late October 1943, Gable's crew had shot 50,000 feet of film and the team was sent home. Before leaving, Gable received an Air Medal decoration and a bronze battle star to his Europe-Africa, Middle Eastern campaign medal. He was ordered to report to General Arnold in Washington, D.C.

When he met General Arnold, however, he was in for a shock. The general welcomed him back then asked him what he had sent Gable to England for. He had forgotten. Gable answered that it was to make a film about aerial gunners, to help with a problem about them. The general replied that the gunner problem was licked and that Gable could do whatever he wanted to with the film. Gable was devastated.

Gable was assigned to the Hal Roach Studios in Hollywood, which was engaged in producing training films for the AAF. Lt. Ronald Reagan was among those working there. Head of the project, called "Fort Roach" in deference to its military orientation, was Major (later Lt. Col.) Paul Mantz, the famous movie stunt pilot. But when Captain Clark Gable reported for duty, he preferred to work with the MGM people with whom he was familiar.

Capt. Clark Gable (L) goes over some material with movie stunt pilot Major Paul Mantz, his commander at "Fort Roach" (Charles A. Watry collection)

Gable, from the footage he had shot mostly with the 303rd Bomb

Group, produced a 63-minute feature entitled *Combat America*. As luck would have it, the film came out at about the same time as the popular film *Memphis Belle,* which far overshadowed Gable's effort. Gable's film appeared seldom from then on. Other footage was made into a film entitled *Wings Up,* which had been recorded when Gable was at OCS at Miami Beach. In all, a total of five films were produced from the footage shot by the Gable team.

D-Day arrived and Gable had no further assignments. By now he was a major. He requested relief from active duty, which was granted. He continued work on his films as a civilian, however, until they were all completed.

"Tail Gunner Joe" was the name given to a highly controversial politician — one whose World War II wartime record is shrouded in conflicting accounts. *"Tail Gunner Joe"* was also the title of a three-hour-long 1977 television program that was highly biased against its subject: Senator Joseph McCarthy of Wisconsin. McCarthy, of course, was the Republican senator who led the 1950s investigations into communists in governmental positions.

McCarthy was also the consummate politician and his every action as an adult was geared toward advancing his political goals. He knew when he was quite young that he wanted to be a politician. As a young lawyer he was defeated in a bid for election as a county district attorney, but he learned from the experience. The next time he ran for office it was for a circuit judgeship and he upset the incumbent by a wide margin.

His tenure as a circuit judge was a political boon, since in his travels he got to know many voters across the state of Wisconsin. When Pearl Harbor came along, McCarthy, as a judge, was exempt from military service. But he knew how valuable a combat record was for a politician, so he applied for and received a commission as a first lieutenant in the branch of service known for its heroes: the Marine Corps.

He was soon in the Pacific as an intelligence officer. His duties included briefing and debriefing pilots in his dive bomber squadron. He never trained as an aerial gunner. Evidently he was quite competent as an intelligence officer, but the duty was hardly dangerous or heroic.

How he came to fly combat missions in his unit's SBD Dauntless dive bombers as a rear gunner has two versions: the friendly version, by himself, and an unfriendly version by his detractors.

McCarthy is quoted as saying his rear gunner experience got its start because, as an intelligence officer, he was not satisfied with the quality of the target photos he needed for his briefings. He complained about them so much to his squadron commander that the C.O. one day told him to find someone who was qualified as a radio operator, gunner and photographer. McCarthy knew that there were no men around that qualified, so he quickly learned to operate a camera and began flying missions to photograph Japanese targets. In 1944 he claimed to have flown fourteen bombing missions. He upped the figure to seventeen by 1947 and he topped out at thirty-two by 1951.

The unfriendly version of McCarthy's exploits in combat was generated by a Marine captain who claimed to have been stationed with McCarthy at Bougainville. He wrote a letter to a Wisconsin newspaper alleging that McCarthy's only combat experience were two missions, both flown the same day.

Some reporters decided to follow up the story and check official Marine Corps records. According to them, the missions his squadron was flying from Henderson Field on Guadalcanal in late 1943 were pretty routine and boring. To ease the boredom, pilots tried to set various sorts of records, such as most missions in one day, most ammo expended, and so forth. The back seats of SBDs were open to anyone who wanted to go along, since the real shooting war had moved away from the area. Ground personnel liked to go along for the cool ride in the back seat to get away from tropic heat of the island. It broke the monotony of duty on the island and was not dangerous since few Japanese remained in the area.

One day McCarthy decided he would try to break the record for the most ammo used in a single mission. Up he went in the SBD and was allowed to blast away at the coconut palms, setting a new record of 4,700 rounds expended from his twin .30-calibers. A few weeks later, after the public relations officer had issued a press release on the feat, McCarthy had collected a whole stack of newspaper clippings from his home state, which he said were worth 50,000 votes.

The probable truth is that McCarthy flew about a dozen flights and came under enemy fire at least once. He had no aerial combat, but strafed abandoned Japanese airfields, hit some fuel dumps, and on one occasion put a couple of .30-caliber rounds through the tail of his own plane.

By chance, McCarthy met a young PT boat commander named John F. Kennedy. They hit it off and McCarthy was invited to go along on some of Kennedy's patrol missions. His fascination with machine guns was satisfied on the PT boat when he was allowed to man one and fire away at his pleasure. Even though McCarthy became a Republican senator and Kennedy a Democrat senator, their relationship was always cordial. Kennedy was the only Democrat in the Senate who was consistently neutral on McCarthy, and he attended both McCarthy's wedding and his funeral.

In 1951 there were charges by columnist-commentator Drew Pearson that McCarthy had faked his combat record. A fellow senator obtained McCarthy's service record from the Marine Corps and inserted it into the Congressional Record. Included in the record were three citations. The first was from the Commander in Chief, U.S. Pacific Fleet, Admiral Nimitz. It commended Capt. McCarthy his volunteer duty as a gunner and photographer in the Solomon Islands in late 1943. There are those who say that McCarthy wrote the commendation himself, forged his C.O.'s signature and forwarded it up through headquarters, where Nimitz, who signed hundreds of such citations, routinely signed it.

There was another citation signed by the Assistant Commandant (Air) of the Marine Corps commending McCarthy for his 30 months of service, particularly in a combat area.

The third citation was written by his immediate supervisor, a major. It cited McCarthy's actions as a volunteer gunner, photographer and observer and listed several of the targets McCarthy had attacked. These included Kolombangara, Kara, Ballale, Kahili, Buka and Bonis.

In 1944 McCarthy had taken a 30-day leave from the South Pacific to run for Senator, but was defeated. He learned from this experience and decided in 1946 after he had left the Marine Corps to try again. This obscure circuit judge was going up against a veteran senator with 21 years in office — one who had a real political machine behind him. Senator Robert La Follette thought so little of the challenger's chances that he remained in Washington until just two weeks before the primary, then campaigned only half-heartedly before the election. Meanwhile, McCarthy was campaigning lustily and vocally. The outcome was close, but McCarthy upset a political legend and went to Washington. A notable contribution to his victory was McCarthy's campaign poster: it featured a photograph of McCarthy attired in flying helmet and goggles with belts of machine gun ammunition draped around his shoulders.

☆　　☆　　☆　　☆

While Gable and McCarthy could hardly have been called "career" gunners there are other well-known people who were. One of them would later play such parts in movies as Moses, Michelangelo, and receive an Oscar for his portrayal of Ben Hur. That man, of course, is Charlton Heston.

From high school on, Heston knew he was to be an actor. Everything fell into place for him in the early part of his acting career, which differs from many actors who struggled to make good. Heston acted in plays at his high school and in little theater groups. From one of these groups he was given a scholarship to Northwestern University, which had one of the better drama departments in the U.S. He was lucky in another way, too. He could not have afforded to go away to college, but since he lived in a north shore suburb of Chicago, he could walk to his classes at Northwestern.

While there he met a girl who would become his wife for more than four decades. Heston went into the Army, but just before he was to ship out for overseas, he and Lydia were married. Heston spent the next year-and-a-half as a radio operator/gunner on B-25s in the Aleutians. He says his marriage profited by this separation from his bride because most doomed marriages fail in the first year. He avoided that circumstance, courtesy of the Army Air Forces.

As with most Aleutian assignments, conditions were grim and the duty was boring. Of his wartime overseas service Heston says only, "I succeeded in not getting shot." He was also thankful for the end of the war by the atomic bomb — it meant he would avoid participating in the assault on the main islands of Japan.

He and Lydia went to New York after his discharge to look for work in the theater. Lydia found a part first while Heston posed for art students at a dollar and a half an hour, with free tea and cookies every second hour.

Then his luck in the theater continued. He was chosen for a small part in a long-running play, which got his career off the ground for good. He maintains it was his size that got him the part, because the star, Katherine Cornell, was tall and liked to be surrounded by taller men. The play was *Antony and Cleopatra,* and 25 years later Heston was to star in a film version of the play and to direct the film as well.

Another actor/radio operator/gunner who had luck in his early theatrical career as well as military service is Paul Newman. Prior to the entry of the U.S. into World War II, Newman had started to college. His career goals at this point were not well defined, so he took business and economics classes, when he really didn't see himself as a businessman. The Japanese attack on Pearl Harbor gave him the breathing spell he needed to sort out his goals.

He quickly enlisted in the Navy and volunteered for the pilot training program. He was assigned to the V-12 program at Yale University. He was at Yale only briefly, because it was determined that he was color-blind and therefore could not qualify as a pilot.

Then it was on to training as an aircraft radio operator and gunner. For the next two years he served on torpedo bombers in the Pacific. Of his service, he says he is an adjustable type of person and suffered no traumatic experiences in boot camp, training or in overseas duty at sea. Later, when the Hollywood types tried to make a wartime hero of him, they were disappointed. He had no heroic tales to relate and maintains that life at sea is ninety-nine percent boredom.

Newman says that he didn't see any real combat. Most of his missions were flying from Pacific islands on submarine patrol and other patrol missions that resulted in no action.

Newman's luck, however, would stand him in good stead during his sea service. Each month, on a rotating basis, a torpedo bomber squadron would requalify in carrier landings aboard a convenient carrer. The six planes of a squadron would fly to a carrier for the training. One month, when it became Newman's squadron's turn to requalify, his pilot came down with a severe ear problem and was grounded. So, instead of six planes being sent to the carrier only five went, with Newman's crew remaining behind.

The five other crews were in the crew ready room on the carrier when a Japanese kamikazi airplane struck the ship. The flying suicide bomb penetrated the carrier and destroyed the ready room killing all of the flight personnel from Newman's squadron...except for the crew that had been left behind because of its pilot's bad ear.

Newman was in the radio room of his carrier just seventy miles off the coast of Japan when the atomic bomb attacks on Hiroshima and Nagasaki were made. Like Charlton Heston, he was spared the inevitable invasion of the main islands of the enemy.

Charlton Heston's real name is Charlton Heston, and Paul Newman's real name is Paul Newman. But Slim Pickens' real name was Louis Bert Lindley, Jr. Before he became an actor, Slim Pickens was a working rodeo rider and clown for almost thirty years. He picked up his stage name in his rodeo days at the suggestion of a veteran rodeo rider who told him that was what he could expect to earn. He also wanted to keep his participation in rodeos a secret from his rancher father, who needed his help on the ranch. His rodeo activities earned him a crushed chest, two skull fractures, two broken wrists, a broken elbow, collar bone, left hand, both feet, and back as well as broken ribs beyond count.

When World War II came along, his list of injuries kept him out of the service. Later in the war he was accepted for radio operator training by the Army Air Forces because someone read his former occupation of "rodeo" as "radio". So he became a radio operator/gunner on a bomber.

After his wartime service he was cast in a part in a movie as a rodeo rider. Later more parts came his way, but usually in the role as sidekick to the star in Republic Studio B-westerns. Gradually his acting talent which he considered as just being himself, led to roles in important films, including *Blazing Saddles, One-eyed Jacks* with Marlon Brando and with Willie Nelson in *Honeysuckle Rose.* Probably his strongest role was as an Air Force B-52 pilot in the film *Dr. Strangelove,* when he rode an atomic bomb down to a Soviet target waving his six-gallon Stetson rodeo-fashion as he fell. His performance stood out even when matched against such actors in the film as Peter Sellers and George C. Scott.

Other actor-gunners include Sabu, the little Indian boy who charmed the world with his film debut in *Elephant Boy.* Sabu, whose name was Sabu Dastagir, went on to make films in England and the United States. During World War II, now a U.S. citizen, he had probably the most extensive combat record of any of the notable gunners, flying 42 missions as a B-29 tail gunner.

Norman Fell, the sad-faced character actor whose early film credits include *Bullitt* and *Pork Chop Hill,* but who is probably better known for his role as the landlord in the TV series *Three's Company,* was a B-25 gunner in World War II, serving overseas in Alaska.

Walter Matthau, the prominent character actor who has had many roles in major motion pictures, including *The Odd Couple* and *Hello Dolly,* was a gunner/radio operator in B-24s with the Eighth Air Force. He served with actor James Stewart in the 453rd Bomb Group based at Old Buckenham. During his wartime service, Matthau garnered six battle stars and was discharged in 1945 as a staff sergeant. He won an Oscar for his performance as best supporting actor in *The Fortune Cookie.*

The star of the long-running television western adventure series *Have Gun Will Travel,* Richard Boone, was a rear gunner on Navy torpedo planes during World War II. He served aboard a variety of aircraft carriers, including *Intrepid, Enterprise* and *Hancock* in the Pacific area.

Charles Bronson, the rugged character actor of such thrillers as *Battle of the Bulge, The Great Escape, The Dirty Dozen* and *The Magnificent Seven,* was reported by Hollywood publicity sources to have flown as a gunner in his wartime service. His AAF hitch, however, consisted of duty at Kingman Army Air Field, in Arizona, as a truck driver for the 760th Mess Squadron.

14. Ernie Pyle Meets The Gunners

Ernie Pyle was known as the "GI's War Correspondent" in World War II because he told the story of the war from the enlisted man's viewpoint. He also tried to get as many names of men as he could in his dispatches, and many times included their street addresses in the home towns. In the early part of the war he visited with Army infantry, artillery, armor and engineer units in North Africa, the Mediterranean area and then in England and Europe. Later in the war, he would go to the Pacific and there he would concentrate on sailors and Marines. In 1944 Pyle won a Pulitzer prize for his reporting.

Now and then, however, he would visit a flying group or squadron, to keep, he said, some sense of proportion about the various fighting units. When he visited a flying unit, if it were a bomber outfit he usually bunked with the aerial gunners. From his writings we can get a sense of what sort of people aerial gunners were. Not necessarily in the heat of battle, but in the tent or Quonset hut, or Nissen hut — where the gunners lived. He could then see them as people, rather than as fighting men.

One unit he visited was the 47th Bomb Group (Light) of the Twelfth Air Force. He caught up with the 47th in Italy. But the group had been fighting in North Africa and the Mediterranean area for some time. It had taken part in the battle with the Germans at Kasserine Pass, and had fought through Tunisia. The group had moved to Souk el Arba, then to Cape Bon and on to the islands of Malta and Sicily before arriving in Italy. Their base had been scraped out of volcanic earth by British engineers where three days previously there had been a huge vineyard.

The 47th flew Douglas A-20 Havoc light bombers. There were two aerial gunners on each crew, both manning the rear of the plane. One fired from a top turret, while the other had a retractable gun which he fired through an open hatch in the bottom of the fuselage. At this stage of the war the German fighter force in the area had weakened, so the gunners and the rest of the crew were mainly concerned with flak. Many would complete a combat tour without having seen an enemy fighter.

Pyle said that he found very few gunners who really liked to fly combat. Most of them appeared to him to accept their jobs as just that — jobs. They kept close track of their missions, counting each as a step nearer

9th Air Force A-20s of the 410th Bomb Group (647th Bomb Squadron) on their way to the target in Europe

their goal — going home.

Pyle gave each gunner the rank of sergeant. He did not differentiate among the various grades of sergeant — to him they were all the same — buck sergeants. Some might have been master sergeants and some might even have been corporals, but if they wore flying suits, on which rank was not displayed, he could not have been expected to know what their true ranks were.

In one tent he visited, there were seven sergeant gunners. The tent was the pyramid type which everyone, including officers, called home. The tents were equipped with a stove and the flyers slept in sleeping bags on foldable cots. There was one lightbulb per tent, and the electrical power generators operated from six in the morning until ten at night. So their billet activities were controlled by an outside force and nobody bothered to turn the light on or off.

Pyle had been invited to the tent of the seven sergeant gunners to share an evening snack. Although there was plenty of food available at the mess tent, many gunners liked to cook their favorite snacks in their tent in the evening. Sgt. Alban Petchal, from Steubenville, Ohio, was the gunner who issued the invitation to Pyle. His specialty was eggs scrambled with potatoes, with the potatoes scrambled right into the eggs. Petchal got the eggs from local Italians for twenty cents each.

As they were eating their snack, Pyle listened to some stories about their experiences, and most of the seven seemed to have had at least one that had been hazardous.

Robert Sweigert, of Williamsport, Pennsylvania, had been hit by flak and had spent two months in the hospital. He had also survived a crash landing in which the plane had broken in two and caught fire. The crew survived, luckily.

Guadalupe Tanguma, from San Antonio, had just received his orders rotating him home. He had gone through an experience that all A-20 gunners worried about. Since the fuselage of the craft was very narrow, there was no space for a copilot's position. So the light bomber was flown by a single pilot. If, on a ground attack mission, the pilot were killed, would the gunners in the rear know it, and if they did, would there be time enough for them to bail out? There was no way they could reach the pilot.

This happened to Tanguma and he and the other gunner took to their parachutes. Tanguma hit a tree upon landing, but he was upside down. Some Italians helped him down, and he gave them his parachute in return. Soon he was at a farmhouse dining on fried eggs. Then the Italians showed him the way back to his base where he rejoined the other gunner who also had landed safely. Tanguma's fluency in Spanish had helped him in his relations with his Italian saviors.

Charles Ramseur, of Gold Hill, North Carolina, had his terrifying experience the day of Pyle's visit. It was not in combat, but with his first sergeant, who had railed at him about not having shaved for several days. Ramseur, after he entered the AAF, had taught himself engraving. With a penknife he had engraved everything metal that he owned. His decorations all had designs, his canteen top was covered with names and flight insignia, his photo album had engraved aluminum covers which had come from a downed German plane. Even his steel helmet bore engraved bombs signifying the number of missions he had flown. He was looking forward to a job as an engraver following the war.

Robert Fleming, Cambridge, Massachusetts, and Steve Ujhelji, Salem, Ohio, who were on the same crew, shared a harrowing experience which won for their pilot a high decoration, the Distinguished Service Cross. Their A-20 had been badly shot up on a mission and it appeared that they would have to crash-land when they got back to the base. At the base, a fighter, also heavily damaged, was making a crash landing as well, but in the opposite direction of the A-20. The A-20 pilot brought his wounded bird in, saving Fleming and Ujhelji, but also he did it so well that he managed to avoid the fighter, whose pilot also survived.

Petchal, who had provided the feast of scrambled eggs and potatoes, had probably the most harrowing experience of any of the seven.

It was on the trip from the U.S. to their overseas station in North Africa. His plane became separated from the rest and ended up over the desert with no fuel. They crash-landed in some sand dunes and all three crewmen were injured. They stayed by the plane for three days, but no rescue came. On the fourth day they began walking, after setting fire to their A-20. They had a five-gallon can of water. Petchal had stomach pains and the two officers were semi-delirious.

After several days they found a trail and later in the day a camel caravan came upon them. The Arabs fed them and let them ride on the camels, but the ride was so rough they preferred to walk.

It was after ten days that they arrived at a French army outpost. By then they had walked more than 100 miles. They spent several weeks in a hospital before they recovered. At the time of Pyle's visit, Petchal had flown more than 60 combat missions, had been wounded by flak once, and was soon expected to be rotated to the U.S.

Another gunner without a frightening experience was John McConnell of Cedarhurst, New Jersey. He had flown nearly his complete tour without seeing an enemy fighter and his A-20 had suffered just one small flak hit. He said that suited him fine. He was saving a brown liquid that friends had sent him in a coffee container for his last mission. He acknowledged that it wasn't coffee.

Pyle received another invitation to visit a gunners' tent where the daily entertainment was to blow up the heating stove. It had been known to blow up seven times in one day.

The perpetrator of this feat was a sergeant named Gilford Muncy who hailed from Hyden, Kentucky. Muncy and his tentmates also relished late evening snacks, and their specialty was fried chicken, which they bought in the nearby village for five dollars apiece. One evening when it was Jack Bohn's turn to prepare the meal, the Scranton, Pennsylvania native made chicken soup, which was not up to his normal standard. He discovered he had used GI soap in place of butter in the soup.

Just before the generators were turned off for "lights-out" the stove blow-up ritual was to be performed. Muncy turned off the stove and let it cool. He cautioned Pyle that when guests came to witness the explosion, the stove would often get "contrary" and not blow up. When the stove had cooled, Muncy again turned the gas back on. They waited. Then Bohn got as far as he could from it and threw a lighted match through the open door. Everyone waited but nothing happened. The contrary stove wouldn't blow up that night.

One gunner, Sgt. John D. Baker, from Indianapolis, had flown more missions than anyone in his squadron. He was well beyond the normal number of missions for a combat tour, and his goal was to log 100 missions.

Many other A-20 gunners were about to complete their tours and were looking forward to rotating to the States. Most said, however, that they would be willing to stay and fly additional missions if they were needed.

A few others were almost at the breaking point — one was not only terrified by combat, but fearful of flying at all. Most gunners behaved on the ground just as other airmen who did not have to face combat every day. They joked, wrote letters, listened to the radio and went about their off-duty tasks just like anyone else. It was the man who sat by himself, didn't talk a great deal and began to stare into space that was taken off combat duty by the flight surgeon.

Just before D-Day in France, Pyle left Italy and went to England in preparation for covering the invasion. One of the units he visited was a Ninth Air Force B-26 medium bomber group. His dispatch did not contain the number of the group, probably because of security reasons. Like the A-20 crews in Italy, many of the flyers were beyond the number of missions that would have sent them home, but most were willing to stay on to participate in the invasion.

The crews felt their group and squadron were the best, and all liked to fly in the B-26. The aircraft had gotten over its earlier mechanical problems and the pilots were better trained in operating them, so there were few accidents. The crews liked the speed of their bomber, which got them out of flak quickly and made it more difficult for enemy fighters to catch them.

Pyle was invited to go along on a practice mission, taking off at night and joining up in the dark. They would later do this on D-Day. There were three gunners in the crew of his B-26. Like the A-20 gunners, Pyle gave them all the title of just plain sergeant.

The engineer/gunner was Eugene Gaines who was from New Orleans. Gaines had married an English girl and she lived in their apartment in a town eight miles away. Since Gaines had to be available for wakeup for missions every morning, he could only be with his bride in the evenings. So, every evening he would ride his bicycle the eight miles to the village and ride it back to be at the base by midnight. It was a 45 minute trip each way, and he never missed making the journey regardless of the blackout and the miserable weather that England routinely dished out. Gaines manned the top turret of the B-26, and while he had fired at a few enemy fighters, he had yet to bring one down.

John Siebert, of Charlestown, Massachusetts, was the radioman/gunner on the crew. He manned the two waist guns in the two hatches in the lower rear fuselage. He had a close call when one of the guns was hit by enemy fire and jerked right out of his hands. Siebert had gone to Massachusetts Institute of Technology and expected to return after his wartime duty. He had taken flying lessons and had logged 800 hours of civilian flying time. He had applied for AAF pilot training, but weak eyesight in one eye kept him out of the program.

In most crews, there is a "character", and in this one it was the tailgunner, Kermit Pruitt. He was a cowboy from Pleasant Valley, Arizona who liked to sing western tunes to the crew over the interphone. He would entertain them until just before the bomb run, when his pilot would tell him to knock it off. He also got chewed out by the pilot when he fired his two tail guns at enemy emplacements below. Up to that point Pruitt had never even seen an enemy fighter, so he took his aggressiveness out on flak towers and flak batteries 10,000 feet below the B-26. The rest of the crew was always shocked by his sudden, unannounced bursts, and the pilot always gave him a few words.

The words didn't bother Pruitt at all. He was fiercely loyal to his pilot, whom he had "shopped around" for. Before coming overseas, he had vowed not to be on a crew whose pilot he didn't trust. He conveniently "missed" train connections when he was on his way overseas with a unit and crew he didn't like. His foresight proved correct. The crew he had avoided was wiped out on its first mission. He considered his current pilot, whom he had selected, to be the best, and that suited him just fine.

Flyers who were to be on the day's mission were normally awakened by a duty NCO who came around to the sleeping quarters with a flashlight, alerting those who were to get out of bed. Pruitt, who began talking and telling stories as soon as he woke up, said one morning that when the war was over he was going to hire an Apache Indian to work for him. Then he was going to tell the Indian to wake him up in the morning at two a.m., but when the Indian came into his bedroom, he was going to take his .45 and shoot at him.

Pyle stayed with the officers of the B-26 unit when he first arrived, then he moved in with the gunners. They lived twenty to a Nissen hut, those half-round structures with corrugated steel roofs that went all the way to the ground. There he met other gunners in addition to those in "his" crew.

There was Phil Scheier, a radioman-gunner from Richmond, Staten Island, New York. Scheier considered that, as a B-26 gunner, he had the best job in the AAF. But, he did not plan to make the military a career. He wanted to return to a school of journalism and become a newspaperman like Pyle.

There was Kenneth Brown from Ellwood City, Pennsylvania who had a Purple Heart from flak wounds in the back and arm.

There was Kenneth Hackett, who, before entering the AAF, had helped build the B-26 bombers he now flew in at the Martin plant in Baltimore. Hackett was from North Miami where his father was police chief, but his wife and 12-year-old daughter were still in Baltimore where he had worked. He answered his daughter's plea to be allowed to wear lipstick, not with a letter, but with a telegram. His answer was, "No!", in no uncertain terms.

From Topeka, Kansas was Howard Hanson, an engineer/gunner who was also the acting first sergeant. He had long since completed his combat tour, but he stayed on working with his squadron and flying an occasional extra combat mission. Hanson was 37 years old, and, in the way of all military units, was addressed as "Pappy," the term reserved for oldsters. He had a wife and two children at home, but he considered what he was doing for the war effort was important and he wanted to get the war business done.

Another Kansan was Walter Hassinger, from Hutchinson. He was a radioman/gunner of remarkable talents. Hassinger had spent $400 of his own money in setting up a private radio station which was piped to speakers in many of the Nissen huts in the barracks area. He expanded it until it reached the quarters of 1,700 men. He rebroadcast news bulletins, played the popular music of the day, passed on official announcements, and carried on a monologue about anything from performance of some of the unit's officers to the state of the weather to whatever gossip about his fellow airmen was current. Pyle said that Hassinger contributed more to the unit's morale than any other single person. He also had the most combat missions of anyone in his hut.

Pyle was impressed with the sincerity of the flying sergeants, and although it was difficult for most of them to express what they were fighting for, they all knew it had to be done. They felt themselves fortunate to be fighting in the air instead of on the ground, and they appreciated the fact that their living conditions were much better than many other fighting Americans. Home, of course, was the ultimate goal of most, and almost without exception, each had a definite plan about his postwar aims.

Ernie Pyle went ashore at Normandy on D-plus-one, and followed the troops for three months, until Paris was taken. He then went to the Pacific war area and continued his writing with what has been called humor and sensitivity, making him the best-loved of all war correspondents.

A good friend of Pyle's was cartoonist Bill Mauldin, whose Willie and Joe cartoons expressed the sardonic way dogfaces looked at the war, officers and their own place in the scheme of things. Like Pyle, Mauldin was also a Pulitzer prize winner. Pyle was in many ways responsible for the popularity of Mauldin. When Mauldin was an infantryman drawing a weekly cartoon for his 45th Division newspaper, Pyle saw his work and wrote a couple of stories praising his talent. This led to Mauldin's drawing cartoons full time for the U.S. Army *Stars and Stripes* newspaper, and the freedom to travel to all areas of combat in Italy, often in the company of Pyle.

Mauldin said one thing he and Pyle knew how to do was to be invisible when things got hot on the battle lines. But one day after he had gone to the Pacific, Pyle forgot, said Mauldin, to be invisible. Pyle, covering the assault landings of the 77th Infantry Division, was killed by a Japanese Army machine gunner on the small island of Ie Shima in the battle for Okinawa.

V

15. Uncommon Valor

The 22nd Bombardment Group was the first Army Air Force unit to be equipped with the speedy Martin B-26 Marauder medium bomber, and one of the first units to deploy overseas after the attack on Pearl Harbor. The 22nd was sent to Australia to attempt to help stem the rapid southerly flow of Japanese forces down the chain of Pacific islands, threatening the Australians.

Based in Northern Queensland at an airbase named Garbutt Field, the Marauders began flying shuttle bombing raids against the Japanese shipping that was carrying the Japanese war machine in its systematic process of island-grabbing. One of the early targets was Rabaul, which the Japanese had made into a fortress for protection of its invasion fleets.

But the round trip from the home base of the Marauders was 2,600 miles, a far greater range than the B-26s possessed. So, the bombers flew to Port Moresby, on New Guinea, and staged out of the primitive airstrip on strikes against Rabaul. Even at that, the round trip from the staging base to the target and return was nearly 900 miles.

The first strike was a success, resulting in a troop transport overturning and sinking. The B-26s ran into anti-aircraft fire, but, surprisingly, no Japanese fighters. One of the nine bombers took a hit from flak and was forced to ditch in the sea. One crewmember was killed, but the others were rescued and returned to their base.

And so it went, in those early days of the fighting in the Pacific under primitive circumstances. For the bombers it meant very little support from friendly fighters. Japanese fighters, recovered from the laxness of the first Rabaul raid and now swarmed against the unescorted Marauders at every opportunity. The gunners of the 22nd took their toll, however, accounting for 94 enemy aircraft destroyed in its first ten months of combat — highest scoring bombardment unit of the Army Air Forces at that time.

One of the gunners contributing to this tally was Sgt. Glenn Campbell of Franklin, Pennsylvania. Campbell was the top turret gunner in the Marauder piloted by Capt. Charlie Hitchcock of Winchester, Indiana; his copilot was a Royal Australian Air Force flyer.

Their mission that day took them to targets at Dilli on the island of Portuguese Timor. Leaving the target, the Marauder was bounced by four Zeros, who made a simultaneous frontal attack on the bomber. Already the right engine was on fire from flak received over the target. Now rounds from the Zeros thudded into the left wing. Top gunner Campbell, though, blasted away with his machine guns and two of the approaching Zeros, with their lack of defensive armament and self-sealing fuel tanks, flamed and went into the sea.

Campbell's accurate shooting cut the threat in half, but troubles aboard the Marauder were mounting. Fire now crept along the wing from the engine to the fuselage. Black smoke billowed into the cockpit and pilot Hitchcock had to open a side window to clear the air, causing flames to ignite in the cockpit. The right engine was now shut down, but still the fire came on. Navigator Lieut. Albert J. Lilkington of Mobile, Alabama fought a losing battle with a hand fire extinguisher.

It was now apparent that the Marauder would have to be ditched in the Arafura Sea, and the crew made preparations. Sgts. Pershing A. Arbogast of Dunmore, West Virginia, G. Schank of Throop, Pennsylvania and Samuel Miller of Trout Run, Pennsylvania broke out the life rafts and assumed their assigned ditching positions. Turret gunner Campbell, though, announced on the interphone for his crew to hear that he would stay at his battle position in the turret in case the Zeros, still behind them and threatening, came at the ailing Marauder again.

After the plane hit the water, all crewmembers were able to get out and into the life rafts, except Campbell. His pilot, Hitchcock, dove back into the sinking fuselage, found his way to the top turret and managed to pull the unconscious body of Campbell out of the plane. Once they got him in the raft, though, it was apparent that Campbell had died at his post, courageously, protecting his crewmates to the end.

For the Eighth Air Force, the battle for Europe was conducted at high altitudes, where the flak was less accurate and where enemy fighters would be less efficient. In addition, the higher altitudes gave more time for the bombardiers to track their assigned targets with their bombsights, making the daylight precision bombing more accurate.

But, the high altitudes also had its effect on the crews of the bombers and fighters who had to function in such a marginal environment. The human body does not adapt well to extremes of low temperatures or to an atmosphere that is nearly devoid of oxygen. The bombers and fighters of the day were not equipped with pressurized cabins and cockpits, with easily controlled temperatures, and the crews had to cope with sub-zero conditions for hours at a time with rather primitive warming devices (mostly heavy clothing) and with the rarified atmosphere with oxygen systems that did not always function properly.

Observers of returning bomber crews reported seeing men crawl out of bombers in an almost helpless condition, stiff, numb and sometimes screaming in pain from the effects of frostbite.

Improved warming systems, such as electrically heated flying gear, were slow in coming, and the grounding of crew members for frostbite became a serious problem in the war effort. There were even threats of punishment for crew members who were careless and allowed themselves to be afflicted with frostbite. But what was a gunner to do when he had a sudden gun stoppage while in combat with enemy fighters? His first reaction was to pull off his gloves to clear the jam or to replace a broken part. There were many other reasons for acting incautiously when in the heat of battle.

Even more critical than the problem of freezing temperatures to the crews was that of staying conscious in the oxygen-less environment of the upper atmosphere. Since one-half the earth's atmosphere is below 17,000 feet, it can be seen that when flying for eight to ten hours at between 25,000 feet and 30,000 feet, where consciousness without oxygen is a matter of only seconds, good supplemental oxygen systems were required. All the heavy bombers and fighters were equipped with such a system, with the aircraft system being piped to all the crew stations aboard. The crew member wore an oxygen mask attached to his flight helmet and if all went well, he could fly the mission with no ill effects. In the larger airplanes, if a crew member wanted to move to another part of the ship, he could unplug his mask from his station fitting, and plug into a portable oxygen bottle, called a "walk-around bottle." When he got to the new station, he could plug back into the aircraft oxygen system.

In combat, though, all aircraft systems: oil, hydraulic, electrical, fuel as well as oxygen, were subject to the effects of violent battle. This occurred to the oxygen system of an Eighth Air Force B-17 named *Hard to Get* while on a raid against Kiel, Germany. Just 15 minutes short of the target, flak cut the oxygen line to the tail gun position of S/Sgt. Adolph F. Frydel. At that moment a twin-engine fighter was making a firing pass at the Fortress, so Frydel stayed at his guns until the fighter had gone. Still conscious, he managed to plug his mask into a walk-around bottle. He then returned to his guns, using the bottle as an emergency source for oxygen.

At about the same time the ball turret gunner, Sgt. Marvin E. McManus, was hit in the jaw and the leg with 20-mm cannon fire from a fighter. He, too, stayed in action firing at the fighters until they were gone.

When he could no longer see any enemy planes, McManus crawled out of his turret to get first-aid for his wounds. He unplugged from his station oxygen system, but remembered to hook up to the portable bottle before he crawled out of the turret.

As he made his way forward toward the radio compartment, McManus collapsed from shock and loss of blood from his wounds.

In the meantime, Frydel came forward from his tail-gun position to replace his portable bottle, when he saw that McManus was not in his ball turret. He found him lying by the door of the radio compartment bleeding from his wounds. Quickly, Frydel worked to stem the blood flow from the unconscious man, who was breathing rapidly because of his injuries.

Sensing that McManus was nearly out of oxygen, Frydel plugged his own bottle of oxygen into the mask of the wounded man. Working on the wounds without oxygen, Frydel lasted about 90 seconds and then fell unconscious on the body of his wounded crewmate.

By now, *Hard to Get* was at the bomb release point and the flak was intense around the Fort. At this moment, another gunner, T/Sgt. Steve P. Bowen, saw what had happened. Bowen grabbed several of the portable bottles of oxygen and revived Frydel, who continued with first aid treatment of his pal.

Still, McManus was using up oxygen faster than Frydel, so once again Frydel used his own bottle for his wounded crewmate. And, once again, Frydel passed out.

It was a total of four times that this episode was repeated, Frydel risking his own life to care for his friend. When well clear of the target, other members of the crew joined in the effort, supplying oxygen bottles to the wounded man and Frydel in a constant stream until the plane descended to an altitude where oxygen was not required.

Frydel's action was selfless, but even a hero cannot argue with the laws of the science of physiology.

☆　☆　☆　☆

A gunner who made a name for himself in ground combat was T/Sgt. Robert L. Loomis of Philadelphia, who had as a civilian been a physical training instructor. Loomis was a gunner on the crew of a B-26 Marauder assigned to the 322nd Bombardment Group of the Ninth Air Force.

In March, 1945 as the war in Europe was winding down, combat veterans of the Army Air Forces and combat troops of the ground units exchanged visits to each other's units to see how the other guys fought. T/ Sgt. Loomis was to participate in this week-long adventure, along with his crew.

The flyers left their base at Beauvais, France and went forward for intelligence and war situation briefings, and then were assigned to accompany the 101st Infantry Regiment of the 26th Infantry Division. For a couple of days they watched as the task forces advanced, fighting when resistance was met.

Then the regiment advanced to the outskirts of Fulda, Germany. There a tank commander, only half-seriously, asked Loomis if he wanted to go along when the tank forces assaulted the city of Fulda. To the tanker's surprise, Loomis said yes. He was assigned to take the position of the assistant driver in the medium tank, and would man a .30-caliber machine gun.

Entering Fulda they got as far as the river when they were stopped by a bridge that had been barricaded. When they stopped they were shelled by German 88's but were not hit. The tanks shelled three buildings on the other side of the river where a number of Germans were holed up defending the bridge and Loomis fired his machine gun. As the sun set, the infantry was able to get across the river.

Loomis left the tank, then, because he wanted to go across the river with the infantry troops the next morning. Back at the regimental headquarters he borrowed a carbine and at two o'clock in the morning crossed the river with some troops. During the night, U.S. patrols had captured quite a few German prisoners. At dawn, Loomis took off to see what damage his tank battle had done the day before, but his real quest was to be able to capture a German officer and claim his pistol as a souvenir.

He moved deeper into the city until he reached the leading outpost of the infantry, where he was warned to advance no farther because anything that moved in front of them would be shot at. But visions of a souvenir prevailed and Loomis went ahead anyway.

Soon he met a French civilian (Loomis spoke French) who showed him where there was a cache of German rifles. He picked up six of them for souvenirs and continued advancing with the Frenchman. They met a German girl on a bicycle who told the Frenchman that there was an anti-tank gun just around the corner manned by German soldiers. Loomis decided that it would be a good idea to capture the anti-tank gun, so he circled around and advanced on its position.

When he got close to the site described by the German girl, he suddenly came upon a German soldier. Loomis raised his carbine to shoot the German, when the soldier threw down his weapon and raised his arms in surrender. As Loomis advanced toward the German three more German soldiers appeared and surrendered.

One of the four German soldiers could speak English, so Loomis, still on his quest for a souvenir pistol, asked if there were any German officers around. The English-speaking soldier pointed at a large building and said that there was a German general inside. Loomis told the soldiers to wait where they were and went into the building.

Inside there were four German officers: the general, a colonel and two lieutenants. Loomis determined that the colonel could speak English, so he told him he wanted them to surrender. The colonel just laughed and said to him that he was alone. Loomis tried to bluff his way through by telling the colonel that they were surrounded, but he was beginning to feel uneasy about the whole matter. The German colonel just shrugged his shoulders at the news that they were surrounded.

Then, Loomis tried a new approach. He told the colonel that he would bring his commanding officer to them to accept their surrender but wanted the German general's word that the four officers would stay where they were until Loomis returned. The colonel got the general's word for him. Loomis asked the colonel to get all officers and enlisted men in the building together in the room. Four more enlisted men emerged and Loomis took them prisoner. Before leaving, Loomis collected all of the pistols worn by the Germans, five in all, and strapped his souvenirs to his belt.

Then he marched the eight enlisted prisoners, four from the building and the four that were still waiting in the street, back to American lines. Other American soldiers were herding German prisoners rearward, as well, so Loomis added seven of his own to the column of prisoners, keeping the one who spoke English with him.

He located the American task force commander, a colonel, who assembled a guard force of 25 men, and Loomis led the group to the German general's headquarters. He entered the room first, saluted the general and said that his commander was outside. The German colonel answered, saying that the German officers were ready to meet with the commander. The American colonel entered the building and soon there was agreement on the terms of the Germans' surrender as well as on the terms of the surrender of the city of Fulda.

The four German officers were marched back to the American lines, and then taken by jeep to the 26th Infantry Division headquarters, Loomis accompanying them. After turning over the German general and the other officers at the headquarters, the division commander, a Major General, awarded T/Sgt. Loomis a Bronze Star medal, telling him that the citation would be sent to him through Army and 9th Air Force channels.

After interviews with a number of war correspondents, Loomis returned to his base at Beauvais, burdened down with his coveted and well-earned pistol souvenirs.

Harry Baren was the tail gunner on Walter Greer's B-26 *Heckling Hare*. Both men were assigned to the 19th Bomb Squadron of the 22nd Bomb Group flying out of Townsville, Australia. The distances to Japanese targets were too great to strike from the Australian air bases, so the bombers had to operate using a shuttle system. They loaded bombs in Australia, then carried them to a forward operating strip on the south coast of New Guinea near Port Moresby. There the Marauders would be refueled and could strike targets in the Japanese-held areas of New Guinea and on New Britain as well as Japanese shipping in ports and at sea.

On the morning of June 9, 1942, the crew of *Heckling Hare* was awaiting takeoff on one of these missions at the forward strip, called Seven-Mile Airdrome because it was seven miles from the city of Port Moresby. The crew had spent the night in its usual fashion, sleeping beneath the wings of the bomber since there were no quarters on the field. Two of the crew slept at the controls of the plane, ready to disperse the aircraft in the event of an air attack by Japanese bombers. If the raids came in the daytime, the two-man crew, usually one pilot and one other of the crew, would attempt to takeoff and circle over the ocean to escape falling bombs. In the previous month there had been 21 such air raids by as many as 40 Japanese bombers and escorted by half that many Zero fighters. Sometimes there would be no warning of an impending attack. If the men were lucky, word about a coming raid would be reported by an Australian coastwatcher hiding in the jungle. In that event, the alarm signal of a volley of three shots fired by a sentry during the hours of darkness, or if it were a daylight raid, a red flag flown from the primitive control tower would announced an enemy attack, followed by tower operators bailing out of the tower and hitting the ditches.

The target for the day's mission was one of the toughest the Marauders could attack. It was the airfield at Lae on the north coast of New Guinea. It was tough because the cream of Japanese fighter pilots in that part of the world were based at Lae, and the B-26s could expect no friendly fighter escort to do battle with the Zeros. So the raid was planned to be a coordinated attack, with B-17s and B-25s from other units participating. The main attack force would be the 12 Marauders of the 19th Bomb Squadron, bombing from 10,000 feet. Thirty minutes prior to the Marauder attack, three B-17s were to bomb Lae from 30,000 feet. It was hoped that the fighters would be alerted by the B-17s and a portion of the fighter force would take to the air. Then 15 minutes before the Marauders arrived, a flight of B-25s would cross Lae at 18,000 feet, drawing the fighters away from the target so that the B-26s could bomb without having to fight their way to the target.

A lot depended on precise timing, and the Marauder crews were not happy with having to wait for the arrival of some ranking observers who were to witness the raid. Finally, a B-17 landed and down climbed the three observers, an AAF lieutenant colonel who was a pilot, another Army lieutenant colonel from the ground forces, and a tall, rangy Navy lieutenant commander.

Now, "wheels" such as the three had visited Marauder crews before at Seven-Mile Airdrome. But it turned out that these three were actually going to fly the mission as observers. The Navy officer was assigned to fly with Lt. Bench in the B-26 *Wabash Cannonball* and soon squeezed his frame into the radio compartment behind the pilots. For some reason, the naval officer then got out of the plane for a few minutes, but when he returned to climb back in, he found his seat was occupied by the ground Army officer, who refused to budge from the plane.

The Navy officer then approached the crew of *Heckling Hare* and asked Walt Greer if he could go along in his plane. Greer agreed and then the Navy officer asked the rest of the crew if it was all right with them if he did. The tailgunner, Corporal Harry G. Baren answered for the crew, saying that they did not mind his coming along if he really wanted to. Baren, though, told the Navy officer that he didn't think he should go on the mission, since it was one of the roughest targets. But the Navy officer was adamant that he was going to fly on the mission.

While the crew of *Heckling Hare* was busy getting things ready to go, the Navy officer told them that he and the two other officers were traveling the area visiting units and finding out what problems soldiers, sailors and airmen faced in the area, and that he would do what he could to help solve them. Harry Baren spoke right up when the Navy officer asked what their complaints were. He told him that the thing they needed most were fighter planes that had enough range to be able to escort the Marauders to and from their targets. When the Navy officer asked about the availability of parts and supplies, Baren bluntly told him that the situation was at least doubly as bad as whatever the officer had been told. Baren also told the commander that their intelligence of enemy targets and capabilities was almost non-existent and threw in some barbed remarks about General MacArthur for good measure.

Then it came time to board the plane, and the Navy officer asked if there was a spare parachute he could wear, since one of the rules for making the flight was that the three observers would all wear chutes. Baren handed him a parachute, which the Navy officer donned. What Baren did not say was that the parachute was not an extra, but was his own. He flew the mission without a chute.

One by one the heavily-laden Marauders clawed their way into the air, straining in the equatorial heat to get airborne. *Heckling Hare* was at the back of the formation of twelve B-26s as the formation climbed to 14,000 feet to get across the Owen Stanley Mountains.

The Marauder crews were in for a big disappointment because as they approached Lae they saw that the B-25s were late and were just then crossing over the airfield instead of being some distance off decoying the Zeros away from the target. It did not take the Japanese fliers long to see the five B-25s were decoys after the 12 Marauders were spotted approaching Lae, and most of the 25 fighters switched from attacking the B-25s to chasing the B-26 formation.

With the Zeros swarming all around them, the flight leader, Walter Krell could see that the carefully planned mission had gone awry and the best thing to do was to get to the target and out again as fast as possible. So, instead of making a leisurely bombing run at 10,000, he lowered the nose to pick up extra airspeed and would bomb from a lower altitude.

Before he could get his formation over the target, one of Japan's best fighter aces, Saburo Sakai, who finished the war with the most kills of any living ace, 64, drew the first blood of the battle. He pulled in directly behind a B-26 and began firing at nearly point-blank range and slightly above the bomber. Almost immediately he could see pieces flying from the plane, then flame erupted in the wing near one engine. The plane began to dive toward the water and never pulled out. It hit the water and exploded at about 300 miles an hour. There were no parachutes and no survivors. The plane was the *Wabash Cannonball*, the bomber into which the Navy officer had originally climbed. The Army ground officer observer who had displaced him perished with the crew.

Heckling Hare was next to get the attention of Saburo Sakai. Prior to reaching the target, the right generator of the plane in which the Navy officer was riding failed. Since the propellers of the B-26 used electrical power to control the pitch, the loss of a generator meant big trouble. They could be controlled manually, rather than automatically, but it required constant attention and some loss of power. When *Heckling Hare* began to lose power on the right engine, it fell back from the protection of the formation and immediately attracted Sakai's attention.

Pilot Greer salvoed the bomb load, but still did not have enough speed to stay with the other bombers. Sakai and seven other Zeros got set up to attack *Heckling Hare.* As he made his firing run, the B-26 suddenly turned and skidded in an attempt to throw his aim off. Pilot Greer was no newcomer and gave an excellent account of himself in spoiling Sakai's aim, said the Japanese ace following the war. A lot of the cannon fire from the Zero was finding its mark, but the Marauder would not go down. In the tail, Harry Baren was getting the ride of his life, with the tail swinging in wide arcs as Greer slipped and skidded the bomber. Baren was wielding the .50-caliber machine gun that he had installed to replace the smaller .30-caliber model with which the B-26 was originally equipped. Although he never claimed a kill, the one Zero that was downed almost certainly fell to Baren's gun. The other .50-caliber weapons in the electrically-controlled top turret were nearly inoperative because of the generator failure.

After what was estimated to be about a ten to 13 minute battle between Sakai and the *Heckling Hare,* a long time for an air battle, Greer was finally able to duck into some clouds, and the Zeros went after the main formation of bombers.

The Navy officer took in all the details of the aerial battle between *Heckling Hare* and the Zeros. On takeoff from Seven-Mile he had been strapped in the radio room compartment, but as soon as he could, he moved about the plane, looking out a small side window, standing on a stool and looking out the navigator's plexiglass dome on the top of the fuselage, where he could get a good view of the entire formation. From time to time he wedged in between the pilots to get a look out forward through the windshield. When the eight Zeros began their slashing attack on the bomber, the Navy officer was looking out of the top dome, where he had a good view, as cannon shells exploded against the wings and fuselage and the chatter of the B-26 guns answered its attackers.

Several times during the battle he moved to the waist position to see the action by the top turret and waist gunners. Through all of this the Navy officer appeared to the gunners to be cool, even though it was his first combat and the *Heckling Hare* was taking heavy damage from the enemy. The nose gun operated by the bombardier, Sergeant Claude A. McCredie, jammed and could not be cleared. So, McCredie moved back to the waist position to assist waist gunner, Lillis M. Walker, by taking over one of the two guns Walker was firing. As McCredie passed through the radio compartment, the Navy officer was looking out a side window. He signaled to McCredie that there were three Zeros off the left wing. McCredie took a look and here came three Zeros with all guns firing at *Heckling Hare*. McCredie said the Navy officer was very calm and even gave the bombardier a grin as McCredie rushed past to get to the waist guns.

Later, waist gunner Walker had to come forward to the radio compartment to make one of the required radio calls back to the airstrip. He, too, reported that the Navy officer was unperturbed by all the battle activity. He did make a comment to Walker that it was pretty rough and that a person got kind of scared. Walker answered that he was always scared up there — at this the Navy officer burst out laughing. Walker said he was certain that the Navy officer was as scared as he was, but he didn't show it at all.

Greer managed to control the engines and propellers on the flight home, and their return to Seven-Mile was without further incident. Greer brought *Heckling Hare* in for a perfect landing and the mission was over.

The Navy commander commented to one of the crew that he was sure glad to be back on the ground. Then he told the crew that he appreciated having been with them and said that he found the flight very interesting. Harry Baren said the crew was amazed at how this officer appeared just as calm as he had on the flight.

Then, the Navy officer who had been saved from perishing with the

Wabash Cannonball in a fiery, watery grave by a quirk of fate, turned and walked toward some people who came forward to meet the airplane.

As the crew of *Heckling Hare* watched the receding figure of the tall man, even then they did not know they had flown with a Congressman from Texas by the name of Lyndon B. Johnson who two decades later would become the 36th President of the United States.

VI
16. The Escort Destroyer

One of the weaker aspects of planning of the Army Air Forces force structure in the pre-war days was the lack of providing for a long-range fighter to escort bombers. Although it had been recommended by planners, nothing was done to develop one. The emphasis had been placed on developing fighters for air defense, not escort.

This deficiency would haunt the AAF in the early daylight raids over Europe. In the beginning the bombers had to rely on the Spitfires of the Royal Air Force for escort, but soon the priority targets that needed to be struck were too far for the short-range Spits. Most of the bomber losses were coming from fighter attacks, while only about one-quarter of the losses were due to flak. Longer-range AAF P-38s intended for use by the Eighth Air Force in England were diverted to the land battle in North Africa. Eventually P-47s, which had slightly more range than the Spitfires, arrived, but early problems with the airplane hindered its use. Priority was given to equipping the P-47 with suitable long-range auxiliary drop tanks, but they were a long time in coming. It would be early 1944 before the truly long-range P-51s would see combat.

The decision was made to develop a bomber to provide long-range defense for the bomber force. It was variously called an escort bomber, an escort destroyer and an escort cruiser. It was not a new idea, but modifying an existing bomber was decided upon. The YB-40 was born.

In August 1942 work began on converting 20 B-17F models to the YB-40 configuration. Two additional power turrets were installed, one in the lower nose and a second top turret at the radio room station. The two single waist guns were converted to mount two .50-calibers each instead of one. This gave the YB-40 fourteen machine guns versus nine for the normal B-17F. An aerial gunner's dream, it would seem.

In addition, armor plate was added to all crew stations and provisions for carrying 12,400 rounds of ammunition were made. The YB-40 would carry no bombs, but would more than make up for the loss in bomb weight by the extra armament, armor and ammo.

In May 1943 the escort bombers arrived at Alconbury, England where they were assigned to the 92nd Bomb Group's 327th Bomb Squadron. The first mission using the new escort was to the St. Nazaire sub pens in late May. The mission proved very little about the value of the YB-40 because only light fighter attacks were encountered. In later raids, German fighter pilots quickly learned to stay away from this strange bomber

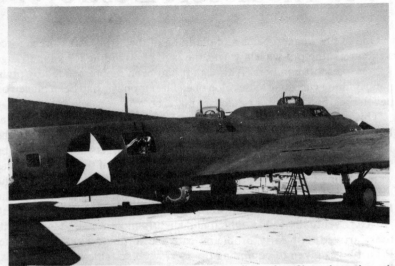

B-17F modified by Lockheed to the YB-40 configuration. Note the twin waist guns and the second top turret aft of the forward top turret. A two-gun chin turret replaced a single flexible nose gun (Lockheed-California Company photo)

with all the black barrels sticking out.

What the Americans learned was that the YB-40 was more trouble than it was worth. The modifications had made the airplane very tail heavy and with its extra weight it could not climb with the B-17s nor could it fly as fast. This meant the whole formation had to slow for the YB-40 to keep up. This was especially vexing to bomber crews whose speed picked up considerably after bomb release when they could head for home in a hurry. With the YB-40, which did not lose any weight at the target, the whole formation was tied to its slow speed.

As a result, the YB-40s were retired after just three months of combat. Some were converted to bomber configuration, but one three-mission veteran was used as a point of interest for visits to the base by British school children. The one high point of the YB-40 program was the development of the chin turret which some late model B-17Fs acquired and which became standard on all B-17G models.

While the YB-40 did not work out well for the Eighth Air Force, in

England, on at least one occasion it served well for the Twelfth Air Force in the Mediterranean theater of operations.

The story — and it is up to the reader to decide how much of it to believe — begins with a bombing raid on the island of Pantelleria. It was June 1943. The B-17s, having made their strike, were returning across the water to their bases in North Africa. One bomber, the *Bonnie Sue,* lagged some distance behind the formation, both left engines shot out. The pilot struggled to control the wounded plane and was seriously considering having his crew bail out.

For nine members of the crew, it was their first mission. The pilot, 1st Lt. Harold Fisher, was a veteran of some 20 missions. Fisher took the normal actions of the pilot of a badly crippled plane, having the crew throw overboard all loose equipment and gear, such as machine guns, ammo, etc., to reduce weight. Then came the dreaded call of a fighter coming at the plane head on. It was quickly identified, however, as friendly by the unmistakable outline of a P-38. To a lagging bomber, a friendly fighter is a welcome sight.

The P-38 joined on the bomber's wing. Fisher switched radio channels to the fighter frequency and asked the fighter pilot if he would escort them to safety. The fighter pilot said he would and dropped back to the escort position behind and above the bomber. Things were looking up for the battered Fortress and its crew.

Their relief was short-lived, however, because suddenly the bomber crew became aware that their plane was being torn apart by .50-caliber and 20-millimeter shells. And the shattering fire was coming from the P-38! Fisher, himself, was able to get a glimpse of the fighter as it made its attack, just before the mortally wounded bomber fell into a spiral, taking it from 4,000 feet to the ocean beneath. Fisher was able to regain some control just before the plane hit the water, but the forces upon impact were fierce. Fisher was able to crawl through the broken windshield and managed to locate an inflated raft. But, he was alone. The nine other members of the crew were either killed upon impact or were trapped in the sinking bomber. He was picked up during the night by a British rescue boat.

His story, which he told in the debriefing the next day, didn't set well with the commanders of the P-38 units. They were furious at him — and he at them. But an intelligence officer stepped between the two sides with a plausible explanation.

Some weeks before, a P-38, low on fuel and lost, had been landed by its pilot at an airport on Sardinia, near Cagliari, which was in Italian hands. The pilot was captured before he was able to destroy his plane by setting it on fire. The Italians test-flew the intact fighter until they had enough technical data for their purposes. Then along came Lt. Guido Rossi, an expert fighter pilot who had an idea of what to do with the plane. His plan was to leave the American markings on the plane and use it to decoy and shoot down straggling bombers. His plan was approved. Rossi himself would do the flying.

Rossi had been successful in shooting down a number of stragglers, but Americans were not aware of his ruse because, until Harold Fisher, no crew member had survived the crashes to report it. All bomber units were warned, of course, but Rossi kept up his hunt, shooting down another B-17 over Naples.

It was Harold Fisher who came up with a plan to outwit the Italian fighter pilot. He approached his superiors with the idea of providing a decoy to lure the Italian into a trap. He recommended using the YB-40, which was heavily armored, bristled with 14 machine guns and carried far more ammunition than the standard B-17s. There were no YB-40s in the Mediterranean theater, but a request to the Eighth Bomber Command produced one on loan. When it arrived in August 1943 Harold Fisher was assigned to fly it, which he had hoped to do.

Fisher and a selected crew began flying missions, taking up the role of straggler as bait for the renegade P-38. But, Rossi did not fall for the plan and added another B-17 to his count on August 19th. A week later Rossi downed another Fort and the same day shot down a P-38 that was on a strafing mission for good measure.

After two weeks of this, Fisher determined to find out more about the Italian through intelligences sources. He found that Rossi had a wife and child who were living in the city of Constantine, which was in allied hands. That night Fisher went to Constantine, to the home of Gina Rossi and her child. He took one look at her face and hurried back to his base, where he had an artist draw a large portrait of the beautiful dark-haired woman on the side of the fuselage of the YB-40. Beneath the picture of the woman's head the artist lettered the name Gina in large letters.

The next mission was against a target at Pisa, Italy, and Fisher took up his position at the rear of the formation. They didn't see the renegade P-38, but were swarmed upon by hordes of German fighters. Two Me-109s singled out the YB-40 and poured cannon rounds into the number four engine, which broke out in flames. When the engine was lost, the heavy, overloaded gunship fell off on a wing, and before the pilots could control it, the plane rolled on its back, plunging toward the sea. For ten thousand feet it fell until Fisher managed to control it at about 5,000 feet. By now, the number three engine was out as well, and it looked as if the heavy YB-40 would never make it home. Fisher would try though, and he ordered all ammunition except that in the guns to be thrown overboard.

At about that time a P-38 suddenly appeared alongside the YB-40. It was flying on one engine, with the other propeller feathered. The pilot of the fighter radioed that he would like to stay with the gunship until they got to their home base. Fisher agreed, but he was not certain whether the fighter was flown by Rossi or not. The altitude of the bomber was now 2,000 feet and the plane was still sinking. Fisher decided he had no choice but to dump the remaining ammo and any guns that could be released.

Then came a voice in Fisher's headset that said that Gina was a pretty name and asked if she were from Constantine. It was the fighter pilot. Fisher called over the interphone for his crew to stop dumping ammo and guns, but the waist guns had already been jettisoned. Then Fisher began to bait the other pilot over the radio, commenting on charms of Gina from Constantine. That was enough. Suddenly the dead engine of the P-38 came to life and, cursing over the radio, Rossi pulled ahead of the gunship. He was going to make a head-on pass at the ship, pouring lead into the cockpit and into the bomber pilot.

As the fighter came at the bomber, all guns that could be trained ahead zeroed in on it, but the gunners held their fire. Then Fisher gave the command to fire, and they opened up, hitting the fighter in the first blast. It began trailing smoke and then flames shot out of an engine. An aileron was gone.

That wasn't stopping Rossi. He set the battered P-38 up for another pass, vowing to ram the bomber if necessary. On the next firing pass the P-38 was again hit furiously, the canopy flying away in the slipstream. This time Rossi could not control the plane as it headed for the water. He managed finally to establish a long, flat glide which continued until the fighter splashed into the sea. As the YB-40 passed over the downed plane, they could see Rossi standing on the wing shaking his fist at them. Fisher called air-sea rescue to have Rossi picked up, although some of the crew would have liked to strafe the fighter and its pilot.

For their efforts, Twelfth Air Force decorated Harold Fisher with the Distinguished Flying Cross and awarded each crewman of the YB-40 an Air Medal for the part they played in that astounding duel in the air.

☆　☆　☆　☆

An Eighth Air Force pilot and crew employed a YB-40 in a similar scheme, but were not rewarded nor was their action officially noted. This was because they did not ask for nor receive approval for their plot. The plot was conceived by Lt. Harry Reed of the 95th Bomb Group, and while he had the cooperation of his squadron lead pilot, no other supervisors were aware of it.

The action began when Flying Fortress groups on a combat mission would be joined by a lone B-17 bomber, like their own. Crew members began noticing that this was occurring fairly regularly and soon began to suspect that the lone Fort was a captured plane being flown by Germans, and that it was being used to direct German fighters toward the formations.

The squadron lead pilot, Captain Glenn Infield, first noted a renegade Fortress in Jaunary 1944. His formation was making a bomb run on a target near Frankfurt when he noticed a single Fort flying directly over the formation. Suddenly, its bomb bay doors opened and a number of bombs were released. They were not larger 500 pounders that the formation was carrying, but smaller bombs, such as the Germans used. Fortunately, they did not hit any of the 95th Group's planes.

It was known that the Germans had been using captured allied planes for a variety of missions, such as parachuting agents and resupplying them, but such missions had little combat effect on American flyers. Now, though, the Germans use of the captured B-17s was indeed a threat to American crews.

It was in early June, 1944 when Lt. Reed came up with a plan to lay a trap for the suspicious bomber. He had been on temporary duty at the home base of the 92nd Bomb Group, to which the YB-40s had been assigned. Since the long-range P-51s now escorted bombers, their YB-40s were not being used and one was sitting idle at the 92nd's airfield.

Reed told Captain Infield of his plan to trap the Germans in the B-17 and down it with the firepower of the YB-40. Infield told Reed that higher headquarters would certainly not approve his plan since they would not even allow fighter pilots to fire at the suspected bomber for fear that it might actually be a genuine American-flown plane. If they were going through with the plan, they had to do it on their own responsibility. Infield grudgingly agreed to let Reed go through with it.

172

Reed borrowed the YB-40 and on June 14, 1944, a few days after D-Day, they put the plan into action.

It was a mission to the Brussels area. Reed and the YB-40 flew in the "Tail-End-Charlie" position in the 18-plane formation of the squadron. Sure enough, as they started over the continent a black spot on the horizon began drifting in toward the formation. Gunners in all the plane swung their guns toward the suspicious speck in the sky. When it got closer most of the gunners identified it as a friendly and went back to searching the sky for other bogies. Neither Reed nor Infield relaxed, however. They were going to check to see whether it was actually a friendly bomber that had become separated from its own formation and was seeking the protection of other bombers and the escorting fighters.

The two pilots, the only two with knowledge of their plan, looked closely at the bomber. It carried no group or squadron insignia, as was normal for Eighth Air Force bombers. Neither did it join in close formation with the group, which would have been usual for an American pilot seeking mutual support.

Then, Infield made the first move to determine whether it was friendly or not. He slowly eased the formation toward the strange bomber, which was on his left side. As the gap between the formation and the loner narrowed, the suspicious Fort suddenly banked sharply away from the fleet. Now Reed and Infield were certain that the plane was being flown by Germans and they put step two of Reed's plan into effect.

Reed eased the YB-40 back from the formation, as if he were having engine trouble. He feathered the number three engine to give the impression his plane was crippled. Just then gunners aboard the bombers called out bandits at 12 o'clock. Dozens of Me-109s and FW-190s came at the formation. The renegade had done its work. Infield called for Reed to bring the YB-40 back into the formation, but the gunship was already too far committed to the plan.

The formation was under attack by fighters clear through their raid on the rail yards at Brussels. And just as Reed and the YB-40 closed to within gun range of the suspected bomber, six Focke-Wulfs left the other enemy fighters and headed for Reed and the other plane. Reed tucked his plane in close formation with the other plane, his wingtip almost in the waist window of the other. He started the number three engine, because he knew he would need all of his resources to battle off the fighters.

Reed's gunners called out that the FWs were starting their firing passes, but they made them without firing their guns. They were afraid, since the YB-40 was so close to the B-17, of hitting their own plane. Then, Reed could feel thumps on his fuselage — the B-17 gunners had opened fire on the YB-40. Reed gave his gunners the order to open up at the enemy-flown plane.

But the first salvo from the other plane had taken its toll. Reed's top turret gunner called out that the number one engine was losing oil all over the wing. Number one's oil temperature was in the red and pressure was zero. It had to be feathered.

Now the B-17 was trying to get away. But each time it turned, Reed stayed right with it, knowing his survival depended on staying close. Gunners in both planes continued blasting at each other. Then Reed put the third part of the plan into action.

Reed's radio operator was a volunteer for the mission who also happened to speak German fluently. He switched to the frequency that the German fighters were using and ordered the fighters to attack the Fort on the left, and, assuming the identity of the German flying the bomber, said he would make a sharp turn to the right. Before the genuine German pilot could protest, the FWs made their attack and three actually fired on the bogus bomber before its pilot could convince the fighter pilots of the trick.

Reed, meanwhile, was making a diving right hand turn back toward England. But, the FWs started after him. Reed could see the Fort above him and decided to make one last attempt to down it. With the extra speed he had picked up in the dive, he zoomed up directly beneath the renegade and all his gunners that could, opened up. The Fort fell off on its left wing and the last Reed saw of it, it was burning and headed down toward the ground.

But now the YB-40 still had to deal with the six German fighters. As luck would have it, Reed's group had completed their attack and was turning for home. Captain Infield in the lead plane noted six FW-190s below the formation and called them out to the escort fighters who promptly dove on the FWs. They happened to be the same ones that were tormenting the YB-40.

Reed looked up and saw the formation of Forts and asked Infield if he could have fighter escort home. So three P-47s joined the YB-40 for the return flight, and all got home safely.

According to Infield, the bombers were never harassed by German-flown B-17s again. Although Reed never received the official recognition he should have, almost certainly many Eighth Air Force bomber crews survived because of his willingness to risk his life in the YB-40.

17. Navy Libs

The mission of Navy patrol bombers during World War II was long-range patrol. They were supposed to seek out and report on enemy shipping, perform anti-submarine duties, reconnoiter enemy installations and then report such vital intelligence information so that attack forces could be dispatched to deal with the enemy. Their mission, even though they many times carried bombs, depth-charges and mines, was not to attack enemy forces. Even their guns were strictly for defense. At times they were forbidden to take offensive action because of the possible loss of vital information that combat might bring.

But the pilots and gunners of VB-104, like the crews of most patrol bomber squadrons, felt that when they could get in a good lick at the enemy, they would not hesitate to do so. They had come to the Pacific to fight a war, not to run from one, and their record in downing enemy planes and sinking ships reflected this zeal.

VB-104 began its combat flying from an airfield in the soggy jungle on Guadalcanal in the Solomons, gradually working its way north as the war progressed. There they endured the mud, odors from the steaming jungle and the nightly attacks from Washing Machine Charlie, the Japanese nuisance bomber whose mission it was to disturb the sleep of the American air and ground crews.

It was there, too, that the gunners of VB-104 got their first enemy kills, flying their PB4Ys that the pilots liked to use as fighter planes against the Japanese transport planes, bombers and float planes. The PB4Y was an unlikely fighter aircraft, since it was the B-24 Liberator with a Navy designation. But, that didn't deter the air crews from jumping a likely enemy aircraft when they could. The Navy flew their Liberators on long-range patrol missions, lasting from nine to 15 hours, singly, rather than in formation as the Army Air Forces did. Therefore, each pilot made his own decisions about what to do when he encountered the enemy, whether the enemy was in the air, on the ground or on the water.

The crew of Lt. John Alley was first to strike pay dirt when his gunners downed a giant, four-engined Mavis seaplane in their Liberator *Open Bottom*. Then the other crews of VB-104 went hunting for Japanese, and six more crews scored, shooting down a succession of hapless twin-engined Betty bombers. The gunners of the Liberator piloted by Lt. John Humphrey got two Bettys in one day.

Although the gunners of Lt. Whitney Wright's Liberator had scored with a Betty, it was on a mission patrolling the area of the Japanese-held island of Nauru, located between the Solomons and the Gilberts, that a Betty got away from them. The mission was considered a hot one, since the squadron had already lost two Liberators that had been assigned to patrol the Nauru sector. So, Wright approached the island from the northwest, hoping the Japanese would think his was a friendly aircraft. The day was bright, just right for observations. Sure enough, there was a freighter loading phosphate at a pier on the west side of the island and a destroyer loitering nearby a mile or two offshore. Tempting targets, but not for a lone Liberator.

Then, suddenly, one of the gunners called out a Betty that was approaching the airstrip for landing, its landing gear down, making it a fat, juicy target. Even though Wright knew that the Japanese defenses were probably alerted by now, he could not resist the temptation and decided to go after the bomber. He dove the large plane and rapidly approached the bomber, flying slightly below its flight path. As the Lib came within range of the Betty, the nose and top turret gunners opened up with a jarring roar, four streams of .50-caliber lead lacing into the Japanese plane. Almost immediately the left engine of the Betty burst into flame, and the Japanese pilots fought to control the bomber on one engine, continuing toward the airstrip. The Navy gunners could not figure out why their devastating firepower at such close range did not blow the Betty's fuel tanks. They had wounded her badly, but she refused to go down. Their musings were cut short by the call that dust trails from the airstrip had been seen, indicating that fighters were probably taking off.

Sure enough, seven Zeros were rapidly approaching the Liberator, Wright wisely broke off the attack on the Betty, but reluctantly, since he had wanted his gunners to down the enemy bomber. Quickly, Wright dove for the water, where they would have the best chance for survival, and firewalled the throttles. Wright, in his haste, forgot to retract the ball turret, and the gunner got the ride of his life, a few feet above the waves. But, the extended turret also cost the Lib about five knots of airspeed, which it could have used in the battle.

The Zeros formed two lines on either side of the Liberator, three on one side and four on the other, staying just out of range of the bomber's guns. Then the fighters came after the bomber, making quartering head-on passes, one from each side. The crew could see the spouts in the water made by the machine gun and cannon shells of the fighters as they walked their way toward the fleeing bomber. But, the Japanese seemed to break off their firing passes before the rounds reached the bomber, probably discouraged by the devastating firepower being poured out by the Navy gunners.

In the waist, gunner Tony Conti was jumping from one side of the fuselage to the other manning the two waist guns as the Zeros bored in from both sides. He was able to put up a good defense because the fighters did not coordinate their beam attacks, and he could take them all on as they came in.

Finally, the Zeros gave up and went home, and the Liberator got home without a scratch. But the crew of the patrol bomber did not consider it a good mission. They had not seen whether their Betty went down, and all of the Zeros got away.

Gunner Tony Conti was to figure in a later mission in Lt. Wright's Liberator. Again, the combat was in the Nauru area where the crew spotted a lone freighter steaming toward the island, unprotected by an accompanying warship. This was a target made to order for the Liberator, and Wright attacked it at low level. A little too low, however, because when the bombs hit their target the ship exploded in a huge burst of smoke and flame. Obviously they had found a munitions ship.

The blast tossed the Liberator about like a feather; the nose glass was broken, giving the bombardier a broken jaw; the bomb-bay doors were blown cockeyed, one of them hanging down, flapping in the slipstream.

The Lib was in trouble. Here they were 750 miles from home, over the water, with a wounded man aboard and a damaged mid-section that was inducing so much drag that it was doubtful if the high power settings that were needed to overcome the drag would allow the fuel on board to get them home. Pilot Wright calculated that they could not make it.

Gunner Tony Conti, who was also the plane captain, decided to see what he could do to help. He managed to hand-crank one of the damaged bomb-bay doors closed, and then tackled the one that was flapping in the breeze — this was the one that was giving the drag problem.

Conti, with another gunner holding him firmly by the ankles, hung out from the narrow bomb-bay catwalk and grappled the injured door into the bomb bay and fastened it in. Now they had a chance to make it back to Guadalcanal.

Several hours later they did. But their problems weren't over. Wright would have to make a landing with no brakes and no flaps. He cooly set the plane down and the mission ended when the big bomber rolled gently to a stop against a grassy gun bunker.

The crew climbed out to count 154 holes in the plane. They also found that the inside of the bomb bay was coated with a sticky, powdery substance. They scraped about a pound of it off to have it analyzed. Sure enough, it was the type of nitrate used in making munitions. Their eventful mission had paid dividends.

It was now a year later, and Lt. Wright, who had been executive officer of VB-104, was now commander of the squadron with its new designation VPB-104. The unit had moved north with the advance on Japan and was now operating from Tacloban on Leyte in the Philippines. In the same tradition, the pilots and gunners sought out the enemy while doing patrol bomber duties.

Lt. Paul Stevens was now the executive officer of the squadron, whose unit nickname was the Buccaneers. It was the day after Christmas, 1944, and Stevens and his crew had been assigned to patrol a sector from Leyte westward across the Philippines and then across the South China Sea to Cam Ranh Bay in French Indochina. Cam Ranh Bay would later figure in the Vietnam war as a major airbase and port for the American forces.

Operating the Liberators from Tacloban was no picnic. Because of the extreme ranges required for their patrol missions, the PB4Ys were loaded to 68,000 pound gross weight, which was 3,000 pounds more than the emergency war overload. In addition, the runway matting at Tacloban field, which was loosely lashed Marston matting, bunched up in front of the airplane's tires, which made every takeoff like an uphill run. In the before-dawn takeoff, Stevens lined the airplane up between the flare pots that served to mark the runway limits. Letting it roll, Stevens trusted that by the time they reached the two-foot dropoff at the end they would have enough flying speed. They did, just barely.

Just as dawn was breaking, the Lib was over Mindoro, in the Philippines, which had been invaded by American troops a few days before. There was an enemy air raid in progress, but the patrol plane sighted no enemy fighters. As they passed Mindoro, they ran into thick weather, with turbulence and heavy rain showers that blanked out their radar. But, as they approached the French Indochina coast, Stevens let down and found the weather more favorable for their patrol purposes.

Steven's Lib had not been loaded with bombs and he was under strict orders to make no attacks on the enemy. He had been chastised previously for engaging the enemy when his mission was solely to patrol. But, like most of the other crew members, he could not in good conscience let an opportunity to hit the enemy pass by. The Lib approached Cam Ranh Bay, which was known to be a major assembly port for large Japanese fleets prior to a major assault on the allies. As the Liberator approached the anchorage, Stevens added full power for a low level pass.

Just clearing the harbor was a small anti-sub vessel, but it was ignored as the Lib pressed on. Ahead were nine twin-float Jakes, one of which was taxiing for takeoff. Stevens cleared his gunners to fire, and the nose and top turrets let the enemy planes have it. The waist gunner strafed facilities along the shore. The three-man crew of the taxiing Jake went over the side into the water, as their idling plane chugged away from them.

Like most prudent combat pilots, Stevens' usual rule was one pass and keep going. But since they had met no resistance, he decided to make a second run on the Jakes. They saw on the second run that one Jake was sinking and one was listing. Again the gunners blasted away adding another listing Jake to their record. A third run was considered, but now Japanese ground gunners could be seen running to their gun positions. Heading north up the coast, the crew spotted a unit of Japanese flyers at Na Trang airstrip lined up in their dress whites, probably for an inspection. Four tanker ships were spotted at anchor. Then it was time to turn back toward Leyte.

As the Lib approached Mindoro again, at 4:10 in the afternoon, the weather suddenly cleared and the PB4Y sighted a Japanese task force headed for Mindoro. This is what they had been sent to find. The force consisted of the heavy cruiser *Ashigara,* along with two light cruisers and five destroyers. They were headed for the invading American force on Mindoro which was now in a vulnerable phase, both at sea and on the beach. The cruiser sent up flak against the patrol bomber, just to discourage any attack. The patrol bomber sent urgent flash messages to let everyone know what they had spotted. As they closed on Mindoro, they were also able to transmit to ground force units, who asked that they land at Mindoro to confirm their sightings.

The airstrip on Mindoro was nothing more than a short, level stretch of terrain that had been bulldozed out a few days earlier. The Liberator was landed in good fashion, but the wheels sunk into the soft dirt so that taxiing was a problem. When Stevens reported to the operations with his sightings, the Army ground commander wanted his plane to attack the task force. Stevens replied that he was under orders to avoid combat. But, eventually Stevens' eagerness to engage the enemy got the better of him and he agreed to take on a load of bombs. Four 500-pound bombs were brought to the plane, but they had to be hefted into the bomb bay by hand, since there was no bomb hoist available.

By the time the bombs were loaded and the fuel tanks filled, it was dark. Luckily there was a bright moon which allowed a takeoff from the unlit airstrip. The ungainly Liberator waddled and lurched as it struggled to gain speed in the soft surface, and Stevens had to horse the bomber over the trees at the end of the runway with brute force.

Once airborne they headed for the Japanese task force. As they spotted the ships in the moonlight, they could see that Army Air Force B-25 bombers were beginning an attack and were receiving heavy anti-aircraft fire. Swinging to the west at 8,000 feet, Stevens told his bombardier to pick out the largest target and they would make their run. As they approached the task force, they too began receiving flak. After bombs away, Stevens swung around to watch where the bombs went. One hit in the wake of the cruiser, but the next two struck the large ship, and the crew could see that oil was streaming from it. In the meantime, the AAF Mitchells had sunk one of the destroyers.

The Japanese task force continued toward the American invasion force, but by the time they got there the ships of the landing support force had had time to slip away, thanks to the earlier sighting by the Navy Liberator. The enemy task force then retired at high speed as the Liberator continued to shadow it. At dawn, they could see that the heavy cruiser continued to stream oil from its bowels and they could confirm that one destroyer was missing from the task force.

Turning for home, the PB4Y arrived at Tacloban after having been in the air for 22 of the past 24 hours. The crew was utterly exhausted. But, there was no rest for Stevens. He was summoned by the commander of the air arm of the Seventh Fleet to give an account of his mission and was asked why he had not seen the fleet on the outbound leg of his patrol. Poor weather was the reason, but what Stevens did not know was the interrogation was to decide whether to court-martial him for engaging in prohibited combat or to give him the Navy Cross for his courageous action. He got the Navy Cross.

Three months later the crew of Stevens' Liberator made like fighter pilots on a mission that began from Clark Field, near Manila. The crew had a specific mission. Intelligence sources had picked up information that a high ranking Japanese naval officer would be making a flight from Batavia on Java to Shanghai, China. The mission of the American crew was to patrol up the eastern side of Formosa, across the straits, and then south down the coast of China.

Passing Formosa and turning for the China coast, Stevens let down through the clouds to just above the water. When they picked up the coast, they turned south and soon spotted a Japanese freighter, the *Koshu,* leaving a harbor. Farther out to sea there was a Japanese destroyer, but Stevens thought the distance was enough that he could safely attack the merchant ship. As they began their low-level bomb run, the destroyer began firing its flak guns, but the Liberator pressed on at 200 knots. The nose and top turrets of the Lib began firing at the freighter and then it was time to lob the 100-pounders. As the Lib swung around to see what their handiwork had done, they were greeted by a furiously blazing ship that was slowly turning in a large circle. They could see crewmen jumping over the side as the sinking ship began its death throes. Scratch one freighter.

More action came just a few minutes later as they resumed their patrol. Two Jake float-planes were cruising serenely along unaware of the approaching Liberator. Stevens joined the formation in the number three position undetected. He told his gunners to hold their fire until they were close enough to make certain of their aim. They were able to get so close that when the Japanese gunner in the rear of one of the Jakes finally looked at the Liberator, they could see the disbelief register on his face. The American gunners opened up and the first Jake went down. The second Jake made a dash for the protection of the destroyer, circling it until the Liberator went away.

Barely 30 minutes after resuming their patrol, the crew of the PB4Y spotted a huge four-engined flying boat coming toward them at three or four thousand feet above them. This seaplane, an Emily, had to be the one they were looking for. It was a spiffed-up version, with guns removed; just the sort that would be transporting a high naval official.

Stevens gave the Lib full power, climbing to the attack. As he swung toward the seaplane the Navy gunners opened up at nearly point blank range, their tracers sparking off the fuselage of the craft. But, now, the climb and the turning attack had robbed the Liberator of its airspeed and it fell off as the flying boat pulled away. Using full power, Stevens finally regained airspeed, but was closing on the Emily, which was in a shallow, high-speed descent, very slowly. The Liberator had used up a lot of its fuel on the attacks against the freighter and the Jakes, and Stevens had to make a choice between continuing the chase and risking a certain nighttime ditching, or letting the Emily go free. He turned for home, dejected that they had not been able to down the Emily. They landed at Clark Field after more than 13 hours in the air.

It was two days later, while he was having lunch, that his squadron and air wing commanders gave Stevens the news that his gunners had been successful — the admiral had gone down. Through intelligence sources it was determined that the fire from the gunners had killed the two Emily pilots and that the navigator had tried to land the flying boat on a river near the China coast. The Emily crashed, but the Japanese naval leader who had been the target of their attack, Admiral Seigo Yamagata, survived the crash. The Emily fell in an area under Chinese army control, and the admiral, realizing he might be captured, took the "honorable" way out and fell on his sword.

So, VPB-104, and Stevens' crew, could chalk up several more victories: a freighter, a Jake, an Emily, and one Japanese admiral.

Not satisfied with its fighter-type attack sorties in the daytime, VPB-104 also assumed the role of night fighter, as well. Intelligence developed information that the Japanese were running what amounted to a scheduled airline at night between Japan and Formosa. Takeoffs were at sunset and landings before sunrise. It was decided to place Liberator patrol bombers over the base on Formosa where the flights arrived and departed, patrolling at 10,000 feet.

Consolidated PB4Y-2 Privateer, the single-tail version of the Navy's PB4Y Liberator, replaced the older version in the later stages of the war (General Dynamics-Convair Division photo)

On April 22, 1945 the crew of Lt. George Waldeck's Lib spotted a Sally twin-engined bomber from 15 miles away. The big Liberator was able to close within 500 feet of the Sally without being observed. Then, the nose and top turret gunners poured 400 rounds into the bomber, setting fire to both her engines. The entire tail section of the Sally broke off as the bomber plunged to its doom.

In all, VPB-104 gunners downed seven Japanese planes in this manner and the airline stopped its operation. The fighter tactics of the patrol bombers again paid dividends.

18. The Night Gunners

As stated earlier in this book, a number of Army Air Forces aerial gunners in World War II received recognition for their victories in published orders. These orders were normally issued by the numbered air forces in the various theaters of operation. Except for a single group of gunners, none received credit in an official USAF post-war compilation of victory credits for WWII.

The exceptions were those gunners who were crewmembers on night fighters, who shared kills with the pilots and radar operators in the fighters. The concept of sharing kill credits by crew members was common in World War I and in the Vietnam conflict as well, where pilots and radar observers in both Air Force and Navy F-4 fighters were credited equally with victories (In fact, the highest scoring "ace" in the Vietnam fracas was not a pilot, but a USAF radar operator with six kills).

The official Air Force document (USAF Historical Study No. 85) which lists all kills by those assigned to AAF units includes only fighter pilots, with the exception of gunners and radar operators flying night fighters.

No night fighter gunner, however, achieved ace status with five confirmed victories. Only four pilots and four radar operators could claim ace status in night fighters, each with five victories apiece.

A total of 26 aerial gunners were credited with shared victories in World War II, with a total of 33 enemy downed, all Japanese. The highest scoring gunner was Staff Sgt. Emil K. Weishar of the 421st Night Fighter Squadron in the Southwest Pacific theater of operations. His three shared victories came all on a single night, November 28, 1944.

Five other aerial gunners had two shared kills apiece. Two were from the same squadron as Weishar, the 421st. They were Staff Sgt. Henry E. Bobo, who scored on September 7th and 9th, 1944 and Staff Sgt. Joseph Mazur who got both his shared victories on the same night, November 10, 1944. Also in the Southwest Pacific with the 419th Night Fighter Squadron was Staff Sgt. Glen O. Deforest who is credited with two shared kills on August 5, 1944 and September 1, 1944.

In the Central Pacific area, two other night fighter gunners shared double victories. Corporal Raymond L. Golden is credited with a victory on the night of January 1st, 1945 and another the next night on January 2nd. He flew with the 6th Night Fighter Squadron. Corporal Jesse V. Tew is credited with two shared victories, one flown with the 6th squadron and

and one flown with the 548th Night Fighter Squadron, both in the Central Pacific.

All of the gunners in night fighters flew the P-61 Black Widow built by Northrop. It was also the first night fighter built specifically for night fighting. All other night fighters of World War II were modified for the job from existing light bombers or day fighters.

The British Royal Air Force was the first to develop night fighters. After the RAF day fighters had driven the German bombers from daylight raids in the Battle of Britain, the Germans turned to blitzing at night. The first night fighters were converted Bristol Blenheim light bombers. These proved ineffective because they did not have enough speed for good interceptions nor the firepower to assure destruction of enemy bombers. They were replaced by two other aircraft modified for the night fighter role.

The first of these was the Boulton Paul Defiant, a two-seat, single engine fighter. The Defiant was unique as a fighter because it had no forward-firing guns. Its firepower was contained in a rear power turret equipped with four .303-inch Browning machine guns, the standard gun for RAF flexible guns and power turrets. Originally a day fighter it had some success because of its unique capabilities with the rear turret. The fighter was very similar in appearance to the Hawker Hurricane fighter, so when it was introduced into combat, German pilots made the standard attacks on what they supposed was a defenseless tail. They were met with the firepower of the four Brownings, which in one three week period saw Defiant gunners accounting for 65 enemy aircraft — 38 of them in one day. It didn't take long for the Germans to change their tactics when encountering the Defiant and they were soon attacking it from below, out of the area covered by the turret. Defiants, which were not the swiftest of fighters, began to suffer heavy losses and soon were removed from day missions. They were equipped with airborne radar and shifted to night fighter operations. In this new role, Defiants were very successful and were credited with shooting down more enemy aircraft than any other night fighter during the London blitz of the winter of 1940-41. One of the ace Defiant gunners was Sgt. F.J. Barker of the RAF 264 fighter squadron, who scored 12 day victories in addition to one night kill. His victories were shared with his pilot, Sgt. E.R. Thorn, who never fired a shot. Both received the Distinguished Flying Medal for their fine teamwork. In one day engagement Sgt. Barker destroyed two DO-17 bombers and was engaging a third when an Me-109 jumped his Defiant and damaged the engine. As the two sergeants were getting ready to make a crash landing near Herne Bay in the U.K., the Me-109 tried to finish them off when they were about 500 feet above the ground. Sgt. Barker fired his few remaining rounds and the Me-109 crashed just a short distance from where the two sergeants crash-landed. Neither RAF flyer was badly injured.

The other Blenheim replacement was the Bristol Beaufighter, a versatile twin-engine fighter that served the RAF in a variety of roles. Its armament consisted of four 20mm cannons mounted in the nose and six .303-inch Browning machine guns mounted in the wing, all firing forward. When it was in production it was the heaviest armed fighter in the world. It, too, was given a radar capability and proved highly effective in the night fighter role. It is credited by many as the plane responsible for ending the German blitz of London in 1940-41.

In 1942, another versatile twin-engine machine, the de Havilland Mosquito, was modified to night fighter duties in addition to its several other roles. It was 40 mph faster than the Beaufighter and the last version had a top speed of 407 mph at 28,000 feet, which put it in a class with many single engine fighters.

When the tables were turned and nighttime raids of Germany by RAF bombers were stepped up, the Germans modified two of their twin-engine machines for night defense. Like the Beaufighter and Mosquito, the versatile Junkers Ju-88 performed a variety of roles for the Luftwaffe, one of which was night fighting. It was somewhat slower than the RAF night fighters, but the final version with boosted engines had a speed of 389 mph, which was quite respectable for a light bomber turned fighter. The other German night fighter was the Messerschmitt Me-110, a day fighter modified for the job. It had speed comparable to the Beaufighter.

In 1940 a team of U.S. Army Air Forces officers had been in England and had witnessed the effectiveness of the RAF night fighters. When they made their report on their observations, they recommended that the U.S. develop a night fighter designed from the very start for the mission. Their recommendation was acted upon quickly and by January 1941 Northrop had a contract to produce its design of the P-61. It wasn't until nearly three years later, in October 1943, that production models began coming off the line. By April and May of 1944, squadrons in combat areas in the Pacific and in Europe began receiving their new fighters. Squadrons in the China-Burma-India and Mediterranean theaters also received the Black Widow.

In the meantime, a night fighter was needed by the AAF, so the U.S.

resorted to the practice of modifying an existing light twin-engined airplane, in this case the A-20 Havoc light attack bomber. Britain had already modified a number of Havocs for night duty, but while the Havoc Is were called night fighters, much of their work was in the night intruder role, carrying bombs in their bomb bays. One version of the Havoc I was equipped with a 2,700-million-candlepower light which would be turned on after tracking the enemy by radar. Then Hurricane fighters that had been flying in formation with the Havoc I would go in for the kill. As may be imagined, there was little success with this tactic.

The night version of the AAF A-20 was designated the P-70, and was equipped with a newly developed radar set from the Massachusetts Institute of Technology. They were rushed to the Pacific in 1942 and were used until the P-61 became operational. The modified fighter was not wholly effective, suffering from a restricted service ceiling. When units began receiving the Black Widow, P-70s were relegated to a trainer status to provide radar instruction for P-61 crews.

Another AAF aircraft modified to help contain Japanese night raids of airfields in the Pacific was the Lockheed P-38M Lightning fighter. A radar pod was slung beneath the nose and the fuselage of the twin-engine fighter was modified to carry a radar operator in a small cockpit behind and slightly elevated above the pilot. Only 75 of this version of night fighters were built.

The U.S. Navy also modified some of its fighters for night defense chores. Some Grumman F6F Hellcats were given a radar pod slung under the right wing and later some Grumman F8F Bearcats were similarly equipped. Some models of the Vought F4U Corsair also had radar pods mounted near the right wingtip. These three single-engine fighters carried no radar observer or gunners, of course. The twin-engine Grumman F7F Tigercat had more extensive modifications in its night fighter version. A large radome was moulded onto an extended nose section and the fuselage was modified to make a cabin for a radar operator who sat behind the pilot.

No American night fighter had provisions for a gunner until the P-61 Black Widow. The gunner's position was designed into the airplane from the very start.

The P-61 was a large fighter, comparable to the B-25 medium bomber both in weight and in size. In shape it was similar to the P-38 fighter, except much larger. There was a central pod between the two engines for the crew and armament. Twin booms extended from behind the engines to

The distinctive outline of the Northrop P-61 Black Widow night fighter is evident in this photo (Northrop Corporation photo)

The awesome firepower of the four fuselage-mounted 20mm cannons and the four .50-caliber machine guns of the top turret is displayed in this photo of the P-61. The gunner's cockpit is the raised one just ahead of the turret (Northrop Corporation photo)

the empennage. The fighter weighed more than 30,000 pounds and had a wing span of 66 feet. It was painted glossy black. Its maximum speed was about 370 mph and it had a service ceiling of more than 33,000 feet.

The crew sat in tandem with the pilot forward and the gunner immediately behind him. The gunner did not occupy a gun turret but had his own cockpit slightly raised above the pilot's. The radar operator sat in the rear of the crew nacelle in a small cabin behind the wing.

Armament consisted of four fixed 20-mm cannons placed in the belly back of and below the radar dome. In addition there was a movable turret on top of the fuselage behind the gunner. The turret mounted four .50-caliber machine guns. The turret could be operated remotely by all three crew members. It could be fixed in a forward position so that the pilot could add the four .50s to his four cannons. The gunner could operate the turret for visual contacts with an enemy aircraft, and usually was the one that would swivel it to catch an enemy in the event of an overshoot. The radar operator could also sight and fire the turret weapons using radar for aiming.

Because of severe buffeting to the airplane caused by the turret, the turret was deleted on the P-61A models after 37 planes had come off the line with turrets installed. The remaining 163 production "A" models and early "B" models did not have turrets and therefore were operated as two-place fighters without gunners. When the buffeting problem was solved, the turret was again installed on the remainder of the night fighter production run, and gunners were once more added to the crew.

Flying night fighter combat missions involved close cooperation with ground radar installations. With their large antenna equipment controllers on the ground could detect enemy penetrators at a greater range than could the airborne radar set in the fighter. Typically, the ground controller would vector a night fighter from its loiter or patrol position to make an interception. The idea was to place the fighter at the rear of the intruder. Then when the fighter's radar picked up the enemy, the radar operator in the rear of the plane would take over in the closing phase of the fight. Usually the pilot would dip down in a ten-degree dive and when drawing near firing range begin a slight climb to the firing position below and behind the enemy. Of course if the intercept did not work out in a textbook fashion, the gunner sometimes got his chance to try his luck.

All of the turret-equipped P-61s went to the Pacific Theater of Operations. One of their major tasks was to help prevent night attacks by the Japanese on B-29 bases during the big buildup of the 20th Air Force for the upcoming last push to Japan.

The squadron with gunners scoring the highest number of kills was the 421 NFS in the Southwest Pacific, with nine gunners scoring 13 victories. In addition to Sgts. Weishar (3), Bobo (2) and Mazur (2) already mentioned, there was Tech. Sgt. Harold L. Cobb, Staff Sgt. Ralph H. McDaniel, Sgt. James W. Pilling, Staff Sgt. Lacy Potter, Tech. Sgt. Brady W. Swinney, and Staff Sgt. Donald H. Trabing each scoring one victory apiece.

The next highest scoring squadron was the 6th NFS in the Central Pacific, which had seven gunners downing eight of the enemy. Protecting the B-29s on Saipan on Christmas night, 1944, crews of the 6th downed six Betty bombers. Corporal Golden was the only gunner to score more than one kill with the 6th. Those with victories in the 6th included Staff Sgt. W.S. Anderson, Pvt. Peter Dutkanicz, Pvt. Patrick J. Farelly, Sgt. Leroy F. Miozzi, Pvt. Otis H. Ohair, and Corp. Jesse V. Tew. The squadron commander must have been some tough customer. Whereas most of the gunners in other squadrons who had kills held the rank of staff sergeant or better, in the 6th those with victories included three privates, two corporals, one buck sergeant and one staff sergeant.

Flying from Iwo Jima, and later Ie Shima, was the next highest scoring squadron, the 548th. With one victory apiece were Staff Sgt. Benjamin J. Boscardin, Master Sgt. David E. Meech, Sgt. Raymond C. Ryder, Master Sgt. Reno H. Sukow, and Corporal Jesse V. Tew, who must have transferred from the 6th (where he got his first of two) to the 548th which at least had some master sergeant gunners.

The 419th NFS was the next highest in scoring with four gunners credited with a total of five kills. Staff Sgt. John O. Graham, Staff Sgt. Frank A. McCormack and Sgt. John C. Snyder added one apiece to the two scored by Staff Sgt. Deforrest.

There were two squadrons with only one gunner victory. The 547th in the Southwest Pacific had Staff Sgt. Ralph M. Knight and the 549th in the Central Pacific had Staff Sgt. William S. Dare. Sgt. Dare shared in the only victory scored by his squadron in the war.

19. Superforts

The ultimate in development of defensive gunnery systems in World War II was the system installed in Boeing B-29 Superfortresses, the very heavy bomber that was to bring Japan to its knees. For the first time in American bombers turrets could be operated by remote control by aerial gunners who were as much as 60 feet away from their weapons.

The heart of the system was a computer-aligned central system which allowed remote controlling of as many as three turrets, two at a time. The "black box" system, built by General Electric, was protected by armor plate, the only part of the B-29, other than protection for the pilot, that was armored. The gunner no longer had to figure windage or lead or lag his target — neither did he have to worry about ballistics; it was all done for him by the computer. Using his remote control electric sight the gunner was free to aim directly at his target, centering it in a reticle of lighted dots. It would be a brave, or foolish, fighter pilot who would face a formation of B-29s with such devasting firepower.

B-29s mounted 12 .50-caliber machine guns, and some added a 20-mm cannon. Ten of the machine guns were in controllable turrets, two upper and two lower. The forward upper turret housed four machine guns. The other fuselage turrets held two guns each. The tail turret mounted two .50-calibers, and, early on, a 20-mm cannon as well. Later the 20-mm cannons were removed because the trajectories were not compatible with the machine guns.

The GE system was controlled by Central Fire Control "gunnery commander" who was stationed just in front of the rear upper turret and used a plexiglass dome for viewing the air battle. He could control both upper turrets, although the bombardier could take over the forward upper turret on demand. The bombardier could also take control of the lower forward turret under certain circumstances, such as frontal attack. Both the bombardier and the CFC commander could take command of as many as six .50-calibers on demand. Gunners in the waist blisters had primary control over the lower turrets. The blister gunners could change control of both lower turrets back and forth between them, controlling one or both depending on which side the attack was coming from. The blister gunners could also take over the tail guns if the tail gunner became incapacitated. They could not, however, sight directly astern of the bomber, except just to spray the general area.

All B-29 gunners went through normal AAF aerial gunners schools,

B-29s of the 29th Bomb Group head out for a strike against Japan in 1945 from their base at North Field, Guam

and in addition were given training in the operation and light maintenance of the GE gunnery system. The CFC gunner, who was responsible for the maintenance of the entire system in his plane, also took a six-week course on the electronic and mechanical design, maintenance, and operation of the system. This course was given at Lowry Field, in Colorado.

Aerial training was given in B-24s, both in flexible guns and turrets. Those destined for B-29 units then received training in the GE system which had been mounted in B-24s modified to adapt the system.

In operational B-29 units, ground crew armorers were primarily responsible for the maintenance of the guns, while technical specialists performed most of the repair and checkout of the CFC system. Aircraft gunners were responsible for the preflight and loading of ammunition in the guns. Although in theory, inflight maintenance, such as clearing gun jams or repairing inoperative turrets, could be performed by gunners while on a mission, in actual practice this proved to be almost impossible. Jammed guns and malfunctioning turrets usually stayed that way until the bomber returned to its base.

In late 1944 a new model B-29, the B model, began to take shape. They would be equipped for radar bombing with an AN/APQ-7 "Eagle" radar antenna mounted beneath the fuselage. The antenna was an 18-foot long rod mounted perpendicular to the fuselage, which rotated from side to side through an arc of about 60 degrees. Since the mission of the B-29B was to bomb from well above 30,000 feet where it would be faster than the Japanese fighter planes, there was little need for armament and guns. The 315th Bomb Wing, which was to be the first to be equipped with the B-29B, began modifying their old bombers to a training configuration until the Bell plant at Marietta, Georgia began turning out the B-models. All four bottom and top turrets were removed and all the Central Fire Control system was taken out. The 20-mm cannon was deleted from the tail turret and most armor, except that in front of the pilots and in back of the tail turret gunner were removed. Three of the gunners were deleted from the crew and replaced by crewmen who acted as scanners. Later many of the 315th's training airplanes were equipped a radar tail turret system, the APG-15. The APG-15 featured three .50-caliber machine guns.

When the 315th began receiving their new B-models, they started deploying to Guam. They were assigned oil refining targets which were located near coastlines and made radar bombing more accurate. The rather primitive radar bombing set worked fairly well and the bombers were able to get good strikes against the fuel producing plants. The radar tail turret, on the other hand, gave all sorts of problems and never did live up to expectations. The occasional gunner who reported his APG-15 was in good operating order was looked upon with some suspicion.

While B-29s were not exactly airliners, they had some of the creature comforts associated with more modern air travel. With cabin pressurization, heated crew compartments and air conditioning, gunners were freed of the encumberance of the heavy clothing, gloves, boots and helmets that kept gunners on B-17s and B-24s from absolute misery. Even the tail gunner had an airconditioned, pressurized compartment, although he was sealed off from his compatriots by an air lock when above pressurization altitudes.

Pressurization also had its drawbacks as a blister gunner in the 479th Bomb Group found out. It was on a mission to Nagoya, Japan on January 3rd, 1945 in which the Superforts underwent 346 passes by Japanese fighters. Sgt. James R. Krantz was at his left blister station in the B-29 *American Maid* when suddenly cannon fire from a fighter blasted the plexiglas blister and Krantz was literally blown out through the blister. The sudden change in pressure, high on the inside of the plane and low outside sucked the gunner through the broken blister.

Luckily, Krantz had foreseen such a possibility and had fashioned a home-made safety harness which restrained him. He was fortunate, too, that his oxygen mask stayed on his face. As he hung there, at 29,000 feet above Japan, held by the harness and one leg hooked inside the plane, frantic efforts were made to bring him back inside the bomber. The other blister gunner attempted to pull him in, but the forces of the strong, frigid slipstream were too much to overcome. The Central Fire Control gunner joined the effort, but again it was unsuccessful. Finally, after the copilot made his way back to the waist, the three were able to get Krantz back into the plane, after more than ten minutes of trying. 100% oxygen was applied to Krantz and after about 20 minutes he began to show signs of recovery. He survived his ordeal, but suffered the effects of severe frostbite. B-29 gunners claimed 14 kills on the mission, along with 14 probables and 20 damaged Japanese fighters. The Japanese, in turn, downed five Superforts and damaged one lucky gunner.

The B-29 had been designed to carry the war to the Japanese homeland. But at the time units had trained in the bomber and were ready for combat, the allies still had not captured enough island bases in the Pacific close enough to Japan to allow the Superfortresses to reach their targets. So, the bombers got into the war through the back door. Instead of flying across the Pacific Ocean, in April 1944 they crossed the Atlantic to reach China, from where they had the range to allow them to bomb Japan.

The bases being built for them in China, however, were primitive fields, built by the hand labor of thousands of coolie Chinese. There were no facilities other than crushed rock runways.

This meant that the bombers would have to stage out of bases in India, near Calcutta, where supply and fuel depots had been established. It was up to the bombers to fly their own supplies to the forward bases in China, and some were even converted to tankers to haul fuel needed on the raids. This "trucking operation" went on for five months.

It was on the second day of the trucking operation that a B-29 got its first taste of aerial combat and gunners were pressed into service. A B-29 of the 444th Bomb Group piloted by Major Charles H. Hansen was carrying a load of fuel to the forward Chinese staging bases and as his B-29 was over the India-Burma border, he spotted twelve enemy fighters at three o'clock and two thousand feet below his altitude of 16,000 feet. They were Oscars. The B-29 crew members manned their battle stations.

Six of the Oscars climbed toward the bomber, while the other six continued on course toward the Hump. When they reached the bomber, they split into two groups of three, forming on either side of the B-29. They flew along with the bomber, out of range, for at least 15 minutes, probably sizing up this new warplane which they were seeing for the first time. The B-29 gunners nervously waited, tracking the Oscars.

Then the lead fighter suddenly curved in from the right side on a firing pass hitting the midsection of the bomber with eight rounds. Blister gunner Sgt. Walter W. Gilonski was wounded in the attack and both upper turrets were put out of commission. As the other Oscars began making their attacks, the 20-mm cannon and the twin .50-caliber machine guns in the tail turret jammed. Tail gunner Sgt. Harold Lanhan was able to clear the jammed machine guns however. Lanhan got good hits on one of the Oscars and it was seen smoking. The enemy fighters made a total of twelve passes before giving up the fight, but only the first pass had resulted in damage to the bomber. A B-29 had survived its first air battle and gunner Lanhan came away with a probable, the first B-29 gunner to score against the enemy.

The first confirmed victory by a B-29 gunner went to another 444th Bomb Group tailgunner, Tech. Sgt. Harold C. Edwards. The kill was registered on one of the early night missions to Japan. The targets were military installations at Nagasaki. Staging out of Chinese forward bases, 33 bombers headed for Japan. Over the target the bombers were met by flak and fighters; none suffered any damage. Tailgunner Edwards, however, firing his 20-mm cannon at a night fighter at a range of 600 yards, scored a kill, the first confirmed in the 20th Air Force.

What might have been the most enemy planes downed by one Superfort during a mission went to a B-29 of the 498th Bomb Group, although the crew did not survive the battle to savor the victories. The date was December 27, 1944 and the bombers were now flying out of island bases that had been wrested from the Japanese on Guam, Tinian and Saipan. The target was Tokyo.

Uncle Tom's Cabin was the lead aircraft in the third element of nine aircraft on the 72 ship raid. The formation's altitude ranged from 28,800 feet to 33,800 feet. Flak was meager to intense and fighters would make 272 passes before the raid was over. Just one minute from bombs away a Tony made a head-on pass at *Uncle Tom's Cabin,* getting hits in the right blister. It kept coming at the bomber without breaking off, and its wingtip ripped a gash in the right side of the bomber's fuselage which ran from the nose to the leading edge of the wing. A yellow flame came from the gash and pieces of the plane's equipment flew out of the hole.

The wounded bomber could no longer hold formation and began to drop down and behind the group. As it did, it was swarmed upon by hordes of fighters. One minute after it left the formation it was rammed again by a second Tony, and pieces of the right wing and parts from the two right engines were knocked off.

Now, *Uncle Tom's Cabin* began falling faster, when yet another Tony rammed the plane, this time from below, hitting the belly. It began to spin, but somehow the pilots managed a recovery and the bomber resumed its course below the formation. At least 30 fighters continued making attacks on the hapless bomber. Finally, seven minutes after the attack began, the bomber went out of control and plunged straight down from 20,000 feet. No parachutes were seen before the bomber hit the ground a few miles outside Tokyo. But witnesses confirmed that the gunners of *Uncle Tom's Cabin* had taken a total of nine Tonys with them.

Ramming of Superforts by Japanese fighters became an accepted tactic as the Japanese, with their backs to the wall, used desperate measures to defend their homeland. The ramming was not always fatal to the Japanese pilots, many of whom would bail out of their crippled fighters and live to fight another day.

The 497th Bomb Group would get a real taste of the ramming tactic on a mission to the Tokyo area on January 27, 1945. The 497th was the lead group of the wing and bore the brunt of what was a maximum defensive effort by both Japanese Army and Navy fighters. An estimated 900 fighter attacks were made during the mission, with about half of those directed at the 497th.

In one of the 200 fighters that took on the 497th was Capt. Teruhiko Kobayashi, a 24-year-old commander of a Tony squadron. With ten Superforts to his credit, he would become the top ace against B-29s. His unit met the formation of bombers when they were between Mount Fuji and Tokyo. Kobayashi fired at the lead bomber, but missed. He continued to the next bomber and rammed it. Kobayashi was knocked out by the collision, but when his Tony had spun down to 12,000 feet he gained consciousness and bailed out. His wingman also rammed a Superfort, but was not so lucky and was killed. Three others in the unit, however, did survive rammings.

A Superfort with the name *Thumper* on the raid played tag with a rammer and survived. The crew later said that the bomber must have undergone at least 100 enemy attacks. Leaving the target with just three engines operating *Thumper* was soon all by itself. The masses of fighters that had been coming at *Thumper* from all sides suddenly were gone — all but one persistent Tony. The three turrets in the rear of the B-29 were empty of ammunition, but possibly so were the cannons in the Tony, because the fighter made no firing passes at the bomber. Instead, the enemy plane made slow, methodical passes at the top of the bomber's vertical stabilizer, trying to slice it with the fighter's propeller. As the blister and tail gunners would call to the pilot the position of the fighter, the pilot, Col. Robert Haynes, would wait until the Tony was close in, then kick the tail up, down, right or left, attempting to keep it away from the Tony. This cat and mouse game lasted for about one hundred miles before the Tony finally broke off and headed for home in frustration.

Sgt. Charles Mulligan, tail gunner in the B-29 *Irish Lassie,* had even a closer call with a ramming fighter that day, as the Superfort was rammed twice in quick succession. It all happened on the bomb run, where the leading 497th Group took most of its punishment. The gunners on *Irish Lassie* had already dispatched four enemy fighters when diving down from directly overhead was a Zeke. Sgt. James McHugh, the CFC gunner, had all six top turret guns bearing on the Zeke, but the fighter came on anyway, slamming into the left wing and tearing away eight feet of the aileron as well as rupturing a fuel tank. All four of *Irish Lassie's* engines kept running, though.

Irish Lassie continued on the bomb run as more attacks came, wounding the radio operator. Then just before bombs away, Sgt. Mulligan, in the tail, called out a Jack coming at them fast from six o'clock low. Mulligan held down the triggers of his turret even though an enemy bullet nicked his right hand. Pieces flew off the fighter as it bore in, but it continued straight for the tail section.

When Mulligan saw that the fighter was going to ram, he threw his arms up over his face. Then the Jack hit, ripping a large hole in the left side of the tail compartment. Just before he passed out, Mulligan had enough presence of mind to put on his oxygen mask. He might have fallen out through the hole in the side, except that jagged strips of the torn fuselage caught in his flying gear and held him in the plane.

The collision ripped out all the control cables on the left side of the fuselage leading to the tail — those of the pilot. As *Irish Lassie* started down, out of control, the copilot tested his controls and found that they were still intact. The copilot was able to regain control of the wounded bomber.

Irish Lassie's troubles were still not over. Fighters stayed with her until she was 60 miles out over the ocean. But, the rugged Superfort had survived the two rammings and many other firing attacks to make it back home with what was left of the rest of the 497th.

On raids against the Japanese mainland, B-29s flew two types of missions. At night they flew singly in bomber streams like those used by Royal Air Force bombers in Europe. In the daytime, they flew in massed formations, like the American AAF B-17s and B-24s in Europe.

Tech. Sgt. Raymond Pritchard, Jr. was a Central Fire Control gunner on the last large daytime B-29 raid of the war in which considerable opposition from Japanese fighters was mounted. He flew in B-29 *Myas' Dragon* which was assigned to the 6th Bomb Group based at Tinian in the Mariana Islands. Their targets were in the Yawata area on Kyushu Island with aiming points of the Sasebo Naval Base, shipyards and the nearby steel mills. A massed formation of 221 B-29s loaded with 1,302 tons of bombs flew at altitudes ranging from 15,000 to 18,000 feet. The date was August 8, 1945, two days after the atomic attack against Hiroshima and one day before the second atomic bomb was unleashed on Nagasaki.

For the first seven hours of the mission, gunners had little to do, since the target was 1,700 miles away and the flight was across open water. Once within 100 miles of Japan, gunners became alert because they could expect an attack by fighters at any moment. They donned their flak vests and steel helmets as the bombers circled over the water, forming up in the bombing formation. This would have been an ideal time for fighters to attack, but at this stage of the war the fuel supply was critical for Japan's forces and defensive fighter forces waited until the bombers were close to land.

As the formation turned toward land, two twin-engine fighters, Nicks or Irvings, joined the formation, flying about two miles to one side. They were probably radioing the B-29's course, altitude and speed to those on the ground. Once over land, anti-aircraft artillery tracked the formation with white phosphorous shells, the smoke trail pin-pointing the bombers for defensive fighter units. Pritchard said he felt that the Japanese Fighter Command appeared to be setting the Americans up for the kill.

Now the radio began to come alive with sightings of fighters. Then the first attack came against Pritchard's group. A lone twin-engine Nick diving out of the sun flashed through the middle of the formation so fast that no gunner had a chance to fire at it — the Nick got no hits either. Then, another Nick came at them head-on, but again no hits by either side. But, now the gunners knew that they were in for some work, and their adrenalin was up.

The formation was scheduled to have fighter escort, P-51s and P-47Ns from bases on Iwo Jima, but so far they were not in evidence. Then, the navigator of the *Myas' Dragon,* called out a P-47 at 10 o'clock high. Pritchard strained to see the fighter, but at first could not pick it up. He began to feel a touch of panic. Finally, when he did sight the fighter he found himself staring at a large red meatball on the side of the fuselage. Pritchard called that it was a Frank, not a P-47 and got ready to engage it. The Frank was about 1,000 yards out and pulling ahead to begin a pursuit curve attack.

As the fighter rolled in, Pritchard just had time to acquire it in his sight. The B-29 gunners always set their wingspan at 37 feet for Japanese fighters. As the Frank came at them, all his cannons winking red and rolling inverted, Pritchard clamped down on his trigger firing the six guns in both upper turrets. As soon as he did he knew he had hits on the Frank. The engine cowling of the Frank flew off and a plume of black smoke gushed from beneath the fighter's fuselage. As the Frank passed below the bomber still diving inverted, the blister and tail gunners joined the fray. Then the tail gunner called out that the Frank was now spinning toward the ground, still trailing black smoke. There was no parachute and although the tail gunner kept the Frank in sight, as long as possible, the formation was out of visual range before the Frank could be seen hitting the ground.

The gunner's joy was short-lived, though, because almost immediately the B-29 off their right wing called that he had been hit and was shutting down the number three engine. At first, Pritchard felt that their Frank had gotten some hits on the other bomber after all, but it turned out the hits came from a Nick that dove vertically through the formation before any gunner could pick it up. The wounded B-29 quickly fell behind the group and began to descend as the formation accelerated toward the IP. The damaged bomber managed to make it back to Okinawa on its own fighting off enemy Navy Georges most of the way. But its gunners downed five of the enemy while the B-29 sustained heavy damage itself. Luckily none of the crew was injured, but that B-29 never flew again.

As the rest of the formation reached the IP, the flak began and the fighters pulled off. Two cruisers anchored in the harbor joined the ground-based AAA in putting up a thick barrage. Most of the bursts were beneath the bombers, however. After bombs away, they were again under fighter attack.

At Pritchard's nine-o'clock position, five black Tonys pulled up in echelon, about 1,500 yards out. They flew along with the group for several minutes, and the gunners tensed up, waiting for the attack. Instead of a coordinated attack, though, only the leader rolled in for a run at the bombers. He got a fierce reception, as every gunner in the formation opened up on him. Pieces of airplane flew off the fighter as it broke down and away inverted.

Then it was number two's turn, and his reception was the same. The fighter pilot had enough caution to break away his attack farther out than the leader, however. The other three hesitated, probably getting up nerve to face the ferocious firepower that the B-29 gunners could dish out. Even though the three were still 1,200 yards out, Pritchard hosed a squirt at the number three fighter, seeing his tracers, about every 12th round, flash by the nose of the Tony. Suddenly number three dove away and to the left, followed by number four.

Only number five remained, thinking it over. But, he waited too long as from overhead a P-47 dove on the Tony from behind. The Tony made a quick break with the Thunderbolt hard on his tail. After three turns or so, the Tony suddenly stalled and fell into a tight spiral, then began to spin down and away.

That was the only Thunderbolt that Pritchard saw on that mission, but a formation of P-51s flashed under them headed for Yawata long after the fighter threat was gone.

The gunners of the XXI Bomber Command that day had battled off 175 individual enemy fighter passes. It was a tribute to the gunner's skill and the firepower of the B-29 fire control system that only four bombers were lost on the raid, just one to fighters and three to mechanical problems.

As the formation of bombers turned away from their targets, they passed close to Hiroshima and were able to witness the incredible destruction that had taken place two days before. Their force of more than 200 bombers that day had done far less damage than one atomic bomb dropped from the B-29 *Enola Gay*. No one aboard the *Myas' Dragon* said anything over the interphone for more than five minutes as they reflected upon what they had seen.

VII
20. Johnny Zero

(Interview, Banning, Calif., April 4, 1985)

John Foley was always small. Born prematurely and sickly in his early youth, he nevertheless, at just over five feet tall and weighing about 110 pounds, was in good enough shape for the draft board to call him into the service. So, at 23 he entered the Army Air Forces from his home town of Chicago, where he had worked at a cardboard box factory. To insure that he would be assigned to the AAF, he enlisted in the Regular Army six days after he was called up in November 1941.

Sent to Sheppard Field, Texas for basic training, he was there when Pearl Harbor occurred and his training was cut short. He said all he got was the Article of Wars read to him and he practiced marching. He said, "Thirty-four of us were chosen from throughout the base, and they told us to pack our gear and go down to the train station. When we got down there, we looked at each other and we were all five foot or a little over. And I was among the tallest at five foot four. And one guy, you know how they snafu in the Army, was six foot four. They must have thought his card said five foot four, and he stood out like a telephone pole.

"We got on the train and they didn't tell us where we were going or what we were going to do. We got to Muroc Dry Lake (now Edwards AFB, California) on Christmas Day, 1941. All they did was just disconnect the car from the train and leave us there. There was nothing around but dust. Finally, after three or four hours we could see a little speck of dust way out, and it got bigger and bigger and then came a little jeep. Two guys jumped out...and said that there would be some trucks out. Two trucks came out and took us to the camp. It was Christmas Day, but by the time we got to the camp it was nine o'clock at night. We thought we'd get something to eat, but there was nothing to eat — everything had been put away. They gave us some tents, but none of us knew how to put a tent up. But, the tall guy began to put up the poles, while the strong guys pounded stakes with axes. The brave guys held the stakes. Finally, many of the fellows gave up and just lay down and went to sleep in the sleeping bags we had been given. The next morning the area looked like a cyclone had hit it with one tent up, another partially up, and others just lying there."

When the rookies roused themselves the first sergeant said ten of the group would go on KP. He had nine of the group picked out, when Foley decided he didn't want that duty and moved behind a heavy-set rookie to hide. The first sergeant said, "I'll take that guy that just moved." So, Foley ended up spending the entire month he was at Muroc on KP. He thought he was being trained as a cook, and that was the last thing he wanted to be.

The purpose of the 34 rookies being shipped to Muroc was never revealed to them. The people at Muroc asked the group why they had been sent there and what were they supposed to do, but the rookies told them that the people at Sheppard Field had never told them.

After a month, Foley and the others were deployed to Australia as part of the 22nd Bomb Group, Foley still convinced that he was doomed to be a cook. The group went by ship, taking 26 days to make the trip. Foley's bunk was four levels below the deck, so rather than spend nearly a month sleeping in the depths of the ship, he slept each night beneath a truck lashed to the deck.

On the ship he talked to some of the others about how he could become a member of a combat crew. The answer was that it was impossible, because he hadn't been to any schools to be trained as a flight engineer, radio operator or armament man (Schools for gunners were just being established when Foley left for overseas).

Not giving up, he asked again about becoming a combat crew member after his squadron, the 19th, arrived in Brisbane. He was told, again, that it would not be possible, but that he should try to be assigned to the armament shop and possibly work his way up from there. He was told to see "Pappy" Robinson, who was the sergeant in charge of the armament shop. Robinson told him that he was too small for the heavy work of loading bombs, lifting guns and the like, but Foley told him he sure would like to try. To his surprise, the next morning he and another of the rookies were picked by Robinson for duty in the armament shop. He was put to work removing cosmoline from machine guns.

Then one day Robinson sent Foley down to clean the two .50-caliber and five .30-caliber guns on a B-26 named *Kansas Comet*. At this time the 19th was still at Brisbane and the crews were flying practice missions, including firing the guns. After a little instruction, Foley became the armorer whose duty it was to clean the *Kansas Comet's* guns. Unbeknownst to him, Foley's work was being watched by the *Kansas Comet's* pilot, Walter Krell, who was to become a legendary figure in the early combat days of World War II in the Pacific.

"One day on a practice mission," said Foley, "one of Krell's gunner's machine guns fired prematurely, with the breech open, and part of the casing of the shell went into this kid's eye and they grounded him. Then Krell came down to "Pappy" Robinson and said, 'I need a gunner, and I want that little kid that has been cleaning my guns.' "Pappy" said, 'He's never flown in an airplane and doesn't know which end of a gun to shoot out of— he's real green and I don't think you'd want him as a gunner.' Krell said, 'Let me leave it up to Foley.' So, he told me he'd like to have me fly with his crew. I said, 'I'd sure like to fly with your crew.' So, I moved my gear down to the flightline to join the *Kansas Comet.*

"As I was starting to pack up my gear, Robinson asked me where I was going, and I told him down to the flightline. He asked me if I had ever fired a gun and I said, 'No.' So, Robinson said, 'Foley, come along with me.' He took me out in a back area where there were some tall ant hills and gave me a .45 automatic. Robinson showed me how to hold it and asked me to fire seven shots at a hill. I took the seven shots and missed it completely because the weight of the gun made me fire into the ground. Then he gave me a Tommy Gun and told me to hit the same ant hill. Well, it did just the opposite (of the automatic) and it went up in the air when I fired it, and I missed the ant hill again because I was shooting up. Then he gave me a carbine and I hit the ant hill with the carbine. I was pretty good with the carbine."

Afterwards, Robinson marked his personnel records that Foley was qualified in the .45, the Tommy Gun and the carbine.

Foley said, "The very next day they took me up on a practice mission. They gave me 200 rounds of ammunition, 100 for each gun (the .50-calibers in the top turret)." After he was shown how to use the interphone and how to operate the turret, his pilot, Krell, briefed him over the interphone on the clock system of calling out bogeys and bandits. He told Foley that he was going to call out the little, puffy clouds in the area and Foley was to fire at them as if they were enemy fighters. The reticle in the gunsight bothered him, so he dimmed it and used the tracers in his ammunition to adjust his aim. After the mission, Foley was in the back of the airplane picking up empty shell casings, Krell came to the back of the B-26, shook hands with him and said, "Foley, you're my gunner."

When the training at Brisbane was completed, the 22nd Bomb Group moved to the northeast coast of Australia, the four squadrons of the group being based on four separate airfields in the vicinity of Townsville. The combat missions were not flown out of Townsville because of the distance to Japanese targets. The B-26s were loaded with bombs at Townsville, then they flew to Seven-Mile Airdrome, so-called because it was seven miles from Port Moresby in New Guinea. From this primitive base, the bombers refueled, then struck targets in Japanese-held areas of New Guinea, New Britain and Japanese shipping in the same areas. Then, the B-26s flew back to Seven-Mile, refueled and returned to Townsville for more bombs. Although this was a rigorous method of operations under appalling conditions of heat, humidity, disease and insects, it constituted the first sustained offensive action against the Japanese by Americans. Until the first raid against the Japanese stronghold at Rabaul by the 22nd in April 1942, all American combat efforts had been defensive, and unsuccessful to boot.

Although Foley's gunnery experience was extremely limited, his first combat mission, which occurred just two days after his first and only practice mission, was a forecast of what was to come for him. The small formation of B-26s ran into a gaggle of Japanese Zeros on an attack against Japanese shipping near Rabaul, and Foley had his baptism of fire right from the start. It was May 24, 1942. When the 19th squadron got back to Townsville the crew went through its first intelligence debriefing. When pilot Krell was asked if anyone in *Kansas Comet* had knocked down any of the enemy fighters, Krell answered that they had not. Another crew nearby cut in with the remark that they had seen a Zero go down in flames from the fire of the top turret of *Kansas Comet.* Krell asked Foley if he had downed an enemy and Foley replied that he thought he had. The shy gunner was too bashful to claim a victory for himself. He continued to refrain from claiming kills, and all of his subsequent victories were confirmed by crew members of other B-26s in the formation.

But, while Foley was off to a good start, "I missed a lot of planes, too," he said. Since he had never been taught to use the gunsight reticle and depended upon tracers for aiming, he had no way of estimating range. His twin .50-calibers were the longest range weapons on the early model of the B-26, so it was up to him to try to discourage attacks at as far a range as his own guns were accurate. He figured this was about 600 yards. He and two others measured a tree limb and cut it off at 36 feet, the wingspan of the Zero. Then his buddies stood on two fuel barrels placed 600 yards from the *Kansas Comet,* and Foley sighted the 36 foot limb that they held in the air. Foley painted two black marks on the combining glass of his gunsight at each end of the limb. Now, he had a measure of distance for attacking Zeros and could begin firing when their wingspan matched the two black marks.

John Foley (1942) is at the far right. He is pictured with other crew members who had survived crashes and were awaiting new crew assignments. The B-26 is *Heckling Hare* in which Lyndon B. Johnson flew a combat mission (John Foley collection)

"Johnny Zero" in 1985

Two weeks after Foley's first victory the *Kansas Comet* took part in a raid against the Japanese fighter base at Lae, New Guinea. The fighter pilots who rose to defend their airfield were the pride of the Japanese fighter pilots in that part of the Pacific. A number of top Japanese aces were based there. But, they were to meet one of America's top aerial gunners because Foley was credited with two victories that day. It was June 6th, 1942 — Foley would never dream that exactly two years later he would be flying combat again on another of his most memorable missions: D-Day in Normandy, France.

Returning to Townsville after the Lae airfield raid, an International News Service war correspondent by the name of Pat Robinson began to take an interest in Foley. He had known about the small gunner's first kill and now Foley had a total of three. He did some news stories on Foley and dubbed him "Johnny Zero." Later Pat Robinson would include Foley in his book, *The Fight for New Guinea.*

The name, "Johnny Zero" caught the attention of two song writers who were looking for inspiration for words to a tune that one of them, Vee Lawnhurst, had written. Mack David, the lyricist, soon worked out the words which praise Johnny for "getting another Zero." "Johnny Zero" was recorded by a group of singers called the Song Spinners on the Decca label. This was in the era when musicians were striking against the record industry and therefore only vocal music was recorded. But, it became one of the popular wartime songs that helped boost morale at that period in America's history. Another wartime song made popular by the Song Spinners was "Coming In on a Wing and a Prayer."

Foley's firing techniques were to garner him seven confirmed kills and eight probables, all Zero fighters. Foley took good care of his weapons and ammunition, and said, "I never had a gun jam or any other malfunction." He linked his own ammo, alternating armor-piercing, tracer, ball, and incendiary rounds. He said, "I fired only one gun at a time, first one then the other." He also said that he never fired at a fighter unless it was coming at the B-26. He would not shoot at a Zero that was just flying along or one that passed by his plane and was moving away.

Flying with Walter Krell in *Kansas Comet,* Foley was involved in the first of three crashes that he was to experience in his B-26 combat tour. The *Kansas Comet* had received considerable battle damage while flying on a mission out of Seven-Mile Drome. But, the plane was able to make it back to the airstrip, limping through the air. The crew was unaware that one of the main gear tires had also been shredded until the plane touched down on the strip. It suddenly veered off the runway and headed for the trees, and there was nothing Krell could do to stop it. The *Kansas Comet* hit one of the trees nearly head-on and burst into fire. All of the crew except the Royal Australian Air Force copilot (The 22nd Bomb Group had a shortage of pilots and used RAAF flyers, both sergeants and officers, as copilots.) managed to scramble out of the battered plane. When Walter Krell saw that the copilot was trapped in the wreckage, he went back to the burning plane to try to release him. He was not successful and the copilot died in the crash. Krell, however, was seriously burned in the lower parts of his body and had to be hospitalized for a good period of time. While he was recovering his crew was split among the other crews of the 19th Bomb Squadron.

Foley was assigned to another crew, again manning the twin fifties in the top turret. He describes the tactics used in attacking targets, saying, "We did mostly low level bombing, although some bombed from 15,000 feet. The highest I ever bombed was 8,000 feet. On the way to the target we flew in formations of three, with twelve aircraft, usually, but we would go with nine or even six — however many we could get in the air. At the target area, we all had specific targets. We would peel off like fighters — at an airfield target, some would go after the aircraft on the ground, some would have heavier bombs and they'd go after the runway, others would go after the buildings and ammunition dumps, all B-26s flying right on the deck. Then we would head for the ocean, getting down at treetop level and rejoin for the flight back."

It was on one of these airfield attacks that Foley's plane was shot down and he underwent another crash. His plane's specific target was an antiaircraft gun emplacement. After attacking it, though, the B-26 had a bomb that did not release. Foley said, "The pilot asked each one of us (on the crew) if we wanted to make a second run on the target with the hung bomb. Every one of us said, 'Yes.'" They made the second run and dropped the bomb. As they pulled off the target, Foley had his turret facing to the rear of the plane. He said, "I saw the tail-end of our aircraft go swoosh. They shot the tail right off the airplane."

The airplane crashed not too far from the airfield target, which was Lae. Foley says the airplane hit a knoll, or small hill. He was either thrown from the airplane or the turret was thrown from the airplane with him in it, but he awoke eight hours later to find that he was the only survivor. The rest of the crew perished. Foley was saved because he was thrown into some tall grass, four or five feet tall, which cushioned his fall. He did sustain a head injury which was probably caused by hitting a machine gun on the way out of the turret.

Fortunately, some natives reached Foley before the Japanese did and they cared for him, carrying him by night and hiding him from the Japanese during the day. After three weeks they reached an American infantry field station that had a small tent hospital. Foley stayed there overnight and the next day was supplied with a pair of pants and a pair of shoes, which he had lost in the crash. That night at midnight Foley sneaked out of the hospital and walked to his base at Seven-Mile Airdrome. His squadron had already returned to Australia so he bummed a ride on a B-24 to Townsville where he rejoined his squadron. His buddies, of course, thought he had been killed and were shocked to find he had survived. They had to give him back the belongings of his that they had divided among themselves.

After a ten-day leave, Foley returned to duty, awaiting assignment to another crew. With his third crew he underwent his third crash, this time bellying-in at Seven-Mile on the runway. No one was hurt in this crash-landing and the B-26, *Martin's Miscarriage,* survived to fly again.

Foley flew 32 combat missions in the 18 months he was in the South Pacific, from January 1942 to June 1943. He participated in the raid on Lae in which future president Lyndon Johnson flew.

During Foley's combat tour in the Pacific, the B-26s never had fighter escort in the target areas where the Zeros awaited them. The ranges of the P-39s and P-40s, that composed the U.S. fighter force in the area at the time, were too short to accompany the medium bombers all the way to their targets and back. Foley said, "That's how we were able to shoot down Zeros like we did, because we had no fighter escort. Sometimes coming back (from the target) P-39s or P-40s would pick us up, but that was too late (to defend us against the Zeros)."

Toward the end of his tour the B-26s were in a sad state of repair. There was a shortage of parts and no replacement aircraft, because the war in Europe and North Africa held a higher priority for B-26 support. As combat attrition took its toll of the Marauders, there became only enough flying bombers to equip one squadron. Foley's squadron, the 19th, was selected to keep the remaining bombers. Foley had the chance to go to another squadron of the 22nd Group which were being given new B-25 Mitchells, but he elected to stay with his beloved Marauders. In an effort to increase the survivability of the remaining aircraft, it was decided to see what could be done to increase their speed. One method was to reduce weight by getting rid of non-essential radio equipment. Another was both to reduce weight and to reduce drag. All of the camouflage paint was removed, which some claim added 15 miles per hour to the speed of the Marauders. When this was done, the 22nd adopted the nickname of Silver Fleet, which was painted on the vertical stabilizer of each plane.

As with most of his buddies, malaria was taking its toll of John Foley. He was returned to the United States and before receiving his next assignment, "Johnny Zero" was sent, with some other combat returnees, on a speaking tour of defense plants under a program called "Production Incentive Program." In a 30 day period, Foley, now a staff sergeant, delivered 60 speeches to workers in munitions factories, aircraft plants and shipbuilding yards.

Then Foley was sent to the gunnery school at Ft. Myers, Florida as an instructor, but he didn't really want to be an instructor. He said, "One day I was instructing and was telling the kids how I actually learned to fire the gun using tracer bullets. But, there was some captain sitting in the class and he came up after it was over and said, 'Foley, you can't tell these kids that. Here at the gunnery school we're teaching them one thing and you're telling them something else.' I said, 'I don't want to be an instructor.'"

So the captain sent him to the squadron commander to arrange his transfer. Foley told the commander that he wanted to get out of instructing. When the commander asked him what he wanted to do, he said he wanted to go back to combat. The commander said, "OK, we'll fix that for you."

Foley was sent to Peterson Field, Colorado Springs, Colorado, where he joined a B-24 unit that was in its last stages of training before going overseas. He was assigned as a nose turret gunner. When their training was complete, they picked up a new B-24 and flew to England via the South Atlantic ferry route. They became members of the Eighth Air Force and were assigned to the 93rd Bomb Group, 409th Bomb Squadron based at Hardwick.

Here Foley had an experience that reminded him of his unexplained assignment to Muroc Air Base when he first entered the service. Instead of starting to fly missions as a gunner, he was sent to a three-week school at Greencastle, Northern Ireland to learn to become an enlisted bombardier. Foley preferred to call himself a "togglier" rather than a bombardier because his task was to toggle off the bombs on the smoke bombs of the lead bombardier. He did not use the bombsight to make his drops. He was never told how or why he was selected to be a togglier.

Foley began flying his missions in mid-May 1944 when the threat from enemy fighters had diminished. He said his worst missions were to Munich, where the flak was fierce. He went to Munich twice. He also participated in the D-Day landings, striking at coastal guns above the Normandy beachhead. He did not know it, but both of his brothers were taking part in the invasion, one with an armor unit and the other with the paratroopers.

Foley and his crew saw only two Luftwaffe fighters during his combat tour. This happened on a day when the weather in England was very poor. When his B-24 arrived on top of the clouds there were no other American planes around. Then they received a weather recall and were supposed to return to the baes. Foley said, "Our navigator was really green." When the recall came, they began homing on the beacon at Hardwick. But the Germans had activated an electronic device to draw Americans and RAF planes into France or Germany. They set up their own beacons on the same frequency as allied bases, but at a greater power, and the radios in the allied planes would seek out the stronger signal and home on that.

Foley's plane, named *Thunderbird,* was being drawn toward France instead of toward Britain. The pilots decided to drop below the overcast to see if they could determine where they were. Sure enough, as they broke out of the overcast, there were two Focke-Wulf 190s waiting for them. The Germans began firing too far out of range, and when Foley's pilots saw the firing, they ducked the B-24 back up into the overcast. They made a 180-degree turn and were soon headed back to their home base.

"I didn't like the B-24," said Foley. He wanted to fly A-20s, which were then based in France. His former copilot had transferred to A-20s and Foley visited him once and the copilot told him it should be no problem to get transferred. When he asked about it back at his own base, he was told he could, as soon as he finished his tour and took a 30-day leave in the States. So, Foley began doubling up his combat flying. If his crew wasn't scheduled for a mission, he would volunteer to fly with another crew. In this way he flew two or three missions as a waist gunner and one as a top turret gunner.

From mid-July 1944 to the end of the month he flew almost every day. He completed a 31-mission combat tour in just 70 days and was returned to the States for his leave, with orders to report back to Europe for a third combat tour, this time in A-20s, he hoped.

When he reported back in to the embarkation port in New Jersey to return overseas, however, he was told that his orders had been rescinded and that he would not go back for a third combat tour. He was sent to Walla Walla, Washington where he became a bombardier, or togglier, instructor and remained there until the end of the war.

Foley would like to have remained in the Air Force following the war, but there was illness in the family and his mother needed his help in Chicago. He left the AAF and got a job working for the U.S. Treasury in Chicago, where he met and married his wife. After two years he changed jobs and worked at several other jobs in the mid-west. When his brother in California wanted Foley and his wife to atttend a ceremony where they would be godparents for one of his children, they visited California and never returned to the mid-west.

After working for a metal company in Pasadena, Foley and his wife went into business for themselves, acquiring franchises for three convenience market stores in Southern California. Things did not work out for them, however, and they went broke at all three stores.

At Norton Air Force Base, near San Bernardino, California, Foley became employed as a civilian employee of the U.S. Air Force, working first in the base commissary. He then went to three schools to train as a hazardous cargo inspector. He was on call 24-hours a day to certify shipments of hazardous cargo being carried by Air Force C-141s and C-130s. After 17 years of civil service employment plus four years of military service, Foley retired to Banning, California.

While John Foley is retired, his exploits are recorded at the United States Air Force Museum at Wright-Patterson Air Force Base, Dayton, Ohio. Foley was inducted into the Hall of Fame section of the museum and there is a display dedicated to him. In a glass case are reminders of his wartime service which include his uniform, his medals and ribbons, his wings, a copy of the recording "Johnny Zero", patches, photographs of him and his crew, and other items.

The sharp-eyed observer will note that the wings on display in the case are not gunner's wings, but aircrew member wings. That is because Foley never qualified for gunner's wings because he never completed a gunnery school. But "Johnny Zero", even without gunner's wings, was quite a gunner.

21. Gunner for the Veep

(Interview — June 27, 1985, Ramona, Calif.)

A man who has the distinction of being the gunner for a pilot who would later become Vice President of the United States is Leo W. Nadeau. Lee, as he is called by those who know him, served on the crew of a TBM Avenger torpedo plane piloted by Vice President George Bush during World War II. The two, along with a radioman, flew an eight-month combat tour in the Pacific with VT-51 squadron, operating off the light carrier San Jacinto (CVL-30). Both, with the radioman, survived a ditching in the sea, and Mr. Bush also survived a bailout on a mission Nadeau did not fly with him. Their radioman did not survive the bailout.

Nadeau was interested in aviation even while in high school in his hometown of Gardner, Mass. He wanted to attend the Ryan School of Aeronautics in San Diego to become an aeronautical engineer, but his family did not have the funds to send him. So he quit high school after two years and went to work to earn the money to attend. Nadeau said, "I've always liked airplanes as far back as I can remember. I was taught by a young guy when I was about nine years old how to build aircraft models...and I've been building those darned things ever since. I've always wanted to fly but never seemed to get the opportunity. I've always been a passenger but never a pilot." His two years, rather than four, of high school kept him from qualifying for the Navy pilot training program and it wasn't until after the war that he took the training that earned him a high school diploma.

His quest for an aeronautical education was short-lived, however, because of Pearl Harbor. When the draft began to breath down his neck Nadeau enlisted in the Navy and was sent to boot camp in October 1942. "I didn't go far," he said, "I was (sent) down to Newport, Rhode Island for boot training. They gave us what I would call an aptitude test. There were hundreds of us taking that test at boot, and I was in the top bracket. Those who were in the high bracket were given the opportunity to make a choice of what school they wanted to go to. And I chose aviation ordnance. I figured I'd get into aviation one way or another. I didn't want to be a mechanic because I wasn't mechanically inclined."

Nadeau was sent to a naval ordnance school near Memphis, Tennessee for three months of ground classroom training, which he completed. Nadeau said, "Right near the end, just before our graduation, they put out a call for volunteers for aerial gunnery. I figured, oh boy, this is it! I can get into the air this way, so I volunteered. I passed the physical, was accepted and was sent down to Hollywood, Florida to the naval aerial gunners training school there."

The training for Navy gunners, with a few exceptions, was similar to the training received by Army Air Forces gunners described elsewhere in this book. The training consisted of classroom training, field training at the gunnery range with target setups for live firing, malfunction training, and aircraft identification. Skeet and trap shooting were also a part of a Navy gunner's training. A major difference between AAF and Navy training was that the Navy training was all ground training. The training in the air was done only after the gunner joined a combat squadron as a part of unit training in preparation for going into combat. Another difference was that Navy aerial gunners received training on aerial torpedos and aerial mines, rather than training just on guns as AAF gunners received. A third difference was that there were no "career" gunners in the Navy as there were in the AAF. All Navy gunners had another specialty — most of them were ordnancemen, like Nadeau, or aircraft mechanics, while a few radiomen were also trained.

Of the conditions of the training, Nadeau said that there was the good and the bad. The good, according to Nadeau, was that "the school was a military school that the Navy took over, so we were assigned two men to a room with our own bath and everything," which made living conditions ideal, considering what some other training bases were like. On the other hand the weather was hot, said Nadeau, "It was so hot that we had school only in the morning — in the afternoon there were big tractor-trailers with seats in them running students to the beach. We had classes and gunnery training in the morning and spent afternoons at the beach in order to survive."

When he had completed gunnery school, Nadeau was sent to Norfolk, Virginia. "We were assigned to CASU-21, which was kind of a holding unit where we waited for assignment," he said.

Nadeau recalled, "That was where I had my very first airplane ride — I had never been in an airplane in my life, not even a small one. I was hanging around a hangar and an SB2C dive bomber was going up on a test flight. So I went up to the pilot and asked him if I could go along for the ride, and he said, 'Sure, just draw some gear.' So I drew a 'chute and a helmet and got into the back seat and off we went. He took it up to about 12,000 feet, and I was just sitting there watching, and all of a sudden the nose of that (plane) dropped. It so happened that my seat wasn't latched and it popped the seat up two or three notches before it locked in and stuck my head two or three inches above the windscreen. I'm looking over the top of the (canopy) at the water coming at us and we were going! He finally pulled out at about 1,500 feet.

"The pilot started into another climb, and while we were going up he said, 'I'm going to do (that) one more time — will you keep your eye on that right wing, I can feel some flutter out there — keep your eye on (it) and see what you can see.' Geez, I'm just about ready to conk out — here I am, the wing's going to fall off on me! It fluttered all right, but evidently it was nothing that concerned him all that greatly, except that he could feel it in his controls.

"We made that second run, and then he swung the plane right around and touched down and rolled up to the hangar. We piled out and turned in the gear and I felt great! (I was) exhilarated!"

From Norfolk, Nadeau was assigned to VT-51, a torpedo squadron just forming at a field near Charlestown, Rhode Island. Here the crews received their basic squadron training. At first they flew early model Grumman TBF Avenger torpedo planes, but later were given later model TBM-1C models of the plane, the General Motors-built version of the Grumman Avenger.

Nadeau became a turret gunner. The electrically-powered turret mounted one .50-caliber machine gun, which was offset to the left so that the gunner's head could occupy the rest of the small turret. The gunsight was a fixed, illuminated reticle and the turret and gun were controlled by pistol-grip controls. Three cans of ammo were carried containing about 300 rounds apiece.

The TBM was a large, three-place airplane. In fact, in its day it was the largest single-engine aircraft flying. It was so large that one of the final models (TBM-3R) was used as a delivery aircraft among aircraft carriers for supplies and personnel — this model sported a total of seven seats in its cavernous fuselage.

It was here that Nadeau was crewed-up with Ensign George Bush, recently graduated from pilot training at NAS Corpus Christi. At the time, the future Vice President was the youngest pilot in the Navy. The third crewman was radio operator John Delaney, of Providence, Rhode Island, who was also as young as Mr. Bush and Lee Nadeau. Delaney, also trained as a gunner, would man the ventral-mounted flexible .30-caliber machine gun when his radio and radar duties would permit. This was the first operational assignment after schooling for all three crew members.

At Westerly, Mass., Nadeau got his first chance to fire at towed targets while in the air. He recounted, "An unusual experience that happened in our squadron. It happened that I had a pretty good eye and could lead a target well — it just came naturally to me. One day we were up on a training flight for gunners and were flying as wingmen for the squadron commander. The commander made his pass for his gunner and we followed, as second in line, and I shot the sleeve (target) right in half. And that killed (training) for the day — nobody else had a crack at it.

"The next day we were assigned aerial gunnery again, but this time it was for pilots. Again, we were wingmen on the squadron commander. The commander went down and made his pass and shot a few rounds off. Then, Mr. Bush winged over, fired a burst and cut the tow rope right off — we lost the sleeve again. Nobody wanted to go on gunnery practice with us any more because they didn't get a chance to shoot."

VT-51 took its torpedo training at Hyannis, Massachusetts in November 1943. Said Nadeau, "At that time the airport at Nyannis was a dirt runway and we lived in Quonset huts. I remember sloshing around in mud in November — everything was mud there."

Also at Hyannis, radioman Delaney got a chance to practice his skills at dropping bombs by radar as well as with the Norden bombsight. The radioman, who sat in the middle of the aircraft between the pilot and the turret gunner, sighted the Norden bombsight through the bomb bay doors when they were opened, according to Nadeau. The TBM radioman was rather a multi-skilled crewman.

Nadeau said, "The target we used was an old, abandoned Coast Guard lightship that was mounted on concrete pedestals right in the midle of Cape Cod Bay. The last time I saw it was after the war when we were camping on Cape Cod, and it was thoroughly riddled with holes."

Next for VT-51 came assignment to the aircraft carrier that would carry them into combat. The squadron drew a new light carrier, the *San Jacinto* (CVL-30), which began life as a crusier, but as the hull was being constructed, war came along and the *San Jacinto* was completed not as a cruiser, but as a smaller aircraft carrier. The combat plane complement carried by the *San Jacinto* consisted of 24 F6F Hellcat fighters and nine TBM Avenger torpedo planes.

The crews became carrier-qualified in January 1944 off the coast of Rhode Island and went on a shake-down cruise to Trinidad in February and March, 1944. Nadeau said, "We got shore leave, but not the way we had planned it. A couple of the fighters snapped their landing hooks and went into the crash barrier (these were the days before the angled-deck carriers). Our whole squadron was in the air at the time the decision was made that something was definitely wrong with the landing hooks and that they had better not take any more (planes) aboard, so we went ashore and the English put us up." The planes were on the island for three days while all landing hooks were removed and inspected. Several other defective hooks were found and were replaced by good ones.

In late March the *San Jacinto* headed out to sea, traveling through the Panama Canal to San Diego. Then it was on to Kaneohe Bay on Oahu in Hawaii, where the torpedo squadron was based while the *San Jacinto* went on maneuvers with just the fighters aboard.

It was May 1944 before the *San Jacinto* finally arrived in the combat zone of the Pacific; its destination was Majuro Atoll in the Marshalls. On the day the *San Jacinto* arrived, Nadeau and his squadron flew their first anti-submarine patrol mission. Later in the month, the squadron went on its first bombing mission. The target was Wake Island and the Avengers dive-bombed targets on the occupied island.

Then in June 1944, Nadeau said, "That was one of the most interesting months while we were out there. It was in the area of Saipan (in the Marianas). We did a lot of (bombing) missions over Saipan for two weeks, softening it up for the invasion." Even though Nadeau was in on a number of hotly contested battles, such as Saipan, he never had the chance to use his aerial gunnery skills against an attacking enemy. "Too many of our fighters around," he said, which kept the enemy fighters away from the torpdeo planes.

Even though he never sighted an enemy fighter to shoot at, Nadeau was able to fire his machine gun on strafing missions on Saipan. On most bombing missions, turret gunners did not strafe because the movement of the turret caused the Avenger to yaw and slow down its speed, which was critical to evading enemy gunfire on the pullout from the dive bombing run. However, there were some preplanned strafing attacks on enemy installations when Nadeau and other gunners were able to fire their weapons.

The Avengers used dive bombing tactics on most of their missions against Saipan and other target areas. The bomb bay held four 500-pound bombs, or a mixture of other sized weapons. Nadeau recalled that there were no special techniques used to slow the airplane down in a dive bombing attack. He said, "There was nothing high-speed about the Avenger. I think it could fall faster than it could fly."

It wasn't long after the planes of the *San Jacinto* began flying combat that the ship and the U.S. planes themselves became targets of the enemy. About 15 twin-engine and single-engine bombers made low level runs against the carrier, but did not score any hits. It happened just as the TBM of Mr. Bush and Nadeau was about to be launched. They were strapped to the catapult, engine running, when the attack started. The *San Jacinto* began to take evasive action which meant that the carrier no longer was headed into the wind, and planes could not be launched. So, Nadeau and the others sat in their Avenger during the entire enemy raid.

On another occasion when the *San Jacinto* was about to come under attack, Nadeau's Avenger was able to get airborne, which was the method used to insure survival of at least some of the airplanes in the event a carrier was hit badly or sunk.

The Avenger orbited near Guam, waiting for the attack to be over, when suddenly, according to Nadeau, "A cloud of oil went by me. We knew that (losing our oil) meant we had only a limited amount of time to keep the aircraft under power. It was far safer to make a water landing under power rather than deadstick. (Mr. Bush) gave the order to brace ourselves and that we were going down. We were too low to drop our load (four depth charges). As we got lower and lower, I could see the water (behind the aircraft) starting to spread out; the tail hit the water and helped slow us down. When the nose came down it was a dead stop and water cascaded all over the aircraft. It was almost like we were submerged and then we bobbed to the surface.

"I was facing aft, but I didn't have my head tucked firmly back against the armor plate and got a good rap on the back of my head. The radioman (Delaney) faced forward and evidently didn't have his shoulder straps tightened — he went head-forward into his radios and split his head open.

"The blow to my head kind of addled me, because I remember popping the handle on my escape hatch (on the side of the turret) and I tried to get out without unbuckling my belt or unplugging my earphones.

"I got them unplugged and scrambled out onto the wing and over the fuselage. (Mr. Bush) already had the life raft out and inflated, but we didn't have our radioman. I went back over the fuselage and there Delaney was trying to get out of my escape hatch in the turret. He couldn't get his door open down below. He was about half in and half out of my turret, but his chest parachute was caught in my gun equipment and he couldn't get out. He was dazed and stunned and there was blood running down his face. I got hold of his shoulder straps, pulled him out and got him onto the wing. By then Delaney was coming out of it, so we both climbed over the fuselage and got into the raft.

"By that time, Mr. Bush had gotten the paddles together and he started to row away. But the survival kit, which was attached to a long line, and to the raft had gotten tangled up in the (plane's) rudder. It was either lose the gear or have the raft go down when the plane went down, so I pulled out my hunting knife, cut the line and we got away. We had just gotten away when the tail flipped up and down the plane went. Just a few seconds after she went down we heard the depth charges go off with a boom from the pressure.

"Then our concern was whether we had been spotted and who would pick us up, Japanese or Americans. We had been spotted and we weren't in the water half an hour before a destroyer came into view. But we didn't know whose it was, but there was nothing we could do about it anyway. It happened to be the *U.S.S. Bronson*. They threw a cargo net over the side and we went up the cargo net."

It took the Avenger crew five days to get back to the *San Jacinto* and three rides in bosun chairs transferring between ships. From the *Bronson*, they were transferred to the carrier *Lexington*, then to another destroyer which came alongside the *San Jacinto* for the final transfer.

George Bush was on easy terms with enlisted men. While neither could visit each other in their separate quarters areas, Nadeau and his pilot would meet on the flight deck. While checking over their plane, they held conversations on a variety of topics, including the young women they were to marry.

What Mr. Bush did not know was that Nadeau was already secretly married, in spite of Navy regulations which required that enlisted men receive permission to marry. Nadeau had married his wife of more than 40 years, Virginia (Moore) just days before the San Jacinto had sailed from Norfolk for the Pacific battle zone. Mr. Bush married his wife of more than 40 years, Barbara (Pierce), or Bar as she is known, just two weeks after he returned from his combat sea duty. While Navy and Marine flyers did not name their airplanes with the same intensity as did AAF flyers, Nadeau painted "Barbie" in small letters just beneath Mr. Bush's cockpit.

Nadeau remembered that the Bonin Islands were the most heavily defended of any of the targets his crew attacked. The three islands of Chichi Jima, Haha Jima and Iwo Jima were within 600 miles of the home islands of Japan and they represented formidable obstacles, as the Marines were to find out on Iwo Jima.

It was on a mission to Chichi Jima that Mr. Bush had a close call. And it was one of only two of Mr. Bush's missions that Nadeau did not fly with him. At the last minute, just before launching, Nadeau was replaced by an intelligence officer, who wanted to observe the target himself. The day before, Nadeau had flown with Mr. Bush on a mission to Chichi Jima on which they had struck gun emplacements. On the day Nadeau was replaced in his turret the target was a radio station which provided warning of American air strikes aimed at the home islands.

Ltjg. Bush made his dive bomb run and the Avenger was almost immediately hit by intense flak. He continued his steep bomb run, however and released four-500-pound bombs on the target.

But, the TBM was fatally wounded and soon fire and smoke began to pour from the plane. The order to bail out was given, and Mr. Bush and one other of the crewmen got out. Mr. Bush landed in the water near the enemy shore, but the parachute of the other crewman streamered and he died in the fall.

No one knew which of the crewmen got out and which one went in with the plane. Nadeau feels that if he had been on the mission, possibly radioman John Delaney might have survived. The two had drilled on bailout procedures and had worked together for many months — bailout for both would have been routine. Nadeau feels that probably Delaney stayed with the airplane too long trying to help the intelligence officer get out of the turret.

Once in the water, Mr. Bush inflated his life raft and quickly began paddling out to sea. He was only six to seven miles from Chichi Jima and the Japanese had spotted him as he parachuted down. The Japanese sent a boat out to capture him, but a fellow Avenger pilot from VT-51 who was flying cover for Mr. Bush strafed the boat and it turned back to the island.

Fighter planes circling over Mr. Bush's raft radioed to the submarine that was patrolling 15 to 20 miles from the island to pick up crewman of downed aircraft. The *Finback* (SS-230) moved toward Mr. Bush's raft and in four hours the skipper spotted it through the periscope. The *Finback* surfaced and took Mr. Bush aboard.

When Mr. Bush was taken below decks, he found the three-men of a

TBF Avenger that had been shot down and picked up by the *Finback* off Iwo Jima the previous day. The next day, a fighter pilot shot down at Haha Jima joined the other flyers.

If Mr. Bush thought he would soon return to the *San Jacinto*, he was in for a shock. It was a full 30 days that he spent on the *Finback*. The skipper put the five flyers to work as lookouts for enemy aircraft and submarines. They worked in shifts, on deck at night when the sub was recharging its batteries, and in the daytime when it patrolled on the surface.

In the meantime, Nadeau flew three missions with other pilots. But activity during Mr. Bush's absence was minimal, since the carrier was given a break in its combat and sailed to what was by then the back-waters of the Pacific war near the Admiralties.

Then VT-51 returned to action. Nadeau was teamed-up again with Mr. Bush and a new radioman, Joe Reichert of New York replaced the missing Delaney.

The next major battle for VT-51, and what would turn out to be their last, was the invasion of the Philippines. Said Nadeau, "On the sixth of November (1944) was when we started working over the Philippines. Our targets were mostly shipping and ships anchored in Manila Bay. We made a hit on an AK transport. That was where you stood in line waiting your turn to go down (on the targets); there were so many aircraft in the air that the air over Manila Bay was saturated. It was a massive raid with one wave after another, because we were told that the Japanese were trying to land reinforcement troops."

After these raids, the *San Jacinto* started back to Ulithi, where a replacement squadron awaited VT-51, which was long overdue for replacement. Nadeau recalled, "We got within one day of reaching Ulithi when we were turned around and sent back to the Philippines. That was the time when the Japanese fleets were coming in from two or three directions heading for the Philippines. We had to make this last run (against the Japanese fleets) and everybody got scattered. There were so many airplanes in the air that you couldn't find your own squadron. Everybody was forming up on anyone who was still flying. And we were really low on fuel. An SB2C joined up on us and he signalled he was just about out of fuel too. He stayed with us as long as he could and then signalled he was going down. We watched him go into the drink.

"I remember talking to Mr. Bush and asking him what our (fuel) situation was. He said, 'We're low (on fuel). If they're (the *San Jacinto*) not where they are supposed to be, we're not going to make it either.' We

On board the *San Jacinto,* 1944. (L to R) Radioman Joe Reichert, who replaced John Delaney (KIA), Ltjg. George Bush, pilot, and Leo W. Nadeau, gunner (Leo W. Nadeau collection)

Leo W. Nadeau in 1985

broke out of the clouds right over the stern of the ship. Mr. Bush didn't make a circling approach. He got instructions for a direct-in approach and he came in over the fantail and sat that thing down. We used just about all the fuel to get us back in."

That was the last major engagement for VT-51. The rest were subpatrol missions and the like. In late November 1944 their replacement squadron arrived and took over their Avengers on the *San Jacinto*. Nadeau had flown 58 combat missions and participated in seven major Pacific battles. He was disappointed that he never got to use his gunnery training against enemy aircraft. He was always hopeful he would, because, he said, "I was always looking for excitement."

Nadeau and Mr. Bush split up when they arrived in San Diego, and it would be 40 years before they would meet again. Ltjg. Bush was assigned to Virginia Beach as a flight instructor and was released from the Navy in 1945.

Nadeau was assigned to the naval air station at Quonset Point, Rhode Island where he worked in ground ordnance. Then he got the chance to be assigned to an experimental group in Boston that was working on developing an infra-red guidance system for bombs. Nadeau also worked with a professor who was developing a light that could penetrate smoke screens and fog. Most of those working at this experimental plant were civilians and most of the projects were highly classified. Nadeau's main task was to take the experimental ordnance to the two or three Navy planes that were testing the ordnance and load it.

Nadeau, who by now was an Aviation Ordnanceman First Class, was offered the rank of Chief Petty Officer if he would volunteer to stay in the Navy with the experimental group, which was about to move to California. He was tempted, but declined. He was glad he did because the group stayed in California just three weeks and then moved on to Eniwetok Atoll for its experiments. His wife and new baby would have been stranded alone far from home.

After his discharge he returned to his home town of Gardner, Mass., and took a temporary job in a furniture manufacturing plant. Then he decided he would go into home building. Even though he had never built a house before, he built a seven-room house for his family. That was the first complete home he built. From then, he did mainly home remodeling and room additions.

He wanted to learn welding, so at the same time he worked as a welder for a firm. Then he also opened another business, a craft and hobby shop, which his wife and children operated. So, he had three occupations going at the same time.

But, eventually, after 23 years, the business responsibilities and general wear and tear began to take their toll, and after an operation he decided to change his whole lifestyle. The Nadeaus sold nearly everything they owned — businesses, house, most of their furniture and moved from Gardner to West Palm Beach, Florida.

He decided he had had enough of business responsibilities and wanted to become just a plain carpenter. The first construction man he talked to wanted to take him on as a foreman. He was successful in talking the owner into giving him a job as a carpenter, but three months later he was the field superintendent of the company, supervising construction of condominiums and four-plexes.

After five years in Florida Nadeau took a similar position in Ramona, California. After awhile, he decided to go back into business for himself as a construction contractor. He now has a small company in Ramona, again specializing in remodeling and room additions. He plans to retire in a year or two and build a new house on the hills overlooking Ramona.

In September 1984, on the same date as the submarine *Finback* picked up Vice President Bush, 40 years ago, a reunion was organized at NAS Norfolk, Va. for the men of VT-51 and the current and former crew of the new nuclear-powered submarine *Finback*. Eight members of VT-51, including Lee Nadeau and Vice President Bush, were able to attend. The group toured the new *Finback,* had lunch aboard the carrier *John F. Kennedy,* and looked over a TBM Avenger that had been restored by the Confederate Air Force and flown to Norfolk for the reunion.

The Vice President had time to chat briefly with Lee Nadeau, who commented to the Vice President that he hoped it wouldn't be another 40 years before they would see each other again.

22. *Paper Doll*

(Interview, Long Beach, Calif., April 2, 1985)

"This guy comes in, throws his B-4 bag down, turns the seat around and goes to sleep. I think, 'Van, this idiot is going to be on your crew!'" That was how Van Gasaway and Dan Brody met, on a train that was taking them from the gunner's replacement pool in Salt Lake City to their new assignment in Boise, Idaho. They did indeed team up as gunners on the B-24H *Paper Doll* of the 453rd Bombardment Group, Brody at the right waist position and Gasaway in the tail turret. Both fought in Europe with the Eighth Air Force as Staff Sergeants and became close friends that has lasted through the years.

The crew of *Paper Doll* was an elite one, and one that, with one exception, flew its 32-mission combat tour as an integral unit. The crew was a lead crew that led the 453rd Group on every fourth mission. It had no copilot assigned because the right seat was occupied by one of the high-ranking officers of the group who commanded the formation. On several occasions this high-ranking officer was a major named James Stewart, of Hollywood fame. Of Stewart, Brody said, "He exhibited himself as an excellent pilot, even under adverse conditions. We respected him for his contribution and dedication to his role in the mission of the Eighth Air Force."

Staff Sgt. Dan (Sylvan D.) Brody entered the AAF from Shreveport, Louisiana, where he had worked as a manager for a beer distributing company after graduating from high school. He had wanted to enter the glider pilot training program, but things didn't work out for entering the program. So, since the draft was looming in the background, he enlisted in the Army Air Force. Of his decision to become a gunner, Brody said, "In order to take an active role in flying, I had to go to gunnery school." He was shortly assigned to the gunner training program at Las Vegas Army Air Field, and when his training was complete he went back to Louisiana, this time to take part in war maneuver training. The newly trained gunner, who had visions of being assigned to B-24s or B-17s, found himself flying in the rear seat of an L-2 (Piper Cub) liaison plane! Not a machine gun in sight!

The maneuvers were soon over, and Brody went to the replacement pool in Salt Lake City and from there to Boise, where he joined the 453rd as part of the original cadre at Gowan Field.

Staff Sgt. Van (Ovando H.) Gasaway entered the AAF from Santa Monica, California where, following high school, he worked as a welder for North American Aviation in Inglewood. He said he worked on both the early P-51s and B-25s. Of his wartime career in the military, he said, "To tell the truth, I think the minute they saw me come in the Air Force, they decided to get two guys, ten feet tall and weighing 400 pounds apiece and make them MPs, just to look after me." Brody agreed with his friend, saying that Gasaway was certainly very active. As we shall see, Gasaway's activeness made for an interesting, but checkered, military career.

Gasaway had originally attempted to enter the pilot training program of the RCAF under a program that was being promoted by Hollywood actor Eugene Pallette. Gasaway had been taking flying lessons at the old Mines Field, now LAX. But, when America entered the war, the Canadian program was cut off. Although Gasaway did not have the required two years of college to enter the AAF pilot training program, he decided to take the alternative written test to try to qualify. Although only 27% of those who took the test passed, Gasaway was successful and entered the aviation cadet pilot training program. He took classification at Nashville and preflight training at Maxwell before going to the Embry-Riddle primary flight school at Dorr Field, Arcadia, Florida, where he flew PT-17s (Stearmans), Class 42D. Of the Stearmans, Gasaway said, "Damned old things, you could hardly spin 'em out, they'd damned near fly themselves."

"Then," said Gasaway, "I went up to Bainbridge, Georgia for basic, flying Vultee BT-13s and they snapped me halfway through." He washed out of pilot training at the midpoint of basic because of a flying violation. He said, "I went up through an overcast when I wasn't supposed to and damn near clipped the squadron commander. Then I had a series of check flights and that was it."

He was sent to what he considered to be the world's worst base, Biloxi, Mississippi, where he said they had signs that said, "Soldiers and dogs, keep off the grass!" He and seven other washed-out cadets were stripped of their cadet uniforms and were issued fatigues and low cut shoes, even though it was winter. After awhile the eight were sent to Wichita, Kansas to ferry L-5 liaison planes to Fort Sill, Oklahoma where they were to train as artillery spotting pilots. Delays in starting the program led to idle youngsters getting into trouble. "We were bad actors," said Gasaway. The young shavetail in charge finally told him that he was out of the artillery spotting pilot program and that he had a choice of going to Infantry OCS or Armor OCS or remain in the Air Force. He said, "I didn't want the Infantry and those Armor guys were getting shot up in North Africa left and right in those tanks." So, he elected to stay with the AAF. He was told that he had to go to gunnery school and to a technical school, so he chose armament for his technical training. As did Brody, Gasaway went to Las Vegas for aerial gunnery training and then to Lowry Field, Denver, Colorado for armament training. He only got into minimal trouble at Lowry and soon found himself in the Salt Lake City replacement pool. He joined Brody on the trip to Boise and the 453rd.

The two gunners were assigned to a B-24 crew headed by a second lieutenant from Austin, Texas named Wendell D. Faulkner. Both in the States and later in England, Faulkner's crew was to fly more training missions than any of the other crews. It paid off as the crew was designated a lead crew. Faulkner was quickly elevated to the rank of captain and when his combat tour was over, Col. Jimmy Stewart took him up to a staff position in wing headquarters. Faulkner was fiercely loyal to his crew and they to him. He stood up for them against what he felt was unfair treatment and in at least one case the crew was in the doghouse for a short while. But, Faulkner always prevailed.

When the 453rd completed its training in the ZI, it deployed to England, flying the South Atlantic route. They crossed the Atlantic non-stop, flying directly from Natal to Dakar without stopping at Ascension Island. They made their way to England and to their base, Old Buckenham, where the unit remained for the rest of the war in Europe. The base at Old Buckenham was not wholly constructed when the 453rd arrived. Said Gasaway, "When we landed on our field the barracks weren't completed, and we had only one mess hall for everybody."

Paper Doll, named for the Mills Brothers' song that was popular at the time, arrived in England in January 1944 and flew its first mission in early February. This was just in time to participate in what came to be known as Big Week, when the Eighth Air Force, along with RAF bombers, concentrated on striking German airplane manufacturing factories. The weather over Germany was clear for the period of February 19 through 25, and Eighth Air Force bombers and fighters swarmed over the continent. Aircraft plants hit by the second division, which included the 453rd, were at Gotha, Brunswick and Halberstadt. While the effort staggered German warplane production for about a month, the real damage to the Luftwaffe was done in the air. Gunners on the B-24s and B-17s as well as the Eighth

Crew of *Paper Doll* after its first mission, England, 1944. Dan Brody is kneeling at the left, and Van Gasaway is kneeling, third from left. (Dan Brody collection)

Dan Brody and Van Gasaway in 1985

Air Force fighters knocked an estimated 200 to 300 German fighters out of the air, the Luftwaffe losing many experienced and valuable pilots in the process. This changed the whole nature of German air defenses. No longer would American bombers be met with hordes of fighters on every mission. From then on, the Luftwaffe would rise in force only when important targets were attacked. Brody and Gasaway were to benefit from this change, which showed in their scores. Brody was credited with just one probable, while Gasaway, in the tail, claimed 2½ kills.

Brody and Gasaway were to participate in several other memorable air campaigns during their tour, which lasted from February to late July 1944. These included the first raids on Berlin, beginning in March, attacks on Schweinfurt in April, the campaign against the Nazi oil industry which took them to targets in Poland, and missions flown on D-Day, the long-awaited invasion of the continent.

In addition to his gunner assignment, Brody was also the photographer on the lead ship, and was responsible for getting strike photos at the target. He operated one automatic camera which was mounted in the bomb bay and also had a hand-held camera, which he used to take photos from both waist positions. On his 11th mission, he was the only group photographer to get pictures of the strikes on the target at Munster, Germany.

His most memorable mission was the ninth, when *Paper Doll* took several hits from flak. A large chunk of flak tore into the side of the plane right at Brody's gun position, missing his thigh by about seven inches. Brody said, "I thought that we had a lot more missions to fly, and that was pretty close. I felt that the odds were not in my favor." The chunk of flak lodged in the plane — Brody recovered it and took it home for a souvenir.

Brody also had trouble with his heated suit on two missions. On one, it malfunctioned and burned his shoulder. He was hospitalized, but when he heard his crew was getting ready for a mission, he talked his way out of the hospital and made the mission. He said, "The way I saw it, I depended on my crew and felt that they depended on me." On another mission, his heated suit would not function and he spent 11 hours in the frigid air without the warmth of the suit.

Gasaway remembers his longest mission as one that stays in his mind. Enemy defenses were not the problem, but the length of the mission, which took his group to southern France near the Pyrenees Mountains to bomb a German flight training airfield. "We shacked it," he said. However long the mission was, it was a long time to be confined in a tail turret.

Both remember their 14th mission, to a target at Watten, France. The flak really zeroed in on the lead airplane, putting more than 100 holes in a wing panel. The damage was so extensive that *Paper Doll* had to be retired, and they received a brand new aircraft. It was promptly named *Dolly's Sister*. It was the first of the unpainted new Liberators to be received by the 453rd. There was more than a little apprehension that the German fighter pilots and anti-aircraft gunners would zero in on this silver bird at the head of a formation of olive-drab Liberators — was it a new American secret weapon?

Dolly's Sister was not long in receiving its baptism in aerial combat. On its second mission, the 16th for Brody and Gasaway, a gaggle of about 150 German fighters, both FW-190s and Me-109s, met them on their way to a target at Brunswick, Germany. *Dolly's Sister* gunners accounted for four probables that day, one each going to Brody and Gasaway.

Brody and Gasaway differ on their assessment of whether flak or enemy fighters were more to be feared. Brody is inclined to remember that both were a threat, sometimes together on a mission, and other times separately, whichever was encountered in the greatest force. Gasaway, on the other hand, considered flak as his greatest apprehension. Sitting in the tail looking at the formation to the rear, Gasaway said, "I could see the flak catching up with us. And they told us that flak could not track us in a turn. That was not so." Fighters, on the other hand, were something Gasaway could get a handle on. "The thing with fighters," he said, "is you could shoot back, but with flak, you could not do anything about it yourself."

About fighter escort from friendlies, Gasaway said that on early missions their fighter escort was rare. Sometimes RAF Spitfires would take them part way to the target, but their short range meant that they could not stay with the bombers throughout the whole mission. Another problem with the British fighter pilots was that they would approach the bomber formation nose-on. "When a fighter puts his nose to you, you were supposed to shoot," said Gasaway. "American fighter pilots," said Gasaway, "would slide up to you from the side and put their wings up so you could tell what he was." Brody added, "When we had fighter escort, it was always a welcome sight, and very disappointing when they were not around."

By the time of the oil industry campaign, however, the fighter escort situation had changed. "P-47s would take us halfway to the target, then

P-51s would join to take us the rest of the way to the target, where P-38s would be circling overhead. Then more P-51s would pick us up on the way home," said Gasaway.

Both gunners agreed that their toughest target was not Schweinfurt, as was commonly supposed, but was Bremen. "Bremen was bad, because you had naval flak gunners there," said Gasaway. "And they were real, real good," he said.

The only member of the crew of *Paper Doll* who did not survive the combat tour was radio operator/gunner William S. Chappell. He was called upon to substitute for another radio operator on another lead crew and was killed on the mission. *Paper Doll's* pilot Faulkner determined that from then on, no member of his crew would fly with another crew, and he was successful in his stand.

Faulkner was also successful in another stand for fairness to his crew, which had to do with the number of missions to be flown. When *Paper Doll's* crew first started flying combat missions, a tour was set at 25 missions. While they were flying, the tour was increased to 30 missions. When it was further increased to 35 missions, Faulkner balked, saying that his enlisted crew members should fly no more. The crew was grounded for a short time, and then their combat tour was terminated at 32 missions. Jimmy Stewart had a hand in the decision to let the crew stop at 32 missions, according to Gasaway. Jimmy Stewart was a popular man with the crew of *Paper Doll/Dolly's Sister*. Besides flying with them several times, he would often meet them as they returned from a mission. He would also give lifts in his jeep to men who were walking the nearly mile or so from the flightline to the barracks area. Imitating Stewart, Gasaway intoned, "'Hey, fella, lak a ride?', sounded just like he did in the movies."

Since the crew of *Paper Doll* and *Dolly's Sister* flew only every fourth mission as lead crew, it took them longer to complete their combat tour; more than six months. The pilot, Faulkner, was then elevated to a position on the wing staff, and the bombardier was made Group Bombardier. Brody returned to the ZI, but Gasaway remained in the UK for a period.

Brody was assigned to what was then called Will Rogers AAF at Oklahoma City and worked in the base photo lab until his discharge.

Gasaway, on the other hand, continued his adventures in the UK, and his penchant for getting into trouble. He was sent to a training base in England to become an armament officer and win his gold bars as a second lieutenant. But the mistake, he said, "was sending my armorer along with me, and we didn't spend much time in class. So, when we came back they sent me up to Norwich to take the examination and I missed it by one point. But, I was never really enthused about it. I think my navigator and pilot wanted me to be an officer more than I wanted it myself."

Then Gasaway returned to his unit and became gunnery NCO, flying practice missions with new crews coming to the 453rd. Since the Luftwaffe was by this time hurling their new jet and rocket fighters against the bombers of the Eighth Air Force, training was needed against such attacks. The RAF now had their Meteor jet fighters in the air, and practice missions were flown against mock attacks by these new aerial weapons.

In November 1944 Gasaway was returned to the ZI and assigned to Victorville AAF in the Mojave Desert northeast of Los Angeles. He said that, as usual, they had a little trouble fitting him into a job. At first he was detailed to check the bombs on AT-11 bomber-trainer aircraft for the early morning bombardier training missions. But, he said, "They thought that was too easy for me, so they put me swinging the compass on the B-24s. We had to get up in the morning at three o'clock and the guy I was working with didn't like that either. So we pulled off a way to get off the duty. There were three of us: one to drive the tug, one in the cockpit to ride the brakes and another guy on the radio. So, on the taxistrip, just before the morning takeoffs, we would hardly move (the bombers down the taxiway), and you could hear all the engines behind you, and the tower screaming at you, and it didn't take long before they moved us." He became a photogramist, plotting the accuracy of B-24 bombardiers in their simulated bomb drops using radar bombing systems.

After VJ Day, both gunners became civilians. Dan Brody entered the University of Southern California in Los Angeles and received a degree in sociology. He remained in the Air Force Reserve and during his first year of graduate work at USC in social work, he was recalled to active duty when the Korean war broke out. He was assigned to March Air Force Base, Riverside, California where he worked in the base hospital doing clinical social work in the mental health department. By now he had received his commission as a second lieutenant. Following his release from active duty in 1954 he attended the University of Connecticut where he received his masters degree in social work. He returned to California and took a position at the Long Beach Veterans Hospital as a medical social worker. In 1967, he left the VA to go into private practice, establishing his own business doing marriage counseling as well as social work at nursing homes and hospitals. He is still in this business today.

Brody continued his Air Force Reserve service, and was assigned to a number of reserve units in the Southern California area doing the same things he did as a civilian: medical social work. He rose through the grades and retired from the Air Force Reserve as a full colonel in 1981. His last reserve assignment was at SAMSO at Los Angeles Air Force Station, and he continues to assist the unit on a weekly basis as a volunteer. His home is now in Long Beach, California.

While still on active duty, Van Gasaway asked for and received permission to take a part-time civilian job as a welder. So, when he received his discharge, he had a ready job waiting. Then he got into the soft drink distributing business, working for 14 years as a route manager for Pepsi-Cola and 7-Up. Following these jobs Gasaway entered the restaurant business, becoming part owner of a restaurant in Long Beach. He sold his interest in the restaurant in 1969 and then worked as a chef in a number of restaurants until his retirement. He said he picked up his knowledge of cooking by, "just watching." His retirement home is in Manhattan Beach, California.

The two former gunners keep in touch and get together now and then to remember the days of *Paper Doll* and *Dolly's Sister*.

23. From Marauder to Museum

(Interview, Sunnymead, Calif., June 24, 1985)

John C. Caputo decided upon a military career even before his country became involved in a war. He wanted to be a pilot in the Army Air Forces, but excessive overbite would not allow him to pass the rigorous physical exam to qualify for pilot training. He already had his private pilot's license, having taken flight training in a Taylor Cub at a small Virginia airport across the Potomac from his native Washington, D.C. The site of the airport is now occupied by the Pentagon.

Between the time he completed his studies at McKinley High School in Washington and the time he entered the service, he had a variety of jobs, one of which included frequent trips to the White House. His first employment was as a Western Union telegram delivery boy, which led to another, more interesting, job as a messenger in the National Press Building. He was appointed a special Western Union messenger for the White House, and for two years delivered press material to the White House and collected releases from President Roosevelt's staff for delivery to the 400 press people at the Press Building.

Other jobs included running an elevator in an office building, and driving an auto parts delivery truck. But, still the AAF beckoned, and Caputo decided to enlist. If he couldn't fly as a pilot, he wanted to be an airplane mechanic.

Upon his enlistment, in July, 1940, he was assigned to nearby Bolling Field — not as an airplane mechanic, but as an auto mechanic! This led to duty as a driver for the base commander, which did not satisfy him, either. Caputo said, "I kept on him. I told him I didn't get into the service to be a chauffeur to him, and that I wanted to get on airplanes. So, one morning he came out and told me, 'You're transferred to the 2nd Bomb Squadron.' So, from then on, I began polishing airplanes, and learning how to work on airplanes."

The 2nd Bomb Squadron did not have any airplanes of its own, so Caputo's first flying experiences as a flight engineer were in B-10s and B-18s that were borrowed from other bomber units.

After several months at Bolling, Caputo's 2nd Bomb Squadron was transferred to Langley Field, Virginia, where another squadron comprising the 22nd Bomb Group, the 408th Bomb Squadron, was already based. They were joined by the other two squadrons, the 19th and the 33rd, which had been based at Mitchell Field, New York. The four squadrons of the 22nd Bomb Group were the first to receive the new, hot medium bomber, the Martin B-26 Marauder. Caputo arrived at Langley on Thanksgiving Day, 1941.

In the short period he was at Langley, Caputo was to get the only training and practice firing a machine gun that he was ever to get before going overseas. Gunners were sent to Camp Lee to fire a flexible .30-caliber machine gun at targets that moved on small rail cars on the range. Caputo never attended a gunnery school nor a full technical school in his entire 22 years of AAF/Air Force service.

He had hardly gotten settled at Langley when Pearl Harbor occurred, and four days later he was with the 22nd Group at Muroc AAF in California (now Edwards AFB). The group began flying coastal patrol missions along the West Coast, flying from Muroc to San Francisco, then down the coast to the Los Angeles area before returning to Muroc. On one of these missions Caputo's B-26 sank a Japanese mini-sub, which Caputo says was recovered in about 1983.

After just one month at Muroc, the 22nd was alerted for overseas. The aircraft were flown to March Field where they were prepared for shipment on a ship to Hawaii. From there they would be ferried to Australia. There were restrictions on the number of crew members who could be taken with the aircraft, so Caputo got a long boat ride to Brisbane.

Even though it took a month to make the trip by sea, Caputo and the others arrived in Brisbane long before the B-26s. While they awaited the arrival of the planes they took training flights in Royal Australian Air Force aircraft, the twin-engine, fabric-covered Avro Ansons. The Ansons were equipped with a simple manually-operated turret containing a single .303 caliber machine gun.

When the Marauders arrived the units soon moved to the Townsville area and prepared to fly shuttle missions out of Seven-Mile Airdrome at Port Moresby.

Like most of the others in his squadron, Caputo's first mission was against Rabaul, the heavily defended seaport and supply facility on New Britain. And the small .30-caliber machine gun in Caputo's tail gun position scored on his first mission. He poured all 300 rounds of his ammunition into a Tony fighter which had just taken off, and the Japanese plane went down. The tail of the B-26 was now defenseless, except for the Springfield rifle which Caputo used to pot away at other fighters.

Caputo vowed never to run out of ammunition again, so when he returned to Australia he pulled a .50-caliber gun out of a damaged B-17 and mounted it in place of the smaller gun. Now, he not only had more firepower, but also ammunition cans that held much more ammo. Later, he added a second .50-caliber to increase his firepower even more. He designed a track system along the sides of the interior fuselage to feed his guns from cans mounted in the bomb bay. By doing this he was able to load 2,700 rounds of ammunition without upsetting the airplane's center of gravity.

Four of Caputo's 29 missions were attacking Rabaul, which he says was the most dangerous of his targets to attack. He said, "Rabaul was the meanest of them all. Because, you see, we were flying low and they were shooting down at us from the mountains and the ships (in the harbor) were shooting up at us." In addition, the Japanese fighter pilots based at Rabaul were some of the best in that area of the Pacific.

For his victory over the Tony fighter on his first mission, Caputo was awarded the Silver Star, the third highest award for bravery in combat. Later, he was awarded a second Silver Star for shooting down a Japanese plane, but it has been so long ago that he can't remember whether it was for missions to Milne Bay or to Portugese Timor. His fourth victory was scored on a mission against Buna. Of his four kills he said, "Two blew up and two crashed into the sea." In addition to his first kill of the Tony, he had victories over two Zero fighters and one Betty bomber.

Caputo also destroyed three Japanese aircraft on the ground when his plane took part in low level attacks of Japanese airfields. Caputo said, "To me they looked like they blew up. It didn't take much ammo to blow them up because I aimed at where I knew the gas tanks were."

Caputo and his fellow crewmen claimed destruction of several Japanese ships, both freighters and tankers. Some of them were hit in Rabaul Harbor, while others were sunk during the battles of the Coral Sea and the Bismark Sea. He said, "We also got some barges when the Japanese were landing troops at Milne Bay. They were unloading ammo or something, because they made one hell of a big explosion when we hit them with our 500-pounders. They were trying to land 10,000 troops and we mowed the hell out of them that day. We caught 'em on the beach. I burned up two barrels on my guns. That was when the 29th Infantry had called in for air support and we gave them everything available. Those

John Caputo and his crew at Reid River (near Townsville), Australia in 1942. Caputo is second from right. B-26 *Little Audry* was not the plane Caputo's crew flew in combat, but was a training airplane (John Caputo collection)

John Caputo looks at the red "meatball" he saw so often in his gunsight in combat. The replica "Val" is a modified U.S. BT-13 now at the March Field Museum. It was used in the movie "Tora, Tora, Tora"

guys (the Japanese) caught it from them (the 29th Infantry) and us both. There were not many Japanese left to pull out."

Most of the Marauders Caputo flew were not named by the crew. But of his first airplane he said, "I named that one *Columbus* because the tail number was 1492. The second plane I named *Rose of San Antone* because the pilot was from Texas. Tokyo Rose knew all of us by name, crew number and everything."

Caputo flew most of his combat tour as a private first class. But when replacement gunners from the states began arriving at his unit, they were mostly sergeants and staff sergeants. So those who had been flying combat in low ranks were quickly elevated, and Caputo went from PFC to sergeant and to staff sergeant in rapid order.

Caputo flew a total of 33 combat missions logging 113 combat flying hours. But four of the missions were photo reconnaissance over enemy territory rather than bombing missions, so he was given official credit for just 29 missions. During his combat tour he was under enemy fighter attack on 15 missions. His aircraft received U.S. fighter escort by a single P-39 on just one mission. "I almost shot him down" said Caputo, "because we didn't know we were going to get him (for escort) and I didn't know what a P-39 looked like."

While Caputo scored heavily against the Japanese, their fighter pilots and flak gunners were unable to get to Caputo in his Marauder. "I never got a scratch," he said. The Japanese did manage to score slightly against him on the ground, however. A photograph among his many memoirs shows him on crutches. He hurt his leg at Seven-Mile Airdrome during an air raid of the airstrip by the Japanese. He said, "I jumped off the wing of an airplane when it was hit by a bomb."

When his combat tour was over, Caputo returned to the States, but he stayed with his beloved B-26 Marauders. He went first to Avon Park, Florida and became an instructor of aircrews destined for combat in B-26s. He taught both flight engineers and tail gunners and remained on flying status. The unit then moved to MacDill Field, Florida and he continued to instruct. His final move was to Lake Charles, Louisiana where he worked at the same tasks. He took his discharge from the AAF on July 26, 1945, just 20 days before the war in the Pacific, which he had helped win, ended.

He was not long in civilian life, however. Just eight months later, in March 1946, he reentered the AAF. He was assigned first to Andrews Air Force Base, Maryland, and for the next 17 years would be a flight engineer or crew chief in the Strategic Air Command. He spent two years at Andrews, broken by a tour in the Berlin Airlift. At Andrews he flew as a flight engineer on C-54s, which were the mainstay of the airlifting of food, coal and other supplies to the isolated West Berliners.

On the Berlin Airlift, Caputo met General LeMay, who coordinated the aerial supply operation. This meeting would influence Caputo's Air Force career in the future. Caputo was supposed to be on temporary duty in Germany for 90 days, but, he said, "I stayed there for nine months."

He flew out of Frankfurt to Tempelhof Airport in Berlin, helping load and unload supplies for the citizens of the blockaded city and for the allied troops stationed there. "Then," he said, "I was grounded because I got a rupture from throwing coal (sacks) around." He was made an aircraft maintenance dock chief at a base near Munich for the remainder of his temporary duty in Germany.

Caputo returned to Andrews AFB and when the headquarters for the Strategic Air Command (SAC) moved to Offutt AFB, Nebraska, he moved with it. Because of his overseas duty, Caputo was overdue for discharge and had not intended to reenlist. "Then," he said, "General LeMay talked to me and said he needed a crew chief on his B-17. Right off the bat I told him I didn't know anything about a B-17. So, he pulled out all the books on how to crew (a B-17) and a month later called me in to question me. What I didn't know I told him right off the bat, 'I don't know, Sir, but I'll find out.' And I stayed with him for four years." Caputo became one of four flight engineers for the headquarters fleet of aircraft used to transport high-ranking SAC officers in their worldwide travels. He crewed on B-17s, B-29s and B-50s.

After his four years at SAC headquarters, Caputo was assigned to the 8th Air Rescue Squadron at Peterson AFB, Colorado, where he was a flight engineer on rescue-equipped C-47s. He was still in SAC, however, because at that time (1950), SAC had rescue services in conjunction with its aircrew survival school nearby in the Rockies. Among the capabilities of the C-47 that Caputo trained on were short field takeoffs using JATO bottles (Jet Assisted Takeoff) and operating the C-47 in Alaska on skis.

Then it was back to VIP aircraft in SAC for Caputo, serving as flight engineer on plushed-up B-25s both at Davis-Monthan AFB in Arizona and at Mountain Home AFB in Idaho.

Then he returned to Davis-Monthan, where Caputo became a crew chief on B-47 jet bombers. He remained on flying status, however, even though his primary job was on the ground.

In the small cockpit of the B-47, there was a three-man crew: pilot, copilot and bombardier/navigator. Any other person that went along had to sit in the aisle that ran alongside the pilot and copilot. Since Caputo was still on flying status, he had to get his four hours of flying time each month to qualify for flight pay. "I flew 23½ hours for four hours flying time, one time," said Caputo, spending all but four hours of that time on the cold metal surface of the aisle. The pilot took pity on him and let him sit in the pilot's seat for four of those hours. The 23½ hour trip took Caputo from Tucson over such checkpoints as Newfoundland, Greenland, Iceland, England, North Africa, the Azores, Puerto Rico, and Bermuda before returning to Tucson. The non-stop flight required three aerial refuelings.

Then came a hardship overseas tour for Caputo — Bermuda! He was able to take his family with him, and spent three years as a crew chief on KC-97 aerial tankers, servicing B-47s like the ones he had been crewing. This was his last assignment on flying status.

He returned briefly to Tucson (Davis-Monthan) before going to Malstrom AFB near Great Falls, Montana. There he was in flight line maintenance on B-47s and KC-97s at first, then became a shift chief in the transient maintenance section.

Caputo retired from the Air Force at Malmstrom in 1962. He was a master sergeant with 22½ years service, 17 of it with SAC. He had held a variety of responsible jobs in the AF, but never attended a formal technical training (nor gunnery training) school. He had, however, attended a number of mobile training unit courses in the aircraft type he was about to be assigned to.

He then worked for civilian firms that contracted with the Air Force to provide maintenance at Los Angeles International Airport for the aircraft of the Air Force Systems Command that were based there. He was in this position for seven years.

Following this he entered the FAA as an aircraft mechanic, still based at LAX. He was sent to eight different schools on aircraft to prepare him to maintain C-47s, T-39 Sabreliners, Sabre 80s, Convair 580s, T-29s, Queen Airs and King Airs. In addition, he maintained a U-3A for the FBI. The work involved a lot of travel because maintenance people had to travel to wherever an airplane broke down in the nine western states that were the FAA region's responsibility.

He was also used in a number of other capacities including that of air marshal. He was not one of those air marshals used to prevent aerial hijackings of airliners, but he was assigned to ride on airliners whose crew were suspected of drinking while flying.

After seven years with the FAA, he was medically retired in 1976. That seven years, plus his 22 years of military service gave him 29 years of federal service.

After retiring, he moved to Sunnymead, California, which just happens to be one mile outside the east gate of March Air Force Base. Here he could take advantage of the facilities of the base, but more importantly, could continue to serve his Air Force. He actively helped commanders of units on the base by giving talks to visiting groups and presenting awards for various achievements of base personnel on behalf of the Air Force Sergeants Association. He participated in a number of base ceremonies as an invited guest.

Caputo is also one of the more active volunteers in supporting the March Field Museum, which is building to a rather imposing collection of both aircraft and memorabilia. He spends about two hours each morning at the museum, checking on what supplies or other support the volunteers need. On one Saturday a month he spends the day in charge of the museum. Caputo is considered the museum's most knowledgeable volunteer about the airplanes and equipment on display.

John Caputo said, "In total, since 1937, I could say that I have been on about 70 different airplanes. I still like planes."

VIII
24. A Strong Finish

It has often been said that for those who have gone to war, that experience will be the most memorable event of their lifetime. Whatever else a person might accomplish during his or her life, the experience of wartime service will be one that will stand out as a highlight, whether it was one of hardship and terror, or, as it was for many, one of challenging adventure that tested one's personal strength as nothing else can do. Even those who do not see actual combat face ordeals not found in "normal" living.

As noted in the first chapter of this book, pilots, navigators, radio operators, flight engineers and other aircrewmen could be assigned to a variety of flying unit types, both combat and non-combat. Only bombardiers and aerial gunners were destined for the "shooting war" and nothing else.

Since that was so, World War II gunners can be expected to have undergone a number of bizarre escapades, and we have seen a number of those relating to combat encounters in this volume. But, the rigors of flying also offered circumstances which produced decidedly unique experiences while not engaged in combat, as well. Take Sgt. Elias Thomas, for instance. Thomas, the ball turret gunner of B-17F *Joho's Jokers,* flying out of Knettishall with the 388th Bomb Group of the Eighth Air Force in the summer of 1943, decided one day to wear his parachute in his cramped ball turret. This was the first time he had tried wearing his chute in the turret. Everything went well until suddenly the back of Thomas' turret fell off, and Thomas with it. Thomas pulled the ripcord and landed safely enough, after his surprise departure from his bomber. Luckily, his group was on a practice mission over England and he was soon returned to Knettishall, where it is presumed he suffered the taunting of his fellow-gunners.

Then there was 21-year-old Staff Sgt. James F. Jones, a tail gunner on a B-17F also assigned to Knettishall. It was September 1943 and the 388th Group had flown its longest mission until then. The group's primary target, an airfield at Cognac in France, had been covered by cloud, so the bombers diverted to alternate targets. By the time the group returned to England, 11 hours had elapsed, darkness had fallen and a weather front had moved in. The formation diverted from returning to its bases in eastern England and tried to find landing fields in southwest England, where the terrain was unfamiliar. At least three bombers were destroyed when crashing into Welsh hills. Staff Sgt. Jones' Fortress, groping its way beneath the clouds in the dark, glanced off the top of a hill, throwing him out through the escape hatch. Not realizing that it was ground contact that had flung him out, he pulled the ripcord of his parachute. It did not have time to deploy before he hit the ground, with the chute and its shrouds wrapping around him as he rolled. Two hours later he regained consciousness and the first thing he saw was a red flare arcing across the night sky. He had rolled for some 100 yards. Checking himself over, he saw that he had nothing more than a sprained leg and a few bruises to show for his ordeal — plus a memory for his postwar years.

While gunners Jones and Thomas were both fortunate enough to end their inadvertent bailouts in friendly territory, Tech. Sgt. Fred Wagner of the 384th Bomb Group was not as lucky. It was on the first mission of 1944 and the target was the Kiel canal in Germany. After leaving the target it was apparent that some bombs in the Fortress on which Tech. Sgt. Wagner was a gunner had not released and were jammed. Wagner grabbed an emergency oxygen bottle and started for the bomb bay to clear the hung bombs. While working to release them, his oxygen system failed and he passed out, falling through the open bomb bay. He came to in time to pull his ripcord, but he ended up a long way from home.

It is one thing to fall from an airplane by accident, but it is an entirely different matter to be thrown from one's airplane by one's crewmates. This happened to Staff Sgt. Tyre C. Weaver, but it saved his life. It was July 1943 and the target for Eighth Air Force bombers for the day was a synthetic rubber plant at Hanover, Germany. Weaver was at his top turret station of his 92nd Group B-17F *Ruthie II* when the formation was approaching landfall inbound to the target. The formation was met by a frontal attack of FW-190s and *Ruthie II* received a burst of cannon fire that mortally wounded the pilot. The same burst found the top turret and Staff Sgt. Weaver's left arm was severed near the shoulder. He slid from his turret and fell to the rear of the nose section behind the navigator, 2nd Lt. Keith J. Koske. Koske went to his aid, but was unable to give Weaver morphine because of a defective needle on the morphine tube. And because Weaver's arm was off close to the shoulder, Koske was not able to stop the bleeding with a tourniquet. Since the formation was still inbound to the target and it would be many hours before medical aid could attend to Weaver's bleeding, Koske decided the nearest medical aid was directly below them, and made the decision to bail out Weaver. He adjusted Weaver's parachute and placed his right hand on the ripcord. Then

Koske jettisoned the forward hatch and positioned Weaver for the exit. As he was pushing the wounded gunner out, Weaver, in shock, pulled the ripcord too soon and the pilot chute deployed inside the cabin. Koske wedged the pilot chute under Weaver's right arm and gave him another shove and the gunner cleared the aircraft. After the mission, the ball turret gunner reported seeing the parachute open and some weeks later the crew learned that Weaver had survived the ordeal and was recuperating in a German hospital.

This incident was not the only drama aboard *Ruthie II* on that mission. When the pilot was mortally wounded, he slumped over the control column grasping it tightly in his arms. The copilot, Flight Officer John C. Morgan, had to wrestle the controls against the forces of the dying pilot to hold the Fortress in formation. Luckily for the other crewmembers of *Ruthie II,* Moran, who had recently transferred to the AAF from the RCAF, was a strapping six-foot, 200-pound, red-haired Texan who needed all of his strength to fly the aircraft. Morgan made the decision to stay with the formation for the protection it would afford. So, for the next two hours he flew the aircraft through the bomb run and on the outward leg of the mission, all the while fighting off the counter-efforts of the crazed pilot. When the formation was 15 minutes beyond the enemy coastline, Koske left his guns in the nose to check on the crew. The navigator found Morgan still struggling with the controls, and between Koske and Morgan, they removed the pilot from the cockpit. With the bombardier's aid, the pilot was lifted past the open forward hatch and placed in the nose section. Neither Koske nor Morgan had heard any firing from the rear guns, so Koske went aft to check on the gunners. He found them all unconscious because the oxygen system had been cut in the earlier attack by the Focke Wulfes. He managed to revive them with emergency oxygen, but all were suffering from frostbite. Morgan flew the plane to a successful landing, and for his remarkable feat the copilot was awarded the Medal of Honor. Eight months later, Morgan's plane was shot down over Berlin. He was able to parachute from the downed plane and spent the next 14 months, until VE-day, in Stalag Luft 1. World War II was certainly memorable for John C. Morgan: seven months of operations with the RCAF, eight months of combat duty with the Eighth Air Force, 14 months as a guest of the German enemy, plus America's highest decoration for valor!

Two B-26 gunners, Staff Sgts. Jesse Lewis and George Williams, had memorable experiences on a memorable mission that changed the way B-

26s were employed in Europe. They were the only two crewmembers who made it back to England on the second raid by Marauders of the Eighth Air Force, on May 17, 1943. Three days ealier, on the first raid by B-26s, the target, a power plant at Ijmuiden in Holland, had been missed, and the force was scheduled to return to the target. The 322nd Bomb Group had trained for low level attack, but their experience on the first mission left doubt in the minds of many crews about the validity of the tactic, since their aircraft had taken quite a bit of damage. For the second mission, only eleven aircraft could be made ready, and one of these aborted on the way to the target. The force bored on in at low level, but mistakes in navigation put the medium bombers over heavily defended areas. Several crashed on the way into the target, two were lost when they crashed into each other in midair, while four more were damaged so badly that they had to ditch when they reached the Channel. A lone B-26 continued toward its base at Bury St. Edmunds, but after 50 miles of flying, it was attacked head-on by three Me-109s. After two passes by the fighters, the B-26 was forced to ditch, sinking in 45 seconds. Out of the doomed ship clambered Staff Sgt. Williams, the tail gunner and Staff Sgt. Lewis, the turret gunner. They made it into a life raft and awaited rescue. Meanwhile, back at the airfield, commanders and ground crews anxiously waited for the sounds of returning engines, but other than those of the one aircraft that had aborted early, they waited in vain. Five days later, Williams and Lewis were picked up by a Royal Navy destroyer, exhausted but safe, while the 20 of 62 of their comrades who survived the crashes in enemy territory could look forward to more than two years in German POW camps. Their memorable mission caused a change in the way B-26s were employed in Europe. The units were retrained for medium altitude bombing and had some success in the Eighth Air Force with attacks on airfields and other tactical targets. But 8 AF leaders were more interested in the strategic mission of the heavy bombers and relegated the Marauders to back-burner efforts. The 322nd flew only 34 missions in the next six months until it was transferred to the Ninth Air Force, where the group performed its tactical mission with high success.

A number of aerial gunners of World War II set marks for other gunners to attempt to match. Others will be remembered by military and aviation historians for the fact that their feats were the first of their type. One of these was Sgt. Kent West, a ball turret gunner of the 97th Bomb Group, who was credited (at first) with the first kill of an enemy aircraft by a gunner in the Eighth Air Force. It happened on the very first mission flown by the Eighth Air Force; the raid on the railroad facilities at Rouen, France on August 17, 1942. Twelve B-17Es from the 97th at Grafton Underwood were heavily escorted by four squadrons of RAF Spitfires on the mission. The weather was good and the target was hit — flak was light, but two Fortresses received minor damage. The Spitfires kept most of the intercepting German fighters from penetrating the bomber formation, shooting down two of the enemy while losing two Spitfires in the process. One Me-109 managed to penetrate the escorting fighters, however, and made a pass at *Birmingham Blitzkrieg,* the tail-end Charlie of the strike force. When the Messerschmitt came within range, Sgt. West, in the ball turret of *Birmingham Blitzkrieg,* sprayed the enemy fighter with his .50-calibers. At first it was thought that West's defensive fire had downed the Me-109, but later it was determined that there was no basis for awarding credit for destruction of the fighter. Still, Sgt. West can claim to be the first gunner of the 8AF to fire at an enemy fighter and the first to have a kill claim taken away from him. West knew he had been to war, however, because *Birmingham Blitzkrieg* landed at Grafton Underwood with eleven flak holes in its fuselage.

The first Eighth Air Force gunner to down an enemy plane on a raid to Berlin was Tech. Sgt. Harold Stearns. It happened on the first raid to Berlin, on March 4, 1944. It was a big raid, but the enroute weather was very poor, and some squadrons of the formation turned back to England. A recall of all the bombers was made, but three squadrons, consisting of just 31 Fortresses, did not receive the recall and continued on to the "Big B", as Berlin was known to the 8AF flyers. Just prior to reaching the target, a small force of Me-109s intercepted the bombers, concentrating on the high group, the 100th. The 100th had the nickname "The Bloody Hundredth" because of the heavy losses it suffered periodically throughout the European campaign. One fighter made a pass at *Rubber Check,* coming in from 12 o'clock high, but Tech. Sgt. Stearns in the top turret was ready for him, and sent him down in smoke and flames. The kill was confirmed and Stearns chalked up a "first," when he returned to Thorpe Abbots.

The first Eighth Air Force bomber crewman to complete a combat tour (then 25 missions) was an aerial gunner, Tech. Sgt. Michael Roscovich,

306th Bomb Group. At the time, April of 1943, 20 missions were as many as bomber crewman could expect to survive without being killed, badly wounded or captured. Possibly Roscovich's attitude pulled him through. He had a jovial disposition and his penchant for playing practical jokes on his fellow gunners earned him the nickname the "Mad Russian." Hardly a mission went by that he did not throw out of the bomber at the Germans a piece of hardware with a suitable message written on it. At the end of his combat tour, Roscovich did not return to the U.S. but accepted a commission and became a ground gunnery officer at an 8 AF base. He even flew a number more missions in this capacity, for a total of 33 for the war. While his luck against the Germans held out in combat, it ran out when he was returning to the States. He was killed when the airplane taking him home crashed in Scotland.

The man who flew the most combat missions in Eighth Air Force bombers was a gunner. Master Sgt. Hewitt Dunn flew more than three complete combat tours for a total of 104 missions against the Germans. Dunn, who flew in B-17s with the 390th Bomb Group out of Framlingham, was nicknamed "Buck" and flew his tours at a time when the number of missions to complete a tour was set at 30. He began flying combat in January 1944 and hit the hundred mission mark in April 1945. He flew four more missions after that, and was credited with one FW-190 destroyed on a mission to Leipzig. His pace-setting 100th mission was also to Leipzig, one of the heaviest defended targets in Germany, but Dunn said it turned out to be a milk run. Dunn flew 26 of his early missions as a tailgunner, then two as a top turret gunner. Then he moved to the nose of the bomber, flying the remainder as a bombardier (togglier) and nose gunner. Nine of his missions were to the "Big B" (Berlin). Dunn was just 24 years of age at the completion of his combat tour. Other flyers flew missions in other theaters, then completed their hundredth in the 8 AF, but Dunn was the only man to fly more than 100 bomber missions, all of them in Europe.

The highest scoring gunner in the Eighth Air Force with 12 victories was Staff Sgt. Donald Crossley, a tail gunner in the 94th Bomb Group. Flying from Bury St. Edmunds in the B-17 *Brass Rail Boys,* Crossley, who was considered to be a natural marksman, was one of the few gunners who had mastered the art of deflection shooting. He was awarded credit for his 12th kill on his 22nd mission, which was to Frankfurt, after just five months of combat. The next highest scoring gunner in the Eighth was Michael Arooth of the 379th with a total of nine credits. His group (B-

17s) flying out of Kimbolton set records for 8AF bomber units, flying more sorties than any other group, dropping the greatest tonnage of bombs and suffering the lowest abort rate of any unit. In the 379th was the Fortress *Ole Gappy,* a B-17G which flew 157 missions, probably the highest of any 8AF bomber, at a time when the average life expectancy for a bomber was 11 missions.

One gunner who had one of the shorter combat tours was grounded after just six missions when it was discovered he was only 16 years old! Sgt. De Sales Glover, flying in the B-24 *"Big-Time Operator"* had falsified his age records when he enlisted, then being just 14 years of age. Included in his six mission combat tour was one to Berlin.

An Eighth Air Force B-17 ball turret gunner had the distinction of flunking gunnery school but went on to become an ace and then some. Tech. Sgt. Thomas Dye of the 351st Bomb Group flying out of Polebrook had trained as a radio operator, but when the need for gunners exceeded those available, Dye volunteered to become a gunner. On his fifth mission he was credited with two victories, but then was pulled out of flying to attend a "refresher" course in gunnery. He did not receive a satisfactory grade in the course, but when he returned to his squadron, he was welcomed back by his crew, who had faith in his abilities even if he could not pass the gunnery course. Their faith in him was well placed, since Dye went on to chalk up a total of eight kills, one of the highest in the Eighth Air Force for gunners. Dye, who flew in the Fortress *Snowball,* was one of the "Ball Boys" of the 511th Squadron. The squadron's name came from the 511th commander, Major Clinton Ball, and inspired such airplane names as *Cannon Ball, Screwball, Speedball, Highball, Spitball, Foulball, Fireball* and *Spareball.*

Gunners who were probably the first to fire at a rocket-propelled fighter were on the crew of *Outhouse Mouse,* a B-17G assigned to the 91st Bomb Group at Bassingbourn. The date was August 16, 1944 and the target was a synthetic fuel plant at Leipzig. On the way to the target *Outhouse Mouse* was jumped by a gaggle of FW-190 fighters and took several hits. One shell entered the radio room, narrowly missing the radio operator, Tech. Sgt. James R. Knaub. Another shell hit the tail gunner, Staff Sgt. M.D. Barker in a leg, and the same round also put one of the tail guns out of commission. With the remaining single gun, Barker was able to hit at least one of the 190s, which went down in flames. He later was awarded a Silver Star medal for his actions. The real damage to the Fortress was to the number three and four engines, which lost their superchargers. With the loss of power, *Outhouse Mouse* was no longer able to keep up with the formation, so the pilot pulled out and turned for home, after salvoing the bombs. Tech. Sgt. Carl A. Dickson, in the top turret, was also wounded in the face in the attack.

As the plane made its lonely way back to England, the radio operator, Knaub, pulled the wounded Barker from the tail gun position and placed him in the waist. He then took over a waist gun position while the waist gunner, Staff Sgt. Robert D. Loomis, replaced Barker in the tail. The bombardier, Flight Officer O.V. Chaney replaced Dickson in the top turret.

In addition to the FW-190s, tiny Messerschmitt 163B rocket-powered Komet fighters had joined in the attack on the thousand plane raid. The pilot of one of them, Lt. Harmut Ryll, spotted the crippled *Outhouse Mouse* and headed for it. At about the same time, two P-51 Mustang fighters from the 359th Fighter Group also noted the limping Fortress, and the pilots, seeing the contrails of the rocket ships, knew that the Germans would pounce on the hapless Fort. Loomis, in the tail gun position, spotted an approaching 163B and called it out to the crew. Then the rocket ship made a firing pass at the bomber coming in from six o'clock high. Loomis answered the stubby fighter's fire with fire of his own, and as the plane passed beneath the Fort, Staff Sgt. Kenneth L. Blackburn in the ball turret also got off some rounds at the rocket. Knaub at the waist gun and Chaney in the top turret also fired. None of the gunners reported seeing hits because the fighter was traveling too fast for their turrets to track it. Then, the German pilot came back up to the Fortress, but instead of firing, for some reason he flew formation with the bomber. That gave the Mustangs their chance, and Lt. Col. John B. Murphy and Lt. Cyril W. Jones, Jr., made the most of it. Murphy overshot the rocket, so Jones got the first hits on the Komet. Then Murphy latched on to the tail of the rocket ship as it dove for safety, and a long burst from his guns finished the Komet off. It was the first downing of a Komet by Americans. It was fortunate for American aerial gunners that so few Me-163s became operational, because a large force could have proven quite a threat to U.S. bombers.

The first American gunner in Europe to down an enemy aircraft at night was a Ninth Air Force gunner manning the top turret of a B-26 Martin Marauder. It happened on a night NOBALL mission. NOBALL missions were against V-1 Buzz Bomb launching sites near the French coast. 32 B-26s from the 322nd Bomb Group attacked on the night of July 7/8,

1944, using radar-equipped pathfinder lead planes. Flying between 6,500 and 9,000 feet the force was hit by some 20 German night fighters at about the time it crossed the French coastline. The fighters included FW-190s, Me-110s and Ju-88s. The Germans used searchlights as well as airlaunched flares to illuminate the bomber force. An FW-190 made a firing attack on the B-26 of Sgt. Kenneth M. Locke, who returned its fire as it came in from seven o'clock low. His burst was right on the money and the fighter went down, wrapped in flames.

Two other B-26 gunners scored on the same night. The Marauder *Homesick* was jumped by a Ju-88 while the B-26 was caught in a cone of light from four searchlights. On the fourth pass by the Ju-88, the top turret was knocked out, but not before Staff Sgt. J.K. Brandemihl in the turret and Sgt. Robert E. Johnson in the tail scored many hits on it, sending it down in flames. The four passes by the Ju-88 had done its work on the B-26, however, which was forced to crash land at the RAF base at Tangmere and never flew again.

Another Ninth Air Force gunner propelled the AAF into the jet age when he downed two Me-262 jet fighters on the same mission. Sgt. Edward S. Tyszkiewicz a top turret gunner in a B-26 assigned to the 323rd Bomb Group accounted for two of the jets on a raid against a railroad marshalling yard. It was in April 1945 just before the end of the war in Europe when a formation of 43 Marauders was attacked by 15 of the German jet fighters. The fight was savage, with the enemy downing three of the bombers and damaging several others. Sgt. Tyszkiewicz destroyed one of the jets and then another made several attacks against the bomber. The jet wounded the gunner and knocked his turret out of automatic functioning so that he had to track the attacker manually. Even so, the second went down and in spite of the pain from his wounds and the difficulty in handling the turret, Tyszkiewicz stayed at his post and fought off further attacks. He won the Silver Star for his bravery.

But the attacks by jet were an omen of things to come. It would not be long before bombers themselves would be jet-powered. And because of the speed of the jet bombers, the need for gunners would diminish. Soon bombers would have only tail turrets, with just one gunner needed to man them. They would also be remotely operated so that there would be no requirement to maintain cramped and uncomfortable firing positions. The aerial gunner would become a rarity — not an extinct breed, but a breed on the endangered list whose days are probably numbered.

Bibliography

Belote, James H. and William M., *Titans of the Sea.* New York: Harper and Row, Publishers, 1975.

Birdsall, Steve, *Log of the Liberators.* Garden City, New York: Doubleday & Company, Inc., 1973.

Birdsall, Steve, *Saga of the Superforts.* Garden City, New York: Doubleday & Company, Inc., 1980.

Blucher, Jay, "Bill Mauldin Today." *Air Force Times,* January 14, 1985.

Bowyer, Chaz, *Guns in the Sky.* New York: Charles Scribner's Sons, 1979.

Branham, Leo, "Clark Gable Makes Films for Training Air Force." *Los Angeles Times,* June 6, 1943.

Butler, Ron, "Pancho Villa's One-Man Air Force." *Westways,* November 1983.

Caiden, Martin, *Black Thursday,* New York: E.P. Dutton & Co., Inc. 1960.

Caiden, Martin, *Flying Forts.* New York: Ballantine Books, 1968.

Caiden, Martin, *The Ragged, Rugged Warriors.* New York: E.P. Dutton & Co., Inc., 1966.

Caiden, Martin, *Zero Fighter.* Ballantine Books, Inc., 1966.

Caiden, Martin and Hymoff, Edward, *The Mission.* Philadelphia and New York: J.B. Lippincott Company, 1964.

Christmann, Timothy J., "Vice President Bush calls WWII Experience 'Sobering'," *Naval Aviation News,* March-April 1985.

Coffey, Thomas M., *Hap.* New York: The Viking Press, 1982.

Cohn, Roy, *McCarthy: The Answer to "Tail Gunner Joe."* New York: Manor Books, Inc., 1977.

Constable, Trevor J. and Colonel Toliver, Raymond F., *Horrido! Fighter Aces of the Luftwaffe.* New York: Macmillan Company, 1968.

Craven, Wesley F. and Cate, James L., editors, *The Army Air Forces in World War II,* Volumes I, II, III, and VI. Chicago and London: The University of Chicago Press, 1949.

Dickinson, Lieut. Clarence E., *The Flying Guns.* Washington, D.C.: Zenger Publishing Co., Inc., 1942.

Dugan, James and Stewart, Carroll, *Ploesti.* New York: Random House, 1962.

Du Pre, Colonel Flint O., *U.S. Air Force Biographical Dictionary.* New York: Franklin Watts, Inc., 1965.

Ethell, Jeff, "Deadly Interception." *D-Day Over Normandy,* Summer 1984.

Farmer, James H., *Celluloid Wings.* Blue Ridge Summit, Penn.: Tab Books, Inc., 1984.

Francis, Devon, *Flak Bait.* Washington, D.C.: Zenger Publishing Co., Inc., 1948.

Freeman, Roger A., *The Mighty Eighth.* Garden City, New York: Doubleday and Company, Inc., 1970.

Frisbee, John L., "First of the Few." *Air Force Magazine,* April 1984.

Glines, Carroll, V., *Doolittle's Tokyo Raiders.* Princeton, New Jersey: D. Van Nostrand Company, Inc., 1964.

Greenwood, Jim and Maxine, *Stunt Flying in the Movies.* Blue Ridge Summit, Penn.: Tab Books, Inc., 1982.

Gurney, Gene, *Five Down and Glory.* New York: Ballantine Books, 1958.
Halliwell, Leslie, *The Filmgoer's Companion.* New York:
Avon Books, 1978.
Hamblett, Charles, *Paul Newman.* Chicago: Henry Regnery Co., 1975.
Heston, Charlton, *Charlton Heston.* New York: Pocket Books, 1979.
Jablonski, Edward, *Air War.* Garden City, New York: Doubleday & Company,
Inc., 1971.
Jackson, Robert, *Fighter Pilots of World War II.* New York: St. Martins
Press, 1976.
Kitchen, Ruben P., Jr., *Pacific Carrier.* New York: Kensington Publishing
Co., 1980.
Lawson, Captain Ted W., *Thirty Seconds Over Tokyo.* New York: Random
House, 1943.
McCombs, Don and Worth, Fred L., *World War II, Strange & Fascinating
Facts.* New York: Greenwich House, 1983.
Morrison, Patt, "Slim Pickens, Cowboy-Turned-Actor, Dies." *Los Angeles
Times,* December 10, 1983.
Musciano, Walter A., *Corsair Aces.* New York: Arco Publishing Company,
Inc., 1979.
O'Leary, Michael, "Resurrection of the Memphis Belle." *AAF Bombers at War,*
Spring 1984.
Oshinsky, David M., *A Conspiracy So Immense.* New York: The Free
Press, 1983.
_____, *Pilot's Manual for B-25 Mitchell.* Appleton, Wisconsin:
Aviation Publications, 1978.
Pyle, Ernie, *Brave Men.* New York: Henry Hold and Company, 1944.
Roscoe, Theodore, *On the Seas and In the Skies.* New York: Hawthorne Books,
Inc., 1970.
Rubin, Harold, *The Fighting 463rd.*
Rust, Kenn C., *Eighth Air Force Story.* Temple City, Calif.: Historical Aviation
Album, 1978.
Rust, KennC., *Fifteenth Air Force Story.* Temple City, Calif.: Historical
Aviation Album, 1976.
Rust, Kenn C., *The 9th Air Force in World War II.* Fallbrook, Calif.: Aero
Publishers, Inc., 1967.
Rust, Kenn C., *Seventh Air Force Story.* Temple City, Calif.: Historical
Aviation Album, 1979.
Rust, Kenn C., *Twentieth Air Force Story.* Temple City, Calif.: Historical
Aviation Album, 1979.
Sakai, Saburo, *Samurai!* New York: E.P. Dutton and Company, Inc., 1957.
Sims, Edward H., *American Aces.* New York: Harper & Brothers
Publishers, 1958.
Taylor, John W.R., editor, *Combat Aircraft of the World.* London: George
Rainbird Ltd., 1969.
Toliver, Raymond F. and Constable, Trevor J., *Fighter Aces of the U.S.A.*
Fallbrook, Calif.: Aero Publishers, Inc., 1979.
Tornabene, Lyn, *Long Live the King.* New York: G.P. Putman's Sons, 1976.

Ulanoff, Stanley M., editor, *Bombs Away!* Garden City, New York: Doubleday & Company, Inc., 1971.

U.S. Air Force, *The United States Air Forces in Southeast Asia — aces and aerial victories, 1965-1973,* Maxwell AFB, Alabama: The Albert F. Simpson Historical Research Center, 1976.

U.S. Air Force, *USAF Historical Study No. 85 (USAF Credits for the Destruction of Enemy Aircraft, World War II).* Maxwell AFB, Alabama: The Alfred F. Simpson Historical Research Center, 1978.

U.S. Army Air Forces, "Night Fighters." *Impact,* May 1944.

U.S. Army Air Forces, "The Widows Begin Biting." *Impact,* November 1944.

Whitehouse, Arch, *The Years of the War Birds.* Garden City, New York: Doubleday & Company, Inc., 1960.

Index